The Biblical Seminar
26

JESUS
THE LIBERATOR

JESUS
THE LIBERATOR
NAZARETH LIBERATION THEOLOGY
(LUKE 4.16-30)

Michael Prior

Sheffield Academic Press

Copyright © 1995 Sheffield Academic Press

Published by
Sheffield Academic Press Ltd
Mansion House
19 Kingfield Road
Sheffield, S11 9AS
England

Typeset by Sheffield Academic Press
and
Printed on acid-free paper in Great Britain
by The Cromwell Press
Melksham, Wiltshire

A catalogue record for this book is available
from the British Library

ISBN 1-85075-524-8

Contents

Preface	9
Abbreviations	11
INTRODUCTION	13

Part I

Chapter 1
PRELIMINARY QUESTIONS	20
The Unity of Luke–Acts	20
The Genre of Luke–Acts	25
The Purpose(s) of Luke–Acts	38
Theology of Luke–Acts	44
Universalism in Luke–Acts	48
What Occasioned the Lukan Work?	60
Gospel Study and the Standpoint of the Reader	61
Conclusion	65

Part II
First-Century Setting

Chapter 2
THE SOURCE QUESTION	68
The Synoptic Gospels in General	68
The Synoptic Problem	68
The Source Question and Luke 4.16-30	72
Is Luke 4.16-30 Dependent upon Mark 6.1-6?	82
Lukan Redaction and Luke's Sources	83
Do Luke 4.16-30 and Mark 6.1-6 Record Two Distinct Visits?	84
Conclusion	85

Chapter 3
THE COHERENCE OF LUKE'S ACCOUNT 90
   From the Gospels to Jesus 90
   What Really Happened in Nazareth? 91
   Conclusion 98

Chapter 4
THE HISTORICITY OF THE NAŻARETH SYNAGOGUE SCENE 101
   The Term *sunagōgē* 102
   The Origins of the Synagogue 105
   Jesus and the Synagogue 109
   The Functions of the Synagogue 110
   Reading the Scriptures in the Synagogue 113
   A Jewish Lectionary? 115
   Jewish Interpretations of the Scriptures 119
   Conclusion 122

Chapter 5
LUKE'S JESUS AS EXEGETE 126
   Jesus and the Hebrew Scriptures 128
   The Use of Isaiah in Luke 129
   The Liturgical Setting of the Isaiah Texts 132
   Isaiah 61 in Luke 133
   Conclusion 141

Chapter 6
ELIJAH AND ELISHA 142
   Elijah and Elisha: Prophets for Gentiles as Well as Israel 142
   Elijah and Elisha Elsewhere in Luke 144
   Jew First, then Gentile 146
   Conclusion 147

Chapter 7
A LITERARY APPRECIATION OF LUKE 4.16-30 149
   Biblical Literary Criticism 149
   The Literary Setting in Luke–Acts 150
   The Structure of Luke 4.16-30 150
   An Analysis of Luke 4.16-30 151
   Conclusion 161

Chapter 8
THE INVITATION OF LUKE–ACTS—YESTERDAY:
THE SOCIOLOGICAL SETTING OF THE TEXT — 163

Luke–Acts: The Gospel of the Poor? 163
The Standpoint of the Reader 163
The Poor and Oppressed in Luke's Gospel 164
Who are the Poor in New Testament Times? 165
The Meaning of *ptōchos* 165
ptōchos in the New Testament 167
The Rich 171
What Makes a Person Poor? 172
Biblical Overview: The Poor in the Old Testament 175
Rich and Poor in Luke's Community 176
Conclusion 181

Part III
CONTEMPORARY READING OF LUKE 4.16-30

Chapter 9
THE INVITATION OF LUKE–ACTS—TODAY — 184

First World and the Bible 187
The Bible and Contextualized Theology: Three Examples 187
Contextualized Lukan Theology Today 191
Lukan Liberation and Life 195

CONCLUSION — 198

Bibliography 203
Index of References 217
Index of Authors 226

PREFACE

At the end of the last century, when physicists considered themselves to be on the verge of completing the discovery of all the laws of physics, Michelson, reflecting the prevailing mood of confidence in classical physics, said, 'The more important fundamental laws and facts of physical science have all been discovered, and these are so firmly established that the possibility of their ever being supplanted in consequence of new discoveries is exceedingly remote...Our future discoveries must be looked for in the sixth place of decimals' (Richtmyer, Kennard and Cooper 1969: 43). Within twenty years of that claim the scientific world was rocked by a series of epoch-making discoveries concerning the nature of matter and the laws of nature.

Up to recently there has been an analogous confidence in the area of Gospel studies. Beginners learned very quickly that their initiation into New Testament scholarship required a profession of faith in the following dogmas: (a) Mark was the first gospel, and was used by Matthew and Luke, independently of each other; (b) Matthew and Luke used another source, consisting mostly of sayings of Jesus (the so-called *Q Document*), again independently of each other; (c) the gospels contain only snap-shots from the life of Jesus, and should not be considered to be biographies; (d) questions such as, 'Did this really happen?' can be left aside in the quest to discover the intentions of the author.

Most of the books of introduction to the study of the gospels concentrate on the different methods of investigation employed by the community of scholars over the last one hundred and fifty years. Special attention is given to source criticism, form criticism, redaction criticism, and more recently, to the social context of the gospels, and to reader-response criticism. There should be place also for a political criticism. Such books of introduction are not satisfactory, since they leave the impression that the study of the gospels is about method rather than meaning. The examples which these books give to illustrate the methods are too disparate to be of much use to students enquiring into the meaning of texts. On the other hand, commentaries tend to concentrate on details to such an extent that only a dedicated minority perseveres with them.

In approaching a text which has been the subject of investigation for close on two thousand years, one has to be sensitive to the academic arrogance of any one age or place, especially one's own. My experience of teaching the Gospels, at university level in four different Colleges in two countries, convinces me that there is need for a book which examines a text of a gospel and shows the use of the different methods in practice. Such a book would serve as an introduction to gospel studies, and would lead its readers to an examination of a programmatic text.

I have attempted at all times to respect the complexity of the questions under discussion, and to reflect the reality that scholars arrive at quite different conclusions. While I investigate the subject from a variety of perspectives, it is not my intention in this book to attempt to *solve* what are probably insoluble problems, such as those concerning historicity and source criticism.

My goal is more modest. It is to introduce educated readers to the different methods employed by biblical scholars, with a view to discussing one major New Testament text. The reasons I have chosen to concentrate on this text will be clearer to the reader as the book is studied.

The references and bibliography make no pretence to be exhaustive. They contain only those works to which specific reference is made in the body of the text. Those seeking additional reading may consult the bibliography in Schreck 1991. In the interests of making the text more readable I have dispensed with notes. I have attempted to incorporate within the text itself as much information as I consider useful. I use the author–date system of reference, giving the name of the author, the year of publication and the page number.

Lastly, a few words of thanks are due. Family, friends and colleagues in Cork, Jerusalem and London encouraged me greatly. I am grateful to Professor Philip Davies for accepting the work for the Biblical Seminar Series, and for his helpful suggestions, to Webb Mealy for his great care in editing the project, and to the staff of Sheffield Academic Press for their careful production of the book.

ABBREVIATIONS

AB	Anchor Bible
ANRW	*Aufstieg und Niedergang der römischen Welt*
BETL	Bibliotheca ephemeridum theologicarum lovaniensium
Bib	*Biblica*
BJRL	*Bulletin of the John Rylands University Library of Manchester*
BNTC	*Black's New Testament Commentaries*
BZNW	Beihefte zur *ZNW*
CIJ	J.B. Frey (ed.), *Corpus inscriptionum judaicarum* (2 vols.; Rome, 1936, 1952 [vol. I reprinted with prolegomenon by B. Lifshitz, New York, 1975])
CPJ	V.A. Tcherikover, A. Fuks, *et al.* (eds.), *Corpus papyrorum judaicarum* (3 vols.; Cambridge, MA: Harvard University Press, 1957–81)
DBSup	*Dictionnaire de la Bible, Supplément*
EBib	Etudes bibliques
ExpTim	*Expository Times*
HNT	Handbuch zum Neuen Testament
HTR	*Harvard Theological Review*
IGA 2	E. Breccia (ed.), *Inscriptiones Graecae Aegypti*. II. *Inscriptiones nunc Alexandriae in Museo* (Cairo, 1911; reprinted Chicago, 1978)
IGUR	L. Moretti (ed.), *Inscriptiones Graecae Urbis Romae*, III (Rome, 1979)
Int	*Interpretation*
JBL	*Journal of Biblical Literature*
JSNTSup	*Journal for the Study of the New Testament*, Supplement Series
JTS	*Journal of Theological Studies*
LCL	Loeb Classical Library
LD	Leclio Divina
NIGTC	New International Greek Text Commentary
NovT	*Novum Testamentum*
NTS	*New Testament Studies*
PAAJR	*Proceedings of the American Academy of Jewish Research*
PG	J. Migne (ed.), *Patrologia graeca*
RB	*Revue biblique*
SBLMS	SBL Monograph Series

SBLSBS	SBL Sources for Biblical Study
SBLSP	*SBL Seminar Papers*
SBS	Stuttgarter Bibelstudien
ScrB	*Scripture Bulletin*
SNTSMS	Society of New Testament Studies Monograph Series
TDNT	G. Kittel and G. Friedrich (eds.), *Theological Dictionary of the New Testament*
THKNT	Theologisches Handkommentar zum Neuen Testament
TSK	*Theologische Studien und Kritiken*
TynBul	*Tyndale Bulletin*
TZ	*Theologische Zeitschrift*
WUNT	Wissenschaftliche Untersuchungen zum Neuen Testament
ZNW	*Zeitschrift für die neutestamentliche Wissenschaft*

INTRODUCTION

The Text of Luke 4.16-30

Setting the Scene
^{14}And Jesus returned in the power of the Spirit into Galilee, and a report concerning him went out through all the surrounding country. ^{15}And he taught in their synagogues, being glorified by all.

Synagogue Reading and Teaching
^{16}And he came to Nazareth where he had been brought up; and he went to the synagogue as his custom was, on the Sabbath day. And he stood up to read; ^{17}and there was given to him the book of the prophet Isaiah. He opened the book and found the place where it was written, ^{18}'The Spirit of the Lord is upon me, because he has anointed me to preach good news to the poor. He has sent me to proclaim release to the captives and recovering of sight to the blind, to set at liberty those who are oppressed, ^{19}to proclaim the acceptable year of the Lord.' ^{20}And he closed the book, and gave it back to the attendant, and sat down; and the eyes of all in the synagogue were fixed on him. ^{21}And he began to say to them, 'Today this scripture has been fulfilled in your hearing'.

Congregation Reaction
^{22}And all spoke well of him, and wondered at the gracious words which proceeded out of his mouth; and they said, 'Is not this Joseph's son?' ^{23}And he said to them, 'Doubtless you will quote to me this proverb, "Physician, heal yourself; what we have heard you did at Capernaum, do here also in your own country"'. ^{24}And he said, 'Truly I say to you, no prophet is acceptable in his own country. ^{25}But in truth, I tell you, there were many widows in Israel in the days of Elijah, when the heaven was shut up three years and six months, when there came a great famine over all the land; ^{26}And Elijah was sent to none of them but only to Zarephath, in the land of Sidon, to a woman who was a widow. ^{27}And there were many lepers in Israel in the time of the prophet Elisha; and none of them was cleansed but only Naaman the Syrian'. ^{28}When they heard this, all in the synagogue were filled with wrath. ^{29}And they rose up and put him out of the city, and led him to the brow of the hill on which their city was built, that they might throw him down headlong.^{30} But passing through the midst of them he went away.

The Next Pericope

³¹And he went down to Capernaum, a city of Galilee. And he was teaching them on the sabbath; ³²and they were astonished at his teaching, for his word was with authority. ³³And in the synagogue there was a man who had the spirit of an unclean demon; and he cried out with a loud voice.

There are many noteworthy features in the account in Luke's Gospel. The most striking one is that Luke is the only one of the four evangelists to record Jesus' reading from, and comment on, the Isaiah text mentioned here. Moreover, he is the only one to begin Jesus' ministry in Galilee in this solemn way.

Matthew and Mark are close to each other in their description of the transition from the desert temptation of Jesus to the beginning of his public ministry in Galilee: 'Now when he heard that John had been arrested, he withdrew into Galilee, and leaving Nazareth he went and dwelt in Capernaum by the sea...From that time Jesus began to preach, saying, "Repent, for the kingdom of heaven is at hand"' (Mt. 4.12-17). Mark reads, 'Now after John was arrested, Jesus came into Galilee, preaching the gospel of God, and saying, 'The time is fulfilled, and the kingdom of God is at hand; repent and believe in the gospel' (Mk 1.14-15). Matthew and Mark immediately go on to the call of the disciples (Mt. 4.18-22; Mk 1.16-20), which Luke deals with later (5.1-11).

For Luke Jesus *returned* in the power of the Spirit into Galilee. In Luke's Infancy Narrative, Nazareth was the home of Mary and of Joseph before the birth of Jesus, and so Jesus was returning home. A report concerning him went out through all the surrounding country, and he was teaching (imperfect tense in the Greek) in their synagogues, being glorified by all (cf. Lk. 4.14-15). The scene in the synagogue of Nazareth follows immediately.

It is true that Matthew and Mark record a teaching of Jesus in a synagogue 'in his own country', at which the hearers were astonished, and asked where this wisdom came from, and took offence at him. Jesus said, 'A prophet is not without honour except in his own country', and did not do many mighty works there, because of their unbelief (Mt. 13.53-58; cf. Mk 6.1-6a). Mark, however, adds, 'except that he laid his hands upon a few sick people and healed them'.

For his part Luke also has the 'No prophet is acceptable in his own country' response, and follows it with the stories of the Zarephath widow and Naaman the Syrian. While Matthew and Mark record only that they took offence at Jesus, Luke says that all in the synagogue were filled with wrath, and tried to throw him from the brow of the hill (Lk. 4.28-29).

Luke's account, then, is unique in *opening* the public ministry of Jesus in Galilee in the synagogue in Nazareth, and in the manner in which he does it by reading and commenting on the Isaiah text.

I have many reasons for focusing on the scene in the synagogue at Nazareth (Lk. 4.16-30). A study of the dramatic account of Jesus' encounter with the people of his own town in a synagogue on a Sabbath day has much to offer an enquirer. Although the Gospels frequently mention that Jesus preached in a synagogue, with the exception of this text there is little to indicate what he said among his fellow Jews in the synagogue.

The Nazareth text provides the earliest extant account of what went on in a synagogue, and from it one would hope to learn about the practices in the synagogue in the first century. The fact that Jesus is reported to have searched for and read from one text of Isaiah invites reflection on how Jews used and interpreted their texts in the first century of the Christian era. Something might be learned also about Jesus' understanding of his mission, or at least of Luke's portrayal of the mission and his understanding of it.

Virtually all scholars agree that this text is a key passage in Luke's Gospel. Karris' assessment is typical: 'Almost all Lukan scholars agree that 4.16-30 is programmatic: it describes Jesus' nature and mission' (1978: 117-18). However, if there is virtual unanimity on the programmatic character of the text, there is no such general agreement about the nature of the programme it prefaces.

For the majority of scholars, the text introduces the reader in a dramatic way to the movement of the gospel from its original Jewish setting to a Gentile one. Jack Sanders is typical of the consensus in saying that the scene is 'programmatic' for Luke–Acts, 'for it sums up and presents in a dramatic way Luke's theology of the rejection of the gospel by the Jews and of the divine intent to send it to the Gentiles' (Sanders 1987: 165). But in a work published in the same year, R.L. Brawley argued that this standard view must be revised (1987: 7-8).

In addition to the many books and articles which bear on the subject there have been a number of surveys of the scholarly debate. H. Anderson surveyed the scene up to 1964 under the headings, The Historical Approach, Form Criticism, Linguistic Reconstruction, and the Method of Redaction Criticism. J.-N. Aletti discussed the situation under the headings, The Structure and the Logic of the Passage, The History of the Tradition, The Lukan Redaction, The Oracle of Isaiah, The Jubilee Year, and the Synagogal Reading (1985). Most recently Schreck reviews the scene for the period 1972–1989, and does so under three headings: Source Criticism, Internal Coherence, and The Prophetic Kerygma and Universal Mission of Jesus (1989). I acknowledge my debt to these authors, and to those in the bibliography.

The rise of interest in Liberation Theology has coincided with, or has been a stimulus for, an increase in exegetical interest in Luke 4.16-30. Luke's interest in the poor has been the subject of a number of special studies (Brekelmans 1980–81, Busse 1978, Busse *et al.* 1980, Dietrich 1985, Dumais 1984, Dupont 1978), and of doctoral dissertations (Aymer 1987, Liu 1986). Luke's Gospel has been entitled the *Gospel of the Poor*, or the like (da Spinetoli 1982, Davids 1976, Schmitals 1975), while Schottroff and Stegemann describe Jesus of Nazareth as 'The Hope of the Poor' (1978).

The term *to evangelize the poor* is an intriguing one. There are two extremes of interpretation, one giving a purely materialist reading (freedom from all forms of suffering now), and the other giving a purely spiritualist one (announcing an eschatological liberation). There is, of course, a middle position: in the Nazareth pericope, 'The Lukan Jesus promises to alleviate the extreme physical deprivation suffered by the beggars, the blind, the lame, the imprisoned and so forth, without, however, ignoring the spiritual aspects of salvation' (Esler 1987: 183). In dealing with the matter nowadays it is common to stress that evangelization involves the liberation of the whole person.

The seventeenth-century French priest Vincent de Paul chose the phrase, *Evangelizare pauperibus misit me* (*he sent me to evangelize the poor*) as the motto of the community of priests and brothers he founded, and to which I belong. I propose to offer some reflections on that key phrase.

My reflections are offered in a number of categories. I consider some of the questions which a modern biblical scholar would wish to pose. I examine more recent emphases of modern scholarship, namely the efforts to situate the traditions about Jesus and the evangelization of the poor in the life of an early Christian community, in this case Luke's church. Lest we fall into the trap of imagining that an enquiry into the Gospel of Luke concerns only the past, I reflect upon the place of this central Lukan theme in contemporary society. In this way, I propose to offer a study of this key text which not only remains sensitive to the concerns of biblical scholarship, but equally respects the faith perspective that the Word of God is alive and active, and calls for a response in every generation.

It is the intention here to pay particular attention to one section of the Gospel of Luke, namely 4.16-30. However, it is my strong conviction that any section of the Gospel of Luke must be seen as a part of the two volume work, Luke–Acts. Before examining the Nazareth scene, then, it is essential to enquire into its place within the whole literary work. It is to this task that we now turn our attention.

Part I

Chapter 1

PRELIMINARY QUESTIONS

Before attempting an assessment of the meaning of any section of Luke–Acts it is necessary to enquire into the category of literature to which the whole work belongs. But, firstly, we must examine the arguments for regarding Luke–Acts to be one literary production. Then we shall explore the question of the literary classification of the whole work, and enquire into how it relates to literature contemporaneous with it. Then we explore the question of the purpose(s) of Luke–Acts, and probe into some of the theological emphases of the work. Only then do we make our first observations on how these questions relate to our investigation of Lk. 4.16-30.

The Unity of Luke–Acts

One of the real achievements of the study of the New Testament in this century is the insistence that the Gospel of Luke and the Acts of the Apostles be considered as two volumes of one work. The American biblical scholar H.J. Cadbury criticized the practice of his predecessors in treating of the Third Gospel in isolation from the Acts of the Apostles. Since their common authorship and their interdependence was recognized, he suggested that they should be designated by one name, and proposed *Luke–Acts* as the title of the work (1927: 7-11). This designation has met with widespread approval. But already by c. 400 AD, John Chrysostom was in no doubt that Luke–Acts was a two-part work. Chrysostom says that Luke divided his work into two parts for lucidity (*Hom.* 1, *PG* 60.17, *Nicene and Post-Nicene Fathers* 11.4—see Wylie 1991).

It is estimated that the two papyrus rolls which Luke used for the double work were approximately 35 and 32 feet long, for Luke and Acts respectively (Aune 1987: 117). Whereas some ancient authors simply begin the second volume where the first left off, Luke begins the second volume with a recapitulation of the contents of the first volume, writing, 'In the first book, O Theophilus, I have dealt with all that Jesus began to do and teach' (Acts 1.1), and returning to the scene of the Ascension which ends the first volume.

The argument for the unity of the two volumes is constructed from many different elements: for example, common language and theology; tradition; each is addressed to Theophilus (Lk. 1.3; Acts 1.1); the first ends with the Ascension of Jesus, and the second recapitulates the Ascension scene, and continues the story.

The Principle of Duality
The case for viewing the two volumes as one composition conceived from the first is formidable, and has been made very impressively by C.H. Talbert (1974). He draws attention to the author's use of the principle of balance (between Acts and Luke, between Peter and Paul in Acts, etc.), which had been noted by several scholars before him: 'Whether the explanation of the data was in terms of tendency, sources, or style, from Baur through Cadbury the correspondences were regarded as highly important to a proper understanding of Luke–Acts' (p. 2). Yet this feature of Luke's structure has been virtually ignored in scholarship up to now.

Clearly, the overall architecture of a literary work contributes to its literary identity, and plays a part, and perhaps a major part, in establishing the significance of the composition. This significance may be illuminated when the literary pattern is viewed against the literary background of the period of composition. The connection between the form and content of a literary work rightly is considered to be so vital that it is unwise to consider one without reference to the other. Having stressed the importance of examining the literary structure of a work before considering its meaning, one is left with the task of defining the structure. What is the structure of Luke–Acts?

For Talbert the principle of balance is one of the major architectonic features of Luke–Acts. He claims that Acts has the logical priority in the Lukan scheme, and he poses the question, 'Why did Luke prefix a Gospel to Acts?' (1974: 30 n. 3). Within Acts itself he draws attention to the balance between the Jewish Christianity reflected in Acts 1–12, and the Gentile brand in Acts 13–28. He examines the balance between the Galilee context of Lk. 9.1-48 and the Jerusalem one of Lk. 22.7–23.16.

The architectonic character of the double work is reflected also in smaller sections: Lk. 4.16–7.17 and Lk. 7.18–8.56; the John and Jesus cycles in Luke 1–2; the comparison of John and Jesus in Luke 3–4; Acts 1.12–4.23 and Acts 4.24–5.42. The correspondences are inverted in Lk. 10.21–13.30 and Lk. 14.1–18.30, and in Acts 15.1–18.11 and Acts 18.12–21.26. There are correspondences too between Luke 24 and Acts 1, and Luke 9 and Acts 1.

In all of these cases Talbert argues that the correspondences are the intentional achievement of the author of Luke–Acts who modified his sources to produce this architectonic effect of balance (1974: 22, 26, 29, 48). Talbert asks whether this is an indication of the unique character of Luke's literary genius, or whether one is dealing with a typical literary pattern of the period and place. He shows that the principle of balance is apparent also in other works of the period, and also in the visual arts: in Homer's *Iliad* and *Odyssey*, in the plays of Aeschylus and Euripides, and in the histories of Herodotus and Thucydides; in the *Odes* of Horace and in Vergil's *Aeneid*, and so on. The pattern in the *Aeneid*, Talbert argues, is particularly close to that of the Lukan work. At the beginning of the Christian era, the Greco-Roman world saw the principle of balance as rooted in the nature of reality, and expressed this both in literature and in the visual arts. It is not surprising, then, that Luke–Acts employs the same form.

Talbert points out that the principle of balance is found also in Jewish literature (Exod. 7.8–10.27; Exod. 10–14; 1 Kgs 3–11; *1 En.* 93; 96.12-17; 1QS 3.13–4.26 and in many of the Qumran Psalms; Ruth; Jonah; Habbakuk; and Micah), and in particular in the book of Jonah, which provides a striking example of similarity of structure to Luke–Acts (with its eight parallels between Jon. 1.17–2.10 and 4.1-11, the four between chs. 1 and 2, and the four between chs. 3 and 4). The principle of balance is reflected also in Solomon's Temple (see especially Ezek. 12.18-19), in the Tobiad Palace in the Ptolemaic Period, and in Herod's Period in the triangular tymphanon, and also in the golden candelabra of the Jerusalem Temple.

The principle of balance (symmetry), then, is deeply rooted in Near Eastern mentality. Hebrews argued by assurance and repetition, rather than by abstract reasoning. Hence the Hebrew love of *parallelismus membrorum*, for example:

1. *Preliminary Questions*

> Have mercy on me Lord, in your kindness
> In your compassion blot out my offence
> O wash me more and more from my guilt
> And cleanse me from my sin...(Ps. 51).

According to Talbert, the Near Eastern mentality expressed itself in terms of balance. Each literary work was organized so as to establish a balance between the parts, and in such a way that each part manifests the whole, and the whole is diffused throughout the parts. An Israelite-Jewish writer would first see any projected work as a balanced whole and would then proceed to compose the work accordingly. Scholars have found the pattern of duality also in 1 Corinthians 8–10; Galatians; Romans 9–11; Philemon; Rev. 1.13–2.18; and in other non-canonical Christian literature.

Talbert, however, seems to need to have it both ways. He accounts for the asymmetries in Luke–Acts by insisting that the ancients, like nature itself, abhorred pure form. He poses the question as to whether the author of Luke–Acts had a ground-plan for his work, and he answers affirmatively, and he illustrates how Aristotle, Vergil, Lucian and Pliny also had. To the question of whether the readers of such a work would have recognized the complexity of the ground-plan, Talbert suggests four possibilities:

1. the architectonic character was a secret of the author;
2. some readers, after long reflection, became aware of it;
3. the pattern was felt immediately by most, but was only consciously perceived after long reflection;
4. the pattern was recognized at the conscious level at the time of hearing/reading.

Talbert points to the principle of duality in the human body itself: contraction and relaxation of the heart; breathing in and out, and so on. This, he claims, helps the reader/hearer to discover the duality scheme of a text. Talbert suggests that the reader/hearer would first encounter the balance of the preface (Lk. 1.1-4), and would be led to expect more. This expectation is then satisfied by the balancing of John and Jesus in Luke 1–2. 'In becoming receptive so far, he (the reader) would become receptive to still more. He would *feel* with the author in this rhythm' (Talbert 1974: 80). The architectonic pattern would have been immediately sensed or felt, if not necessarily consciously and rationally perceived (p. 81).

The Ascension as Hinge

One of the most noteworthy features of the double work of Luke–Acts is the presence of two accounts of the Ascension, one at the end of the first volume, and the second at the beginning of the second. As the following chart indicates, a strong case can be made for seeing Luke–Acts 'hinging' on the Ascension scene according to the principle of duality.

The Ascension as hinge

Ascension
Luke 24
Acts 1

Mission in Jerusalem	Mission in Jerusalem
Lk. 19.41–24.49	Acts 1.12–8.1a
Mission in Samaria and Judea	Mission in Judea and Samaria
Lk. 9.51–19.40	Acts 8.1b–11.18
Mission in Galilee	Mission to 'ends of earth'
Lk. 4.14–9.50	Acts 11.19–28.31

This scheme, however, does not take account of the Infancy Gospel of Luke or of the incidents before Lk. 4.14. We shall return to the Ascension account as we consider one of the major features of the double-work.

Luke–Acts as a Single Two-Part Work?

The view that Acts completes the story begun in the Gospel of Luke is stressed by Tannehill (1986–89) and Johnson (1991–92). Neither part is complete without the other. While the Gospel alone could be classified as an ancient 'biography', and the Acts alone as some kind of 'history' of significant events, the fact that the two form one work subordinates each half to the literary whole.

General acceptance of this insight should be followed by an insistence that any part of either volume should be viewed against the background of the whole work. Despite the enthusiasm with which scholars agree that the two books are two volumes of one work, much of the work done on one volume does little more than pay lip-service to the other. Up to very recently, for example, the major series of commentaries on the New Testament have Luke and the Acts examined by two different scholars. The recent commentaries on both books by Tannehill (1986–89) and

Johnson (1991–92) mark a welcome development in recognizing the unity of the two volumes and respecting their literary coherence.

If Luke–Acts is a narrative unity, telling one story, then each section of the two volume work is related to the overall story. But in what sense are the two one work? Did Luke compose the whole work as a unity, but in two volumes? Or did he first write the gospel, and subsequently the second volume? Or, thirdly, did he compose Acts first, and then a volume dealing with the life of Jesus? It is only if Luke composed the whole work as a unity that we can talk of his overall purpose in writing the two volume work.

Moreover, a number of features force us to question the validity of the literary unity of Luke–Acts. If it is a narrative unity, it is unique in the history of Early Christianity. While there are several examples of the genre of gospel, in addition to the canonical ones, and there are several different additional acts, there is no other example of a two volume gospel–acts. Moreover, there is no support in the manuscript tradition for the narrative unity of Luke–Acts. Thirdly, some explanation must be found for the stylistic differences between the two volumes, for example, those most recently examined by J. Dawsey (1989).

Notwithstanding the strength of the evidence from both the content of the work and the tradition, not all scholars are convinced by the arguments which are advanced in favour of the literary unity of Luke–Acts. In addition to Dawsey (1989), Parsons regards the two as interrelated but independent works (1987), and Pervo (1987) argues for a separation of the two parts into two different literary classes.

The Genre of Luke–Acts

Are the Gospels Biographies?
In 1978 C.H. Talbert attempted to classify the Gospels against a background of literature contemporaneous with them. He designated them as biographies in the Greco-Roman sense. A librarian in antiquity, then, would have catalogued Mark and John with the *Type B* biographies, which aim at dispelling 'a false image of the teacher', and provide 'a true model to follow' (1978: 94). They would share a shelf with Xenophon's *Memorabilia*, Philodemus' *Life of Epicurus*, Philostratus' *Life of Appolonius of Tyana*, and so on. Matthew's gospel would have been catalogued along with *Type E* biographies, which validate the teaching of a philosopher or ruler, and would be on the same shelf as

Porphyry's *Life of Plotinus*, Andronicus' *Life of Aristotle*, and Philo's *Life of Moses*, all of which are concerned with the teaching of the master and the exegesis of that teaching.

Finally, Luke–Acts, because it deals with the life of Jesus (Gospel) and his continued presence in the work of his successors (Acts), would join, among others, the anonymous third-century BC *Life of Aristotle*, and Diogenes Laertius' *Lives of Eminent Philosophers* (Type D). The purpose of such works, giving first the life of the founder of the philosophical school, and then the lists, or narratives of successors, was to demonstrate the identity of the true followers of the founder (Talbert 1978: 106).

The fact that Luke–Acts deals first with the life of the founder of a (religious) community, and that the second part, the Acts, deals with his disciples and successors suggests that the work belongs to that category of Greco-Roman biographies of philosophers which may be designated *succession narratives*. Such works arose in a milieu in which there was a struggle over where the true tradition was to be found in the present (Talbert 1978: 108).

While Talbert's views are a welcome challenge to the notion that the Gospels and Luke–Acts represent a unique literary form, and his categorization of the work respects its two-volume character, his designation of it as belonging to the category of *succession narrative* needs more support than he adduces (see the critique in Aune 1987: 79). For example, Diogenes Laertius, the author of what Talbert sees as the chief 'parallel' for Luke–Acts, wrote two centuries later than Luke–Acts.

Talbert's attempt to verify the existence of a specific, identifiable genre into which to fit Luke–Acts is not altogether convincing: 'There are many other analogies on the market: memoir, apologia, encomium, aretalogy, false history, novel or romance, however these various types be severally defined; on the Jewish side, we have midrash or lectionary as possibilities' (Hemer 1989: 39).

Burridge's recent work concentrates on the genre of gospel, and compares the four canonical Gospels with the literary characteristics of Greco-Roman biography. He shows convincingly that, in the matters of the titles, the opening formulae, the subject, the external features such as their prose character, their size, structure, scale, literary units, use of sources and methods of characterization, the four canonical Gospels reflect the same *family resemblance* as one finds in the Graeco-Roman biographies (1992: 191-206). His examination of such internal features as the settings, topics, atmosphere, quality of characterization, and range of purposes, style and social setting convinces him that there is a high degree of correlation between the generic features of Greco-Roman biographies and the synoptic Gospels. He concludes, 'While they may well form their own subgenre because of their shared content, the synoptic gospels belong within the overall genre of *bioi*' (pp. 218-19). The same is true for the Fourth Gospel (pp. 220-39).

Acts as 'Novel'
Richard Pervo deals with the genre of Acts in isolation from Luke. In his estimation Luke and Acts represent different genres (1987: 4). Pervo's aim is to elucidate the *entertaining* nature of Acts (p. xi) and to show how pervasive that element is (p. 11). He takes the title of his work from Horace: 'The one who combines profit with delight, equally pleasing and admonishing the reader, captures all the plaudits'

> Omne tulit punctum qui miscuit utile dulci,
> Lectorem delectando pariterque monendo (Ars Poetica 343-44).

According to Pervo the Acts should be classified as one type of *historical novel* (1987: 122), and not as history. Its purpose is to edify its readers, showing in an entertaining way that virtue is superior to vice. It shares with ancient novels a fascination for escapes which often require miraculous intervention (e.g. the escape from prison in Philippi, Acts 16.16-40). Pervo focuses attention on the fictional elements of the arrests and imprisonments (e.g. 3.1–4.31), persecutions and martyrdom (e.g. 21.27–22.29), mob scenes (e.g. 16.19-23), trial stories (e.g. 25.6-12), and on travel and shipwreck (e.g. 27.1–28.16).

Pervo's designation of Acts as a *historical novel* is not very helpful, especially since there is no agreement about what constitutes the genre of novel. His definition of the *novel* as consisting of material + manner + style + structure (1987: 114) is much too vague for defining genre. He admits in his conclusion that 'the essence of the novel resists rigid classification' (p. 136). While Pervo's work itself is novel, it suffers from the limitation that its argument consists in piling up claim upon claim. Moreover, it does not help us to distinguish between the conventional methods of a dramatic historian and those of a writer of fiction which are tied to quite different purposes. In exaggerating what he regards as the fictional element in Acts he dismisses the factual. In any event, one could not legitimately extrapolate from an examination of the marvellous elements in Acts to draw conclusions about the character of Lk. 4.16-30.

Luke–Acts as 'History'
The preface of Luke has appeared to many to offer substantial indications of the author's interest in historiography, with its reference to accuracy, research and investigation. The style of the preface, together with its construction and vocabulary, was considered to be reminiscent of the prefaces of (some, at least) historians in antiquity (see Aune 1987: 90). However, Luke's statement of interest in following the methods of historical investigation of itself could not guarantee historical reliability, since he may have been merely conforming to a convention. Moreover, even if Luke could be compared to historians of antiquity, e.g., Thucydides, this would not satisfy questions about factual accuracy, since, especially in the case of speeches, one must allow for the possibility that reported speech may reflect the rhetorical skills of the historians, rather than merely the more passive transmission of what actually was said (Alexander 1993: 4).

Luke begins his work with a preface to the two volumes (Lk. 1.1-4), and the second volume with a secondary preface (Acts 1.1-5). Josephus' *Against Apion* is similar to Luke in that respect (1.1-5 and 2.1-2). The preface of Luke–Acts describes it as a narrative (*diēgēsis*) (Lk. 1.1), a term which suggests that the author was determined to write an account of what happened. The preface has a dedication, mentions the author's predecessors, states his appropriate methodology, and refers to the intention of his writing.

Since Luke–Acts reacts comfortably to the traditions of the Old Testament, we know that the author shares with it the central notions that God is the Lord of History, and that his dealings with Israel involved the promise of descendants, deliverance from slavery, settlement in the land of Canaan, the Sinaitic Covenant, and the Covenant with David. His fascination with Jesus, and with the developments after his Ascension, of course, is obvious. But the question remains, whether Luke–Acts is a work of history, approximating to our criteria of historiography? Allowing for the fact that there is no such thing as objective history, and that all accounts are interpretations, can we have any confidence that its accounts of words and deeds are close to what actually happened? Or are we dealing with some kind of imaginative reconstruction of history, which has more to do with fiction than with biography or history?

The achievement of any historian in antiquity must be judged in accordance with the criteria agreed to be normative at the time. Writing

1. Preliminary Questions
29

history in antiquity involved many different elements and skills. In general, ancient historians preferred oral over written sources. First-hand evidence had pride of place, but, of course, reliance on others was dictated when the historian was not present at the relevant events. Eyewitnesses and other reliable authorities could be interviewed, making whatever checks as were necessary. Documentary sources when available were used. It appears that it was normal for a historian to write a draft of the work, into which many details were added later. With regard to the faithful recording of things, Aune concludes, 'Ancient historians freely abridged, omitted, or expanded material, made substitutions from other sources, shaped and coloured the narrative and invented minor improvements in detail' (1987: 82). However, such a general assumption is not a reliable basis on which to judge specific cases, such as the relationship between the record of the Nazareth scene and what actually took place.

When one examines the attitude of historians to speeches clearly there is a divergence in practice. Thucydides says of his own practice, 'My habit has been to make the speakers say what was in my opinion demanded of them by the various occasions, of course adhering as closely as possible to the general sense of what they really said' (1.22.1). Later historians moved away from the rational historicism of Thucydides, and some included speeches which were the historian's inventions which displayed his own rhetorical skills. Polybius, in his turn, criticized this practice, and insisted that the peculiar function of history was to discover the words actually spoken, whatever they were (12.25a.5-25b.1). Nevertheless, 'Apart from Thucydides and Polybius, speeches composed for historical works were not based on actual speeches but were rhetorical compositions judged "suitable" (*to prepon*) for the person to whom they were ascribed in the particular situation envisaged' (Aune 1987: 93).

Greco-Roman historians were committed to writing history that was true, useful and entertaining. In his manual, *How to Write History*, the second-century AD satirist, Lucian of Samosata, complained that history has but one function, usefulness that is the product of truth. He complained that every person was writing history, 'nay more, they are all Thucydides, Herodotuses and Xenophons' (1.2-5). Lucian set out to describe the criteria for history writing.

Pervo claims that 'Although it would be relatively simple to demonstrate that Acts violates every single canon advanced by Lucian, that is not material. Lucian ridiculed works he regarded as poor specimens of history writing. A book like Acts did not even meet the standards of the works he despised...Acts was simply falsehood through and through' (1987: 7-8). Pervo's submissiveness to the exaggeration of his own valuable insight is not to be recommended.

If Luke was a historian, what kind of one was he? The author of Luke–Acts set out to narrate (aspects of) the early history of the Christian Church, from its origins in Judaism and in the ministry of Jesus, to its penetration into various areas of Asia Minor and Greece, finally ending up in Rome. There is no reason to imagine that he sought to give a complete picture of the expansion of Christianity. He says virtually nothing about the advance of the Gospel east of the Jordan, in Egypt or even its establishment in Rome. His achievement should be credited with what it is, the first attempt to provide a history of the early church, and one which was a model for imitators down to the more complete Church History of Eusebius (c. 325 AD).

For my particular purposes, I wish to enquire whether the account of Lk. 4.16-30 comes close to describing what was said and done one Sabbath day in the synagogue at Nazareth when Jesus came. Or, is the account better understood as some kind of historicized fiction? Are we dealing with history, or with some mixture of fact and fiction (*faction*), in which the author employed some of the features of fiction-writing, giving the scene a dramatic quality that nobody present on the day would recognize as a fair description of what happened? Did Jesus actually say what is reported, did the events take place as described, or are we dealing with the literary creation of the author, or his source?

Historicity and Luke–Acts: A Historical Survey
The question, 'What really happened?' is a perfectly legitimate one, even if there will be considerable difficulty in answering it satisfactorily. It is a question of historicity, and no amount of investigation into such questions as the literary or theological purpose of the work can give the answer to it. Scholastic investigation moves from one emphasis to another. The overwhelming interest that has established the consensus in this century has not been on matters of historicity, but rather on the sources of documents, and on the editorial skills and especially the theological interests of the author.

The reflections of John Chrysostom, who was much closer to the mind of Hellenistic historiographers than we are, are instructive. He preached fifty-five homilies on the Acts of the Apostles in Constantinople (400 AD) and saw the work as a type of history. He casually refers to the author as an historiographer *(historiographos, Hom.* 21, *PG* 60.163; cf. *Hom.* 28, *PG* 60.211; *Hom.* 35, *PG* 50.254).

For Chrysostom, the authenticity of Luke's history is guaranteed by his sources, among which the oral are preferable to the written, and the eyewitness ones the best of all. Luke showed his credentials in the Gospel, the source of which was the eyewitness of the apostles. His credentials in the Acts, he claims, are even more impressive, having himself been a companion of Paul, and hence an eyewitness of some of what happened.

Chrysostom echoes the conventional view that 'in matter of belief, the very thing that gives one a right to be believed, is the having learned from eyewitnesses: whereas the other appears to foolish persons mere parade and pretension' *(Hom.* 1, *PG* 60.18). He notes that Luke does not hide details even when they might not be flattering. On the other hand he does not give too much information which would make the reader dull.

Chrysostom believed that God acts in all events of history, and that the purpose of history writing is primarily didactic, since we learn from the record of events, as we do from the events themselves. The paraenetic function of history, an aspect of the theme of the usefulness of history, common in Hellenistic historiography, is vital for him. Acts teaches us by providing pictures of worthy persons in the earliest church, ancestors of the Christians of Chrysostom's generation, who are to be emulated (Wylie 1991: 68).

Wylie concludes her study of Chrysostom's view of Acts as a work of history as follows:

> John was reading the book of Acts in the context of the Hellenistic (not the modern) sense of the word. Many of the methods and values of Greek historiography influenced John's reading of the text...Although ultimately John was still a Christian preacher whose main goal was to interpret the biblical text for his church, his interest in moral interpretation should not be divorced from his recognition of the text as history and his Hellenistic perspective on what that means. His reading of Acts as the story of the church's ancestry provided the means to relate the history to his congregation (p. 72).

Against the background of nineteenth-century scepticism concerning the reliability of Luke as a historiographer, a number of scholars changed their assessment of the author in the course of their investigations. For example, the English scholar W.M. Ramsay judged him to be meticulously accurate in his historical setting of Acts 14. His subsequent studies and field-work led him to the conclusion that Luke's history of early Christian origins was unsurpassed for its accuracy (1915: 37-38, 80, 89). Although Ramsay's meticulous field-work was of the highest quality (see 1890; 1895–97), his general conclusions go well beyond the evidence (e.g. 1930: v). For even the greatest accuracy in some details (e.g. 1915: 96-97) is no guarantee of general reliability.

Adolf von Harnack, the celebrated German historian of the Early Church, was also a convert to the assessment of Acts as a reliable historical source. He devoted three volumes to Acts (1906; 1908; 1911) and concluded that from the standpoint of historiography it is a solid, respectable, and in some respects an outstanding work. He went on to say that it is a true work of history, not only in its major features, but in the majority of its details (1911: 222). Moreover, Eduard Meyer, one of the great masters of the history of antiquity, put Luke on the same level as the great historians of ancient times, such as Polybius and Livy. A significant stimulus to enquiry into the linguistic, geographical, archaeological and historical background to Luke–Acts was provided by the monumental five-volume work on the beginnings of Christianity, edited by Foakes-Jackson and Lake (1920–33).

But more recently, when it comes to investigating the two-volume work of Luke–Acts, there is a surprising lack of interest in what really happened. Since scholars deal with the two volumes separately (while paying lip-service to their unity), and since most of the relevant studies are on the Acts of the Apostles, an overview of the most significant scholarship of Acts will be of value for our purposes also. One will notice, from about 1950, the total eclipse of Luke as a reliable historian, coupled with a very positive assessment of him as a theologian. The scene began to change in 1970, with the appearance of several works reopening the question of the value of Luke as an historiographer.

Martin Dibelius, one of the most influential figures in the study of the Acts this century, effectively bypassed the question of historicity. He claimed that such a matter was fraught with subjectivity, whereas the form-critical method led to results which were universally valid, and was capable of leading to less subjective and more verifiable criteria for the historicity of the tradition (1961: 91). If Luke was a historian at all, he was a 'literary historian'—that is, someone who was not above abandoning the exact reproduction of a tradition 'for a higher historical truth'—rather than a historian in our modern sense (pp. 97, 107). The author of Luke–Acts, in his view, was a creative writer who invented speeches, and was not a person primarily interested in communicating what really happened, but one whose orientation was fundamentally influenced by his post-apostolic theology.

Haenchen went further in his skepticism concerning the historical value of Acts. His commentary on Acts (1971) marks a turning-point in the interpretation of the book. He abandoned Dibelius' view that the author was a companion of Paul, and regarded the 'we' passages of Acts as a literary device to add more credibility to the account, and to give the reader the impression that a fellow-traveller had written it. He allowed Luke great literary scope in embellishing at will the tradition passed on to him, since he had the pious purpose of influencing more effectively the church of his own day. Although he granted that the author was indeed a historian, and did write a historical work, he could not compare it with the works of a Xenophon or a Thucydides, since the author lacked adequate historical foundations. Moreover, Haenchen suggests that his readers seem to have been gluttons for edification, who would not object to the suppression of fact, nor to the 'dramatic technique of scene-setting in an episode where, untrammelled by tradition, he enjoyed freedom of movement' (1971: 107).

Luke was driven by his theological purpose, which, according to Haenchen, was concerned with the expectation of the imminent end of the world, and the mission to the Gentiles (1971: 94). The author enlivened bare facts by transforming a simple report into action, and by weaving a speech into it (pp. 104-105). Haenchen's understanding of the motivation of the author decides for him the historical value of the author's traditions, and of the work itself. He regards the Acts as some kind of first-century 'faction', in which there is a good deal more of creative fiction than historical fact, since he allows the author to suppress, change, or even invent facts in order to advance the purpose which Haenchen assigns to him. Pervo judges that Haenchen's method results in a two-headed Luke, 'who was bumbling and incompetent as a historian yet brilliant and creative as an author' (1987: 3).

Conzelmann went further still in his disregard for the author of Acts as a recorder of what actually happened. In his view the whole of Acts

27, the account of the voyage and shipwreck, for example, is the author's invention (1963: 72-81, 249). Every part of what might otherwise be regarded as having historical value is relegated to the category of creative invention, for reasons of literary and theological effect.

While there is an increasingly louder chorus of voices calling for a more critical view of Luke as a historiographer, it is often the case that only lip-service is paid to the view that Luke is a historian as well as a theologian. On changing from reading History to Theology, Drury was led 'to a certain bafflement', in that 'History was much pondered and invoked in New Testament studies but practised in a less pervasive and delicate way' (1976: xii), a charge of which he is not himself altogether innocent (see Prior 1979: 5-6). The reader expects from an author who castigates New Testament scholars for their neglect of Luke as a historian more evidence for his refusal to acknowledge the possibility that Jesus was a story-teller comparable to Luke. For a work that professes to enquire into Luke's Gospel with the nose of a historian there is an unfortunate agnosticism on the very question of historicity: 'Little will be said here of the factual value of Luke's work' (Drury 1976: 12).

Unlike C.K. Barrett, who regards Polybius and Plutarch, Josephus and Tacitus as Luke's fellows (1961: 9), and C.H. Talbert (1978), Drury places Luke firmly within the tradition of Jewish historiography with its great love of midrash and story. Luke is 'one of the greatest narrative midrashists' (Drury 1976: 12). His fascination for a midrashic interpretation tends to force conclusions on the evidence. His failure to deal with I.H. Marshall's important study (1970) betrays a serious weakness in the work. Although Marshall puts more stress on Luke as theologian he does show that the two roles go together (cf. Hemer 1977–78).

Nevertheless, until the recent challenge to the consensus, the historical value of Luke's work has been considered to be extremely low. 'It is as preacher (following Dibelius) and writer (following Cadbury) that Luke is viewed today. The understanding of Luke as a historian, whether good, bad, or indifferent, occupies only third place in today's thinking about Acts' (Pervo 1987: 2). This tendency is illustrated in one of the most recent commentaries on Luke–Acts. Johnson provides a literary analysis. 'I do not take up issues concerning the origin of a story in the life of Jesus, or the development of a tradition before it reaches Luke' (1991: xi). Alexander's study of the Lukan preface argues that it lies outside the category of Greek historiography, but belongs to the category of *scientific* or technical explanatory prefaces, with specific

Christian elements (1993: 147-48). However, although it is very insightful on the nature and function of the preface, her work does not advance the case significantly, either for or against the wider question of the historicity of Luke–Acts.

There are several signs of a change in the estimation of Luke as a respectable historian. Among the recent works which seek to place Acts within the ambit of Hellenistic historiography are Plümacher (1972), Gasque (1975; 1989), Hengel (1979), van Unnik (1979), Aune (1987), Bovon (1987), Donelson (1987), Hemer (1989) and Lüdemann (1989).

Gasque (1975) surveyed the scholarship on the historicity of Acts, and his work was followed by Hengel's stimulating survey (1979). This then was followed by Lüdemann's book on the historicity of Acts. However, the most comprehensive challenge to the prevailing view of the author of Luke–Acts has come posthumously from the pen of Colin J. Hemer. He insists that 'The question of Acts' relationship to the history which it purports to relate is too important and fundamental not to be re-opened' (1989: 29). One of the major factors which accounts for the obvious neglect of the question of historicity is 'the current all-pervasive interest in Lukan theology' (p. 2).

The three major works of Dibelius, Conzelmann and Haenchen, which focused on Luke the Theologian, had the inevitable effect of casting scepticism on the historicity of Acts. This consensus has been challenged, particularly by Hengel (1979). Elsewhere Hengel affirms: 'We are concerned only with the *truth*, theological and historical. Truth is our sole obligation; we have to seek it and present it, and in the end it will prevail against all our conjectures, all our desires to be right, our imaginative constructions, and our anxiety' (1983: xiv). Hemer insists that both history and theology must be brought to bear on the question. The questions posed by the non-expert, such as, 'Did it really happen?', or, in a more sophisticated fashion, 'Is Acts historically trustworthy?' are questions of some import, and attempts should be made to address them (1989: 25).

For Hemer, Acts was written by Luke, a companion of Paul. For that reason, as well as many others, Hemer has considerable respect for Luke as a faithful witness of what happened. Inevitably his work will be undervalued because it will be considered to be overtly apologetical. However, all reconstructions operate in terms of a particular hypothesis, and what distinguishes Hemer's hypothesis from the prevailing ones is the fact that it supports the more traditional view.

Hemer ends his study:

> The conclusions which result from all this work may be regarded as unfashionable as, indeed, only a few years ago, with the enquiry itself; clearly the time has come for a change. Much good work has been done in the area of Luke's theological interests, but the historical questions are not thereby answered, nor can they be thereby ignored. As our knowledge of Hellenistic history continues to grow through the discovery and publication of new inscriptions and other evidence, our picture of early Christianity and the documents it inspired will naturally grow accordingly (Hemer 1989: 414).

According to Aune, Luke–Acts is a popular 'general history', written by an amateur historian with credentials in Greek rhetoric. He adds that historians were trained in rhetoric, not in historiography: 'Using his rhetorical skills, Luke adapted the genre of general history, one of the more eclectic genres of antiquity, as an appropriate literary vehicle for depicting the origins and development of Christianity' (Aune 1987: 77).

If source and redaction questions have dominated the study of the Acts up to recently, it is clear that the value of Luke as a historian is being considered afresh. The future investigation of Acts will have to take much more account of the historical value of Acts, and this will have to be done in conjunction with the closest attention to matters of form and redaction criticism. 'Unless redaction critics pay more attention to the relation of the gospels to the historical ministry of Jesus their readers may be forced into opting for a form of gnosticism in which Luke, rather than Jesus, is proclaimed as Lord!' (Prior 1979: 6).

The Genre of Luke–Acts: Conclusion
The recent scepticism regarding the historical reliability of Acts is strongly influenced, if not altogether determined, by decisions taken by scholars regarding the intention of the author. A clear distinction must be made between the conscious intention of an author, and what readers consider it to be on the basis of their reading of the text. This distinction is all the more apposite when one considers the great diversity of scholarly opinion regarding the intention of the author.

I have argued elsewhere that Luke–Acts was completed before the death of Paul. The most compelling argument is the failure of the author to mention the death of Paul, the persecution under Nero or the destruction of Jerusalem (Prior 1989: 72-73). I have exposed the implausibility of the prevailing view of a much later date, and have exposed the weakness of the arguments which regard Luke 13.35a; 19.43-44; 21.20-24 to have been written in the light of the destruction of Jerusalem in 70 AD. The Lukan texts predicting the destruction of Jerusalem reflect no more than the most general prediction of commonplace military strategy and consequent devastation. Had the Lukan texts the kind of detail one finds in Josephus' account of the siege (the number, location and dimensions of the platforms, the flames, the famine, the details of Titus' strategy, the bandits, the faction-fighting, or the like—cf. *War* 5), one might be more inclined to conclude that Luke's predictions were written in the knowledge of what actually took place. Luke 13.35; 19.43-44; 21.20-24 do not at all require a dating after the destruction of Jerusalem (Prior 1989: 195-56).

Aune concludes his discussion:

> Luke was a dramatic historian who framed his first book with two dramatic episodes, the Sermon at Nazareth (Lk. 4.16-30), prefiguring Jesus' rejection, execution, and resurrection, and the story of Jesus' resurrection appearance on the road to Emmaus (Lk. 24.13-35). Luke included many more dramatic episodes in Acts, where he was less constrained by his sources (Aune 1987: 128-29).

Talbert is both realistic and hopeful:

> The jury is still out on the issue. If the verdict can be reached, the genre of Luke–Acts might provide the clue for the relative ordering of the various themes isolated by redaction criticism and of the primary occasion that prompted the document. This methodology, moreover, need presuppose no source theories for Luke–Acts (1989: 310).

Burridge's work, which was undertaken with the expectation of exposing the untenability of regarding the gospels as belonging with the category of Greco-Roman biographies (1992: 105), illustrates the generic identity of all four gospels, and situates them firmly within that category. The association of Luke with Acts, however, complicates the issue. Maddox designates the double work as a *theological history* (1982: 16). Hengel, concentrating on Acts, prefers the category of *historical monograph* (1979: 36). Aune settles for *general history* (1987: 77). Burridge has shown that the borders between the genres of ancient historiography, monograph and biography are blurred and flexible. Moreover, he shows that the intention to entertain and edify, which inclined Pervo to place Acts outside the category of historiography, is to be found in ancient historiography also. He regards the insistence that Luke–Acts must be treated as one genre to be problematic, and agrees with Parsons that Luke could have produced two works, belonging to two distinct genres of literature (Burridge 1992: 245). The fact that no manuscript tradition puts the two volumes together, despite the four Gospels always being found together, weighs against regarding the two volumes of Luke as of the same literary genre. Acts reflects a wider scene than that of the Gospel, and if the Gospel can be seen to be a life of Jesus, elements of other genres such as history, monograph or romance start to appear in Acts (Burridge 1992: 246).

In the past Luke–Acts has been considered to belong to the genre of ancient history. Recently the case has been established that the Gospels belong to the category of biography. Claims continue to be made that Acts shares the characteristics of a third genre, popular in Greek antiquity, a romance novel. Little is to be gained by forcing the complex work into a single determinative genre. To regard it as of a mixed genre brings us closer to the truth, since it allows the critic to respect the variety of characteristics of the double work.

My primary interest in enquiring into the genre of Luke–Acts is in the implications of the discussion for an assessment of Luke as a faithful reporter of what happened in the synagogue of Nazareth. Although one can never answer such questions with certainty, I am of the view that nothing in Luke–Acts should predispose one to presume that Luke's account of that occasion is unreliable as a witness to what really happened. Before moving on to a consideration of Lk. 4.16-30, however, it is necessary to enquire into the questions of the purpose(s) and theology of Luke–Acts.

The Purpose(s) of Luke–Acts

The difficulty in separating the notion of the purpose of Luke–Acts from that of the genre can be gauged by noting how frequently *purpose* occurred in our discussion of the genre. It is no less difficult to discuss the alleged purpose(s) of Luke–Acts independently of its alleged theology. The discussion of the purpose of Luke–Acts is very often confused with that of the putative theology of the work, and vice versa. Insofar as it is possible to do so, the two areas of investigation should be examined in a fashion which respects the diversity of the two questions, and the different methodologies appropriate to the two searches.

Whether it is possible or not to settle the question to a degree of satisfaction, the enquiry into the purpose of Luke–Acts is likely to bear much fruit in our understanding of the work. It is widely accepted that the composition of the writings of the New Testament, and of most writing, ought to be viewed against the background of the period of their composition. Each writer wrote in a particular social, cultural, religious and political context. If only we knew with some degree of assurance the circumstances of the composition of Luke–Acts, we would be in a better position to evaluate it as a document of its own period, and to discuss its relevance for today.

Unfortunately we know so little about the circumstances of the early Christian communities between the years 60–95 that the interval is sometimes spoken of as the *tunnel period*. Since very little is known from outside the text about the circumstances of its composition, we are left enquiring into the information which the text itself provides.

Although the great Tübingen biblical scholar F.C. Baur was not the first to recognize that authors exhibit a particular tendency in their writing, it was he who first insisted that any age can be understood only against a knowledge of the central problem of that age. In his view the problem of the New Testament period was the legitimacy of the Gentile mission outside the law. In Baur's estimation, the author of Acts sought to reconcile the opposing views of those who supported the Pauline gospel, and those who supported that preached by the other Apostles.

Historical Overview
As soon as scholarly criticism abandoned the idea that the author of Acts was merely reproducing what happened, there was a drive 'to appreciate the impulse which drove the author's pen' (Haenchen 1971: 15). The diversity of views reflecting the tendency of the author, as surveyed by Haenchen (pp. 15-24), ought to guard us against any dogmatism in the question:

- 1777 J.D. Michaelis: Acts had two intentions: 1. to give a trustworthy report of the first outpouring of the Holy Spirit, and the first miracles corroborating the truth of the Christian religion; 2. to recount the circumstances which proved the validity of the Gentile mission over against the Jews. Luke is said to have written during Paul's Roman captivity.
- 1798 J.J. Griesbach: Acts intended to defend Paul against the attacks of Jewish Christians.
- 1817 S.G. Frisch: Acts was attempting to convince Jews and Jewish Christians that the worth and standing of Jesus

Messiah was greater than that of Moses, and that it was the will of God and of his Messiah Jesus that all men should share in the Christian salvation.

1836 K.A. Credner: As a disciple of Paul, the author of Acts selected only what was important for Pauline doctrine. The whole work is a historical commentary on Rom. 1.16; 3.9; 10.12. The author intended to write a third book, and that is why he fails to mention Paul's death.

1836 Karl Schrader concluded that the Paul of Acts was different from the Paul of the Epistles. 'He therefore ventured to suggest that the apologetic purpose of Acts had compromised its historical reliability' (Haenchen 1971: 16).

1836–38 F.C. Baur: He proposed three theses: 1. Paul preached a different gospel from that of the other Apostles. There were, then, two forms of early Christianity: Paulinist and Judaist. 2. Acts was an attempt to reconcile the two. 3. Any age can be understood only against a knowledge of the central problem of the age. In every age there is a struggle between the old and the new, until they are reconciled in a higher unity. *The problem of the New Testament period was the legitimacy of the Gentile mission without the law.* Acts seeks to reconcile the opposing parties, and therefore it must be considered to come towards the end of the process. Acts is therefore unhistorical, and not the work of Luke. Nevertheless, because of the reliability of (some of) his sources (e.g. sketches or diaries of Luke) Acts was of some historical value.

Tendency Criticism (Tendenzkritik) in scholarship was firmly established by F.C. Baur, who argued that the Acts of the Apostles had as its aim the smoothing out of tensions which in fact existed in the Early Church, the tensions between the Jewish element in the Church, as represented by Jerusalem, Peter and James, and that part of the community more open to Gentiles, and represented by the diaspora Christian communities and championed by Paul, Barnabas and other missionaries. Baur affirmed that the Acts of the Apostles was not a guide to understanding the realities of the life of the Christian community at the purported time, but rather was to be seen as the author's attempt to play down the realities of the tension that existed.

1846   Albert Schwegler denounced Acts as not having any value for the time with which it purports to deal, having some only for the time of its composition, namely 110–150, when the Jewish form of Christianity was supposedly still dominant.

1854   Eduard Zeller argued similarly that Acts had no intention of presenting an historical account, but was striving to influence the conflicting parties of Paulinists and Judaists. It was composed 110–130.

1851   G.V. Lechler opposed the approach of Baur and the Tübingen school. He insisted that the antipathy which Baur proposed existed between the Jewish and Gentile wings of the Church was exaggerated. Paul was no assailant of the Law. On the contrary he observed the Jewish feasts and the Law. Acts, whose author is Luke, portrays him correctly. More seriously for the Baur thesis, Lechler argued that Jewish Christianity had lost its influence after the destruction of Jerusalem and the death of most of the Apostles. It could not have been as prominent in the second century as Baur's hypothesis required it to be. Instead Lechler proposed that the Catholic Church developed within Gentile Christianity itself, and indeed in Pauline circles, by a process of the natural evolution of its structures.

1857   Albrecht Ritschl, similarly, argued that Catholic Christianity was not the result of reconciliation between Pauline and Jewish Christianity, but was a development from Gentile Christianity alone, which incidentally had never been under Paul's complete sway.

1850–52   Bruno Bauer insisted that 1. In Acts, the Paul of the Epistles has undergone a major transformation: 'the religious dialectician, accustomed to fight only with words, is supplanted by the "wizard" who "dazzles his opponents". The Apostle who "fulfils his historical work through sufferings, struggles and trials" becomes the "miracle-worker"'—and, quoting Bauer himself, 'The wizard has nothing in common with the religious dialectician; the miracle-worker contradicts the spiritual hero' (Haenchen 1971: 21). 2. Acts takes away from Paul the honour of the mission to the Gentiles, and hands it over to Peter. It presents the mission as sanctioned by Peter, with Paul becoming a strict servant of the Law. 3. F.C. Baur

	was wrong. The conflict between Paulinism and Jewish Christianity no longer existed. The victor was that 'Judaism' in which the existing church saw itself. The Paul of Acts is no single-handed revolutionary, but one who is absorbed into the holy chain of tradition. Haenchen cannot disguise his disappointment with Bauer's relegation of the Pauline Epistles to 'works of free reflection', and ridicules him for considering Acts to have been a necessary precursor of Galatians (1971: 21).
1882–86	A.D. Loman claimed that the Paul of the Great Epistles, no less than the Paul of Acts, was an idealization of the historical Paul—'the progressive evolutionary stages of a legend of Paul'.
1888	Rudolf Steck declared Loman to be correct. 'We shall have to get used to the idea that no Apostle wrote anything, any more than Jesus himself did.' The Pauline Letters were written by a school. He concluded that the report in Acts is the fundamental datum for the historical situation. Haenchen's own position shines through: 'Thus we come to the grotesque spectacle of "ultra-radicals" transformed into champions of Acts' (1971: 22).
1866	Ernest Renan described the Acts as semi-historical, semi-legendary, which although false in nearly every detail, enshrines valuable truths for the finding.
1870	Franz Overbeck assembled the case against Baur's hypothesis. Acts does not stand midway between the early Christian parties. The Gentile Christianity of Acts is not Pauline, nor is its Judaism that of the first Apostles. With the exception of its universalism, the rest of Paul is put aside, because he is no longer understood. The purpose of Acts is to win the favour of the Roman authorities. The Gentile mission in Acts is not derived from the theology of Paul, but is presented as being part of the programme of the community from the very beginning (Acts 1.8). The conflict Paul has is with the *unbelieving* Jews, not with Judaists. This distorted picture of Paul puts the Acts in the period 110–30, during the rule of Trajan.
1897	Johannes Weiss, similarly, sees the *apologia* before the Romans as central to Acts. Acts presents Christians as

1. Preliminary Questions

guiltless, and Christianity as the fulfilment of the hopes of Judaism.

Haenchen completes his overview of the age of tendency-criticism with the comment, 'After this work of Weiss's, "tendency-criticism" fell silent' (1971: 24).

The inability of scholars to determine the purpose of Luke–Acts with any degree of unanimity is reflected in the modern period also, as can be seen from the selection of modern writers on the subject:

Hans Conzelmann, in his seminal work on Luke's Gospel, argued that Luke's work was his response to the embarrassment of the delay of the parousia (1953). B.S. Easton argued that in protesting the innocence of Jesus in the Passion account, and of Paul in Acts 13–28, and in insisting that Christianity was nothing other than fulfilled Judaism, Luke–Acts was an apologia of Christianity to Rome (1954). A.J. Mattill, Jr on the other hand, argued that it was an apologia for Paul against Jewish Christian charges (1970). J.C. O'Neill, who puts the composition of the work in the period 115–130, concluded that Luke–Acts was Luke's apologia for the Christian faith, which had a burning inner purpose of bringing non-Christian people to the faith (1970). I.H. Marshall concluded that Luke–Acts was primarily for Christian believers, and secondarily for the evangelization of non-believers (1970, 1978).

Several scholars have avoided the temptation to restrict the purpose of the work to one single item, and have suggested a combination of purposes. E. Earle Ellis argued that Luke–Acts has a triple purpose, namely, 1. to combat the gnostic dehistoricizing of the gospel, 2. to correct the view of those who saw the Kingdom of God solely in terms of an imminent return of Jesus, and 3. to describe the relationship of Judaism to Christianity (1972, 1974). S.G. Wilson concluded that Luke's history writing had a pastoral purpose, namely the offering of counsel to his fellow-believers (1973). In the view of C.H. Talbert, Luke–Acts was written for the express purpose of serving as a defence against Gnosticism (1966).

R. Maddox concludes his study of the subject with the judgment that two words stand out from the preface of Luke as evident markers of his intention: *peplērophorēmena* (those things that have been fulfilled among us), and *asphaleia* (the reliability of the message heard). These words indicate that the work 'aimed at reassuring the Christian community about the significance of the tradition and faith in which it stands...(Luke) writes to reassure the Christians of his day that their faith in Jesus is no aberration, but the authentic goal towards which God's ancient dealings with Israel were driving' (1982: 186-87). His final words are, 'With such a message of reassurance, Luke summons his fellow-Christians to worship God with whole-hearted joy, to follow Jesus with unwavering loyalty, and to carry on with zeal, through the power of the Spirit, the charge to be his witnesses to the end of the earth' (p. 187).

In my view also, the key to the purpose lies in the preface, in which the author indicates his intentions, namely, to give an orderly account of what happened in the ministry of Jesus, who was empowered by the Spirit of God, and of the continuation of that ministry by the disciples, also empowered by the same Spirit of God. The author carries out his task beginning with events in the temple in Jerusalem, detailing the ministry of Jesus in Galilee (4.14–9.50), after which he sets his face for Jerusalem. The climax of the Gospel occurs in Jerusalem. However, it is clear from the words of the ascending Jesus that Jerusalem is not to be the permanent abode of the Christian Church. Its destination is to extend to the capital of the Roman Empire, the city of Rome. Luke–Acts, then, charts the progress of the Gospel from Jerusalem, the capital of Judaism, to Rome, the secular city.

Theology of Luke–Acts

It is obvious from examining the literature on the subject that the question of the Theology of Luke–Acts, or of the Acts of the Apostles, is one which has not been decided upon with any degree of unanimity among scholars. The reasons for this failure to identify the Theology of Acts are multiple. Perhaps one of them is the relative neglect of the book in many scholarly circles. It has been said that the Acts has not received the same attention in Protestant scholarship as has been gained by Pauline studies, because the Acts is considered to be a document of triumphalism, whereas the theology of Paul is very much related to the Cross.

Another factor influencing the modern assessment of the Acts is the seminal work of Hans Conzelmann who, in his study on Luke (*Die Mitte der Zeit*, literally *the mid-point of time*, but translated into English as *The Theology of Saint Luke*, 1960), set the tone for much of the subsequent debate on the theology of Luke. In general terms, he regarded the theology of Luke and the accompanying volume of Acts to reflect a very significant diminution of the eschatological fervour of the Christian message. Eschatology was pushed into the distance, and the in-between time was to be effected through a long process of acclimatization within, and, to some extent, conformity with, the drive of secular society.

In developed forms of such reflections, it has been claimed that Luke–Acts represents the phenomenon of 'Early Catholicism', that is, a system in which the eschatological fervour of the Christian community has solidified into set dogmatic statements, highly organized ecclesiastical structures, and, in the most general terms, an encasement of the Spirit, preventing it exercising its capacity to blow where it wills. In the judgment of many Lutheran scholars, the documents of 'Early Catholicism' are 'a sad declension from the apostolic—especially the Pauline—gospel', and are judged to be 'not only post-apostolic in date but sub-apostolic in standard' (Bruce 1977: 51—but note that the quotation does not reflect the author's own view). The phenomenon of Early Catholicism is seen to reach its most disagreeable proportions in the Pastoral Epistles.

Many of these reflections derive from the perspective of the scholar, rather than from an unbiased examination of the text. Of course there is no such thing as a purely 'unbiased' reading of any literary text, since each reader sits in a particular context, working within particular presuppositions even before examining any text. To some extent, there will be things in any text which for whatever reason stimulate the reader, and these may be taken to have a power and an authority that does not coincide with the power and authority with which the writer intended to endow them.

When one examines in detail the task of describing the theology of Acts, one has to consider a number of basically methodological factors. First of all, one must be aware of the method of discerning such a theology. For example, is the method to derive from an examination of Luke–Acts in its totality? Or is one justified in searching for a theology of Acts, while only keeping half an eye on Luke? Or is one examining Acts as a free standing element of literature?

Another series of questions needs to be kept in mind.

1. *The Dating of Luke–Acts*
This will indicate something about the theology of the work. Of course one has to be very careful to avoid any kind of circular argumentation

which would run as follows: Acts reflects a late development of such and such, and therefore must be dated to the end of the first century. Then one begins another argument by saying, because Acts was written towards the end of the first century, it must have adapted itself to the conditions obtaining then.

An example of this procedure is provided by Haenchen. In dealing with the treatment of the expectation of the imminent end of the world, he states that 'When Luke wrote Acts, Paul had been executed and James the brother of the Lord had died a martyr; Christians had burned as living torches in the gardens of Nero; the Holy City and its Temple lay in rubble' (1971: 95). But Haenchen had not up to that time provided any argumentation for that conclusion.

2. The Sources of Acts

Since there is no consensus about the sources available to the author of the Acts, it is a matter of great difficulty to apply the same methods of investigation to that work as one applies to the investigation of the Gospel of Luke. Although a lively debate continues on the relationships between the synoptic gospels, the majority of scholars continue to hold the view that Luke had available to him the completed Gospel of Mark, and a sayings source *Q*. Although there continues to be a debate about the sources of Acts, there is no security in identifying them. This makes it extremely difficult, if not virtually impossible, to discern the theological principles of Acts, by way of enquiring into his redaction, or by means of compositional criticism, that is, how the author selected from, discarded, arranged and modified the sources available to him in his efforts to produce the final work.

3. The Speeches in Acts

Another source of supposed information critical to discerning the theology of Acts is the speeches in the work. Although it is not generally acknowledged to be the case, there is an *assumption* in the work of many commentators that the speeches are the composition of the author of the Acts—rather than the author's source's record of what was said. It continues to be the case that that assumption underpins the discussion about the theology of Acts, insofar as the theology is considered to be reflected in the speeches.

A major stimulus to justify this assumption is the comparison between the Paul reflected in the Acts and the Paul reflected in his own letters. No less than a thorough examination of the evidence of the Letters and that of the Acts would need to be undertaken before one could advance securely in the matter. The view taken here is that it is altogether unwarranted to conclude that a person's own expression of his perspectives is the only possible way of arriving at an understanding of his real views. In other words, it is not the case that autobiography contains the totality of the revelation of a person. We readily concede that the views of other people (biographies) are a great source of illumination in understanding a character.

The use of the speeches needs to be examined with considerable sensitivity, for a number of reasons. For example, to concentrate on the speeches as a guide to the theology of the author results in the isolation of the speeches from the overall narrative of the work. Since the Acts of the Apostles is a narrative which intertwines accounts of both incidents and speeches, its theological identity should reflect this structure. The movement within scholarship concerning the speeches has been admirably summed up by Talbert: 'Research on the speeches (of Acts) has moved from taking them as sermons of Peter and Paul, through taking them as examples of the earliest kerygma, to taking them as Lucan compositions' (1989: 310).

4. *Crucial Texts*

Another point of access into the theology of Luke–Acts is the investigation of what individual scholars regard as certain key or crucial texts. Various attempts have been made to identify key texts: for example, the Nazareth scene, the Ascension scene, the speech of Peter at Pentecost, or the closing of Acts. It has to be conceded that the identification and nomination of these key texts is the result of personal and individual predisposition or preference. It is a tendency of human nature, abundantly testified by examining the diversity of scholarly conclusions, that people can elevate into matters of crucial significance those items which they have identified for themselves as being important.

5. *The Tendency of the Author*

Another way to try to discover the theology of Acts is to attempt to identify what a scholar will consider to be the theological tendency or 'agenda' of the author. This approach is attractive, because it appears to offer some kind of answer to a question which is complex. The trouble with this methodology, however, is that an individual reader can discern one particular theme or apparent interest within the text, and then subsequently elevate this individual theme into a position that presents it as virtually *the* theology of Acts.

F.F. Bruce prefaces his remarks by claiming that Luke does not rank with Paul, John, or the writer to the Hebrews, 'but he is a theologian in his own right, bearing witness to the common faith of the church of his day with emphases which are distinguishable from those of the other NT writers' (1990: 60). He organizes his reflections on the Theology of Acts in the following categories: 1. The Doctrine of God; 2. The Doctrine of Christ; 3. The Doctrine of the Spirit; 4. The Church and its Ordinances; 5. The Gentile Mission; 6. Biblical Theology; 7. Soteriology; and 8. Eschatology. Bruce has no difficulty in supporting his statements with a range of textual references (1990: 60–66). The overall statement, however, is rather bland. It is in his comments on 'The Gentile Mission' that he comes nearest to treating a theme in Acts.

In my view, the universal mission of Jesus and the Church is at the heart of the two volumes of Luke–Acts, and it is to this theme that we now turn, not least because of its significance for the interpretation of the Nazareth text.

Universalism in Luke–Acts

The most striking aspect of the double work of Luke–Acts is that it is the clearest expression in the New Testament of the unity between the ministry of Jesus and that of the early Christian community. In outlining the vigorous spirit that animated Jesus and the first generation of the Church, his work may be considered to be an exhortation to his readers/hearers to exert similar energies in moving out into the (Gentile) world.

The Universalism of Luke's Gospel

The Infancy Gospel. The universalism within the perspective of Luke is foreshadowed in the prophetic words of the infancy gospel. Luke 1–2 serves the same purpose in relation to the rest of the Gospel as does Acts 1–2 to the remainder of Acts. Just as Acts 1–2 provides a transition from Jesus to the Church, so Luke 1–2 serves as a transition from the story of Israel to that of Jesus. They are vehicles of the evangelist's theology, rather than statements of history (Brown 1977: 242-43).

In the annunciation to Zechariah in the temple of Jerusalem, the angel

1. Preliminary Questions

Gabriel predicts that Zechariah's son, John, 'will turn many of the sons of Israel to the Lord their God' (1.16). In the annunciation to Mary in Nazareth Gabriel promises that her son, Jesus, will inherit the throne of his father David (1.32). In Mary's *Magnificat* the new stage in God's plan is hailed as help to Israel and to the posterity of Abraham (1.54-55). In Zechariah's canticle (*Benedictus*) also it is God's favour to Israel which is praised (Lk. 1.68-79).

If in the two annunciations and in the birth of John God's favour appears to be restricted to the people of Israel, the opening verses of Luke 2 shift the attention from Herod, Judaea and Galilee, to Emperor Augustus and all the world (2.1). The angelic choir sees in the birth of Jesus a source of peace to all with whom God is pleased (Lk. 2.14).

Soon the significance of Jesus appears on a more explicitly universalistic plane. In the Song of Simeon (*Nunc Dimittus*) we have sentiments indicating that the servant's mission, both to his own people and to all nations, was being ushered in: 'Lord, now let your servant depart in peace, according to your word; for my eyes have seen your salvation which you have prepared in the presence of all peoples, a light for revelation to the Gentiles, and for the glory of my people Israel' (Lk. 2.29-32).

However, Simeon's message to Mary is that the child is destined to occasion the fall and rising of many in Israel (1.34). Moreover, it is the redemption of Jerusalem that Anna also has in mind (1.38). The final scene of Luke's infancy gospel finds Jesus in the temple in Jerusalem, in the company of the Jewish teachers (Lk. 2.41-50).

Luke's Precursors of Jesus. Nevertheless, any suggestion that Jesus' mission would be restricted to the land of Israel is corrected with the time reference to Caesar Tiberius (Lk. 3.1). Luke introduces John's preaching with a quotation from Isa. 40.3-5 (Lk. 3.4-6), ending with '...and all flesh shall see the salvation of God'. We also see John castigating his audience with a critique of salvation by virtue of ethnicity: 'Bear fruits that befit repentance, and do not begin to say to yourselves, "We have Abraham for our father"; for I tell you, God is able from these stones to raise up children to Abraham...' (3.8). Moreover, Luke introduces the public ministry of Jesus by giving his genealogy, indicating that he was not only a son of David (3.23) and of Abraham (3.34), Jewish heroes, but also of Adam, the first human, and of God himself (3.37).

Jesus and the Synagogue. In several places in the Gospels it is mentioned that Jesus visited synagogues (e.g. Lk. 4.33, 44; Mt. 12.9; Mk 3.1), and that he taught in them (e.g. Mt. 4.23; 9.35; 13.54; Mk 1.21, 39; 6.2; Lk. 4.15, 16-30, 31-32, 44; 6.6; 13.10; Jn 6.59; 18.20). The Gospels also record acts of exorcism and healings in the synagogue (e.g. Lk. 4.33; 6.6-11; Mk 1.39; Mt. 4.23). According to Lk. 4.16 it was his custom to go to the synagogue on the Sabbath day.

The Nazareth Scene. As we shall have occasion to verify, the universalism of Luke is highlighted in the Nazareth scene (Lk. 4.16-30), and in several other places in the course of the Gospel.

Luke in General. Although Luke respects the reality of Jesus' virtual restriction to the house of Israel, he stresses more than the other evangelists Jesus' association with those on the fringe of society, such as tax-collectors (the calling of Levi, 5.27-28; Mt. 9.9 and Mk 2.14; eating with them/scandal Lk. 5.27-32; Mt. 9.9-13 and Mk 2.13-17, but in Luke only at 15.1-3; Jesus, friend of tax-collectors and sinners, Lk. 7.34; Mt. 11.19; and Zacchaeus, unique to Luke, at 19.1-10). Attention is also drawn to Jesus' banqueting with the poor, the maimed, the blind and the disabled (only in Luke, at 14.12-14; cf. the parable of Lazarus, only in Luke, at 16.19-26).

His interest in Samaritans is apparent (e.g. the Good Samaritan parable, the incident of the ten lepers, the reference to the Samaritan villages, all exclusive to Luke, at 10.30-37, 17.11-19 and 9.51-55, respectively). Luke also devotes space to Gentiles (Elijah and Sidon; Elisha and Naaman the Syrian, only in Luke, at 4.26-27; the cure of the possessed man in the Gerasene district, Lk. 8.26-29, shared with Mt. 8 and Mk 5; 'Men will come from east and west and north and south, and sit at table in the kingdom of God', Lk. 13.29 and Mt. 8.11; dealings with the Roman centurion, Lk. 7.1-10 and Mt. 8.5-13).

His portrayal of Jesus' concern for women is striking, when one remembers the patriarchal nature of the society. We have the likening of the Kingdom of God to a woman leavening dough, Lk. 13.20-21; a woman's joy as an image of God's, Lk. 15.8-10, and Jesus' ministering women, Lk. 8.1-3; Martha and Mary serving Jesus, Lk. 10.38-42, all unique to Luke, as well as hospitality, Lk. 7.44-50, shared with Mt. 26 and Mk 14, and the widow's mite, Lk. 21.1-4, shared with Mk 12.43.

1. Preliminary Questions

The Cleansing of the Temple. Luke's account of the cleansing of the temple shows in sharp relief his portrayal of the universalism of Jesus: 'And he entered the temple and began to drive out those who sold, saying to them, "It is written, 'My house shall be a house of prayer'; but you have made it a den of robbers"' (Lk. 19.45-46). The reference is to Isaiah 56, a passage in which the foreigners ('who join themselves to the Lord, to minister to him, to love the name of the Lord, and to be his servants, every one who keeps the sabbath, and does not profane it, and holds fast my covenant') are given a privileged place 'in my house of prayer...*for my house shall be called a house of prayer for all peoples*' (Isa. 56.6-7). Note that while there is place for foreigners, it is virtually always by way of their coming to an appreciation of the God of Israel (Isa. 56.7-8); in other words, we are dealing with understandable spiritual colonialism.

In the words of P.D. Hanson, Isa. 56.7 'is a frontal attack on the narrow exclusiveness of the hierocratic tradition with its teaching that the temple priesthood was limited to the sons of Zadok, and that membership in the community was limited to the sons of Israel. The new Universalism is summarized in verse 8' (Hanson 1989: 389). Verse 8 reads, 'Thus says the Lord God, who gathers the outcasts of Israel: I will gather yet others to him besides those already gathered'.

A comparison between the Septuagint text of Isa 56.7 and the version in Luke is instructive:

LXX: *ho gar oikos mou oikos proseuchēs klēthēsetai pasin tois ethnesin*

Luke: *kai estai ho oikos mou oikos proseuchēs humeis de auton epoiēsate spēlaion lēstōn*

In place of the Septuagint's *pasin tois ethnesin*, Luke has *humeis de auton epoiēsate spēlaion lēstōn* (from Jer. 7.11). The charge was that the priests who were responsible for the temple were robbing the Gentiles (nations) of their opportunity of experiencing it as a place of reconciliation between God and humankind. The temple was in a special way a place of atonement, and its largest area was for the Gentiles. Luke's quotation from Isaiah, then, accuses the priests in charge of the temple of usurping the right of the Gentiles, by allowing their court to be taken up by merchants, money-changers' stalls and animals.

The function of this area of the temple is indicated in the Syriac (*Peshitta*) translation of Isaiah: 'For my house is a house of *reconciliation*, to be *explained* to all the nations'. In reality, however, there were no priests in the Gentiles' area, explaining to them that the temple is a place of reconciliation between God and humankind. Indeed there was a notice in Greek and Latin on each of the thirteen gates leading through the barrier separating the Court of Israel from the Court of the Gentiles, warning the Gentiles that they could die venturing in (see Meyers and Strange 1981: 53).

After Jesus cleared the Gentiles' court he taught them, as the place was intended to be used, namely for teaching. *Pace* J.T. Sanders (1987: 34), Jesus' opposition to the temple was not that it was made by hands, but that it was not being used for the purposes for which it had been constructed, namely, as a place of reconciliation between God and all who ventured therein.

The two outstanding and unambiguous pieces of evidence to indicate Luke's portrayal of the universalistic interests of Jesus are the scene in the synagogue in Nazareth, and the cleansing of the temple.

The Resurrection Appearance of Luke 24.44-49. In the climactic account of the resurrection appearance in Lk. 24.44-49 and its echo in Acts 1.3-8 we have a passage that synthesizes Luke's account of the ministry of Jesus, and propels his readers forward into the continuation of that mission in the Church, a mission beginning in Jerusalem, but destined for the ends of the earth. The key passage reads:

^{44}Then he said to them, 'These are my words which I spoke to you, while I was still with you, that everything written about me in the law of Moses and the prophets and the psalms must be fulfilled'. ^{45}Then he opened their minds to understand the scriptures, ^{46}and said to them, 'Thus it is written that the Christ should suffer and on the third day rise from the dead, ^{47}and that repentance and forgiveness of sins should be preached in his name to all nations, beginning from Jerusalem. ^{48}You are witnesses of these things. ^{49}And behold, I send the promise of my Father upon you; but stay in the city, until you are clothed with power from on high'.

^{50}Then he led them out as far as Bethany, and lifting up his hands he blessed them. ^{51}While he blessed them, he parted from them. ^{52}and they returned to Jerusalem with great joy, ^{53}and were continually in the temple blessing God.

In the first book, O Theophilus, I have dealt with all that Jesus began to do and teach, ^{2}until the day when he was taken up, after he had given commandment through the Holy Spirit to the apostles whom he had chosen. ^{3}To them he presented himself alive after his passion by many proofs, appearing to them during forty days, and speaking of the kingdom of God. ^{4}And while staying with them he charged them not to depart from Jerusalem, but to wait for the promise of the Father, which, he said, 'you heard from me, ^{5}for John baptized with water, but before many days you shall be baptized with the Holy Spirit'. ⁶So when they had come together, they asked him, 'Lord, will you at this time restore the kingdom to Israel?' ⁷He said to them, 'It is not for you to know times or seasons which the Father has fixed by his own authority. ⁸But you shall receive power when the Holy Spirit has come upon you; and you shall be my witnesses in Jerusalem and in all Judea and Samaria and to the end of the earth.' ⁹And when he had said this, as they were looking on, he was lifted up, and a cloud took him out of their sight. ¹⁰And while they were gazing into heaven as he went, behold, two men stood by them in white robes, ¹¹and said, 'Men of Galilee, why do you stand looking into heaven? This Jesus, who was taken up from you into heaven, will come in the same way as you saw him go into heaven.'

¹²Then they returned to Jerusalem from the mount called Olivet, which is near Jerusalem, a sabbath day's journey away; ¹³and when they had entered, they went up to the upper room, where they were staying, Peter and John and James and Andrew, Philip and Thomas, Bartholomew and Matthew, James the son of Alphaeus and Simon the Zealot and Judas the son of James. ¹⁴And these with one accord devoted themselves to prayer, together with the women and Mary the mother of Jesus, and with his brothers.

Several elements of this account, which I regard as the hinge between the Gospel and its sequel, deserve attention:

1. *The mission was inaugurated by the risen Jesus.* This is Luke's presentation of the full-blown universal mission of the Christian gospel. It is inaugurated by the *risen*, rather than the earthly Jesus. Even so, as the development of Acts shows, the universal application of the good news was realized only gradually and painfully by the Christian community, even after the infusion of the Holy Spirit at Pentecost.

But in allying the two volumes together Luke makes clear that there is an essential link between the earthly and the risen Jesus. By uniting the two aspects, the double work also reflects the perspective that the ministry of Jesus in the Gospel serves as the exemplar of the ministry of the community.

2. *He opened their minds to understand the Scriptures.* a. *The mission of Jesus is in fulfilment of the Scriptures.* In line with other writers of the New Testament, Luke sees Jesus' ministry as fulfilling the hopes of the Septuagint Scriptures. Already on the way to Emmaus, he had said to the two he had joined, 'O foolish men, and slow of heart to believe all the prophets have spoken! Was it not necessary that the Christ should suffer these things and enter his glory?' (Lk. 24.25-26). Luke adds, 'And beginning with Moses and all the prophets, he interpreted to them

in all the scriptures the things concerning himself' (Lk. 24.27). From this we see that in the perspective of Luke there is continuity between the experience of Israel and that of Jesus, and, as will be clear later, that of the early church. Even if the leadership of the Jews rejected him, Luke's Jesus and the early church did not abandon them.

'Luke is the most explicit of the evangelists in insisting that to understand what God was doing in Christ one had to know Scripture' (J.A. Sanders 1987: 78). In the parable of the Rich Man and Lazarus, Abraham explained that if they would not read Moses and the Prophets properly they would not accept the testimony of one rising from the dead (Lk. 16.27-31). In the Emmaus and pre-Ascension accounts in Luke 24, as we shall see, great prominence is given to an interpretation of the Law and the Prophets as a hermeneutical key to understanding the suffering, death and vindication of Jesus.

Luke has three quotations of Isaiah with the citation formula: Lk. 3.4-6 (Isa. 40.3-5); Lk. 4.18-19 (Isa. 61.1-2 and 58.6); and Lk. 22.37 (Isa. 53.12). There are also explicitly clear Isaianic phrases at Lk. 2.30-32 (Isa. 52.10; 42.6; 49.6); Lk. 7.22 (Isa. 26.19; 29.18; 35.5-6; 61.1); Lk. 8.10 (Isa. 6.9-10); Lk. 19.46 (Isa. 56.7); and Lk. 20.9 (Isa. 5.1-2).

Probably even more significant than the quotation of and allusions to individual passages in Isaiah is the manner in which fundamental patterns in Isaiah serve as a framework for the central thrust of Luke–Acts. 'Isa. 49.6, which is explicitly cited in Acts 13.47, and is reflected in Lk. 1.79 and 24.47, as well as in Acts 1.8 and 26.20, apparently influenced the shape of the whole of Luke's work' (J.A. Sanders 1987: 80).

The Song of the Servant of Isaiah 49 encapsulates many of the striking features of Luke–Acts:

> But now the Lord says, who formed me from the womb to be his servant, to bring Jacob back to him, and that Israel might be gathered to him, for I am honoured in the eyes of the Lord, and my God has become my strength—he says: 'It is too light a thing that you should be my servant to raise up the tribes of Jacob and to restore the preserved of Israel; I will give you as a light to the nations, that my salvation may reach to the end of the earth' (Isa. 49.5-6).

The salvation is described in terms of establishing the land, apportioning the desolate heritages, and freeing the prisoners (vv. 8-9).

b. *The mission of the church is in fulfilment of the Scriptures.* But in Luke's vision, it is not only the ministry of Jesus which is in conformity with the Scriptures, but also the ministry of the Church: 'Thus it is written...that repentance and forgiveness of sins should be preached in his name to all nations, beginning from Jerusalem' (Lk. 24.47).

Luke's perception of the compatibility between the ministry of Jesus, which is, by and large, confined to Israel, and the universalist thrust of the early church, is reiterated in Paul's defence speech before King Agrippa:

> To this day I have had the help that comes from God, and so I stand here testifying both to small and great, saying nothing but what the prophets and Moses said would come to pass: that the Christ must suffer, and that, by being the first to rise from the dead, he would proclaim light both to the people and to the Gentiles (Acts 26.22-23).

What distinguishes Jesus and his followers in the early church from other Jews is not the Scriptures themselves, which all Jews shared in common, but his interpretation of them. This involved seeing in the Scriptures that

> the Christ was destined to suffer and to rise from the dead on the third day, and that

> repentance and forgiveness of sins should be preached in his name to all nations, beginning from Jerusalem.

Certainly the empowerment to effect the universal mission, if not also the very acceptance of the necessity of it, would have to await being 'clothed with power from on high'.

3. *Prophecy and suffering and rising from the dead.* From Lk. 9.51, when Jesus sets his sights on Jerusalem, the reader's attention is on the fate that will befall the prophet Jesus. He will go on his way today, tomorrow and the day following, 'for it cannot be that a prophet should perish away from Jerusalem'. He adds,

> O Jerusalem, Jerusalem, killing the prophets and stoning those who are sent to you! How often would I have gathered your children together as a hen gathers her brood under her wings, and you would not! Behold, your house is forsaken. And I tell you, you will not see me until you say, 'Blessed is he who comes in the name of the Lord' (Lk. 13.33-35).

Opposition to the prophetic message of Jesus is mirrored in the treatment of the preachers of Acts (5.40-42). The martyrdom of Stephen brings the message to Samaria (Acts 8.4-5) and the Greeks (Acts 11.19-21). The imprisonment of Paul does not hinder the free preaching of the Word (Acts 28.30-31).

4. *The gospel is to be proclaimed to all nations, beginning from Jerusalem.* The message of repentance and forgiveness of sins should be preached in his name to all nations, beginning from Jerusalem. Here Luke reveals the dynamic movement from Jerusalem, the place where his Gospel begins and ends, to the capital of the Empire. That Jerusalem has a particular prominence in Luke is clear. It frames the infancy gospel (Luke 1–2), and is the goal of the journey begun at 9.51. It is the location of which the reader is given many reminders within the narrative of the gospel (9.53; 13.33-35; 17.11; 18.31; 19.11, 28). It is the place of the final ministry, death and resurrection of Jesus, and, with the exception of the Emmaus scene, is the sole place of his resurrection appearances (contrast Mt. 28.16-20). If Luke propels the gospel to the mainly gentile city of Rome, he recognizes the seminal function of Jerusalem, the capital of the Jewish faith. The link between the *missio ad gentes* and that *ad Judaeos* is intimate. Nevertheless, Luke respects the restricted nature of the mission of Jesus, which, with such noteworthy exceptions as Lk. 4.16-30, is mainly to his own people.

5. *You are witnesses of these things.* In both Lk. 24.47-48 and in Acts 1.8 the witness to Jesus will begin in Jerusalem, and be carried forward into all Judaea and Samaria, and finally to the ends of the earth. The twelve apostles provide the continuity between the ministry of Jesus and the preaching of the early church, as is clear from the qualifications required of Judas's replacement: 'So one of the men who have accompanied us during all the time that the Lord Jesus went in and out among us, beginning from the baptism of John until the day when he was taken up from us—one of these men must become with us a witness to his resurrection' (Acts 1.21-22). Peter and James are prominent in the first half of Acts, and although Paul does not fulfil the conditions of replacement for Judas, he is the one most closely associated with the spread of the gospel to the ends of the earth, or at least as far west as Rome.

6. *Jesus and his followers are empowered by the Spirit.* The role of the Holy Spirit both in the life of Jesus and in the missionary activity of the church is critical for Luke. Twice the witnesses of the Ascension are promised the Spirit: 'Stay in the city, until you are clothed with power from on high' (Lk. 24.48), and, 'But you shall receive power when the Holy Spirit has come upon you' (Acts 1.8).

1. *Preliminary Questions* 57

The Universalism of Acts
The empowerment takes place at Pentecost (2.1-11), and soon afterwards we read the chronicle of the spread of the Gospel in Judaea and Samaria (Acts 8.1b–11.18), in which the tentative mission is vetted by the Mother Church of Jerusalem. There follows the conversion of the Ethiopian eunuch, the conversion and mission of Paul, the conversion of Cornelius (Acts 10.1-48), and the missionary preparations in the church at Antioch.

Pauline Missionary Activity
We learn from the Acts of the Apostles that Paul went to the synagogue, as was his custom (Acts 17.2; cf. Lk. 4.16), and that he used them as the bases for his missionary work. Although there is no reference to Paul's visits to synagogues in the Letters, the account in Acts is consistent with Paul's view that the good news of salvation was to be brought to the Jews first, then the Gentiles (Rom. 1.16; 10.14-16; 1 Cor. 9.20-21, etc.). In a very real sense, Acts presents Paul more as an apostle of the Jews than of the Gentiles. But, as the text of Acts makes clear, in addition to meeting Jews in the synagogues, he also encountered those on the fringe (e.g. Acts 13.16, 43; 14.1; 17.4; 18.4). Paul visited the synagogue in Salamis (Acts 13.5, proclaiming...), Antioch in Pisidia (Acts 13.14, reading, preaching), Iconium (Acts 14.1), Thessalonica (Acts 17.1); Beroea (Acts 17.10), Athens (Acts 17.17), Corinth (Acts 18.4), Ephesus (Acts 18.19; 19.8), and in general (Acts 24.12; 26.11).

It is clear, then, that in Luke's view the universal mission is part of God's purpose, and was foretold in prophecy, and conveyed to the disciples by the ascending Jesus. It was effected through the power of God's Spirit. The gospel was presented to Jews first (Acts 3.16; 13.46), and subsequently to the Gentiles (Acts 13.46; 18.6; 19.8-10). This reflects Paul's carefully worked out missiological position as crystallized in the thematic statement of Rom. 1.16-18, 'For I am not ashamed of the gospel, for it is the power of God bringing about salvation for all who believe, for the Jew first, and then for the Greek, for in it the righteousness of God is revealed...'. The ending of the Acts situates Paul in the capital of the secular city (Acts 28.28).

I have argued elsewhere that Paul's first encounter with the Risen Christ involved both a fundamental turning-point in his spiritual perception, and a mission to bring both Jew and Gentile within the embrace of the gospel (Prior 1989: 125-26). The conversion experience served more to redirect his enthusiasm, than merely provide him with an interior illumination. The revelation involved a commission, which resulted in a necessity being laid upon him (1 Cor. 9.16). The target of the commission was *all the nations*, a phrase used four times in the letters (Rom. 1.5; 16.26; Gal. 3.8; and 2 Tim. 4.17). Although Paul understood his own role to be directed towards the Gentiles (Rom. 11.13), this is not to be understood as if he could turn his back on that to the Jews, even if that interpretation might be read into Gal. 1.16; 2.2, 7-9. Romans 9–11 attests to Paul's concern for the evangelization of the Jews as well as of the Gentiles, and 1 Cor. 9.19-23 shows his desire to identify with both Jew and Gentile in order to win them to Christ. Paul's strategy as reflected in Romans is to win over Gentiles, in the hope that Israel may become jealous (Rom. 11.11), and lead ultimately to the time when *all Israel will be saved* (Rom. 11.25-26).

The letter to the Galatians is invoked frequently as an argument to counter the Acts' presentation of Paul as apostle of the Jews. In my view, Gal. 2.1-10 does not imply any parting of the ways between the mission to the uncircumcized, undertaken by Paul and Barnabas, and that to the circumcized, by the Jerusalem pillars. Rather, we see a division of labour, solemnly sealed by a handshake of fellowship (v. 9), signalling that each side was free to go out as representatives of the same gospel. This division of responsibilities was freely entered into, and the preaching of the same gospel was the shared goal and focus of the energies of both groups. The gospel was one, even if the audiences were different (see Sampley 1980). In examining Galatians, one must not ignore either its polemical nature, or one's own predispositions, which can lead to an exaggeration of the conflict between the Pauline and the Petrine gospels (see Wechsler 1991).

In Luke's perspective, then, the universal mission of the gospel was there to be discovered in the traditions of Israel, as interpreted by the Risen Jesus. As we shall see from a more detailed examination, it was demonstrated in a striking way in Jesus' inaugural preaching at Nazareth (Lk. 4.16-30). After the Ascension it was propelled by the power of the Spirit in the ministry of Philip (Acts 8.26-39), Peter (Acts 10.1–11.18), and dramatically in the missionary activity of Paul.

The Jews in Luke–Acts
Up to recently it was one of the 'assured results' of scholarship that Luke–Acts was a Gentile Christian document, written by a Gentile Christian for Gentile Christians. It is my strong contention that since the

1. *Preliminary Questions* 59

Lukan mission is universal, it is directed also to the Jews. There is considerable diversity of views among scholars on the question of the portrayal of Jews in Luke–Acts. The issue is an important one for many reasons. One is dealing with the interpretation of a text revered in the Christian community, which can be seen most straightforwardly to attempt to give an account of the growth of the Christian faith after the Ascension of Jesus. It is possible also to view the work as an apologetic from a period much later than that being described. It raises the question of whether, and if so to what extent, Luke–Acts can be regarded as anti-Jewish.

Broadly speaking there are three viewpoints:

First, according to Luke–Acts the Jews have been rejected as the chosen people of God, because they crucified Jesus, and rejected the Gospel preached by Paul and other Christian preachers. The rejection of the Gospel by the Jews, then, has opened up the way for its being offered to the Gentiles, with the latter being the real interest of the author of Luke–Acts.

Secondly, against this view of the blanket condemnation of Jews in Luke–Acts others point out that a distinction must be made between those Jews who converted to the Christian Way and those who did not. But even in this view, it is the failure of the Jews to accept the new Way that propels the author forward in his insistence on the Gentile destination of the mission.

A third view makes much of the Acts' depiction of the success of the Jewish mission. In the second as well as the first half of the book conversions of Jews are mentioned as illustrations of the progress of the Way (13.42-44; 14.1; 17.4, 10–12; 18.4-5; 21.17-26; 28.24). It is noteworthy that while there is mention of mass 'conversions' of Jews and God-fearers, there are no such mass conversions of Gentiles. Of course the author is aware also of the reality of the unacceptability of the new order to many Jews, a fact which he mentions almost in the same breath as its acceptance among others (13.45, 50; 14.2-5, 19; 17.5-8,13; 18.6, 12-13; 19.9; 21.27–26.29; 28.24-29). Despite opposition, most of which comes from Jewish groups (but some also from non-Jews, e.g., the owners of the slave girl in 16.19-24, and the Ephesian silversmiths of ch. 19, as well as Christians, 15.1-5), the word continues to spread (13.46-49, 51-52; 14.6-7, 20-23; 15.6-35, 40-41; 17.1-10, 14-15, 33-34; 18.6-8, 14-18, 21-23, 27-28; 19.9-10, 15-20; 26.30–28.16). Finally, Acts ends with the picture of Paul preaching unhindered for two years in the imperial capital (28.30-31).

In my view, the third of the above three interpretations of the evidence comes closer to the broader truth, namely, that Luke–Acts sees the Gospel as being universal in its destination, thereby embracing both Jews and Gentiles, and in the same order as noted by Paul in Rom. 1.16-18. The various movements of the proclamation of the good news detailed throughout Luke–Acts can be seen to come to a climax at the end. Despite adversity at virtually every turn, from Jew, Greek and Christian, the picture of Paul preaching unhindered in the imperial capital shows the Christian message in Luke's eyes as having an unstoppable power.

What Occasioned the Lukan Work?

Having surveyed in 1975 the history of investigation of the Acts, Gasque reached a frustrating conclusion, 'There is no general agreement among scholars on even the most basic issues of Lucan research' (1975: 305). The determination of the locale of the author, as Rome, Ephesus, Achaia, Antioch of Syria, or Caesarea is mere guess-work. There is no agreement on the circumstances occasioning Luke–Acts. Suggestions abound: the delay of the parousia; gnosticism; suffering, persecution; rich and poor; apology for Paul to Romans, or Jews; need to defend continuity of salvation history, and so forth.

Talbert concludes, rightly:

> Redaction criticism has enabled us to see the author as a creative theologian with a perspective of his own and to discern parts of that point of view. It has not enabled us to grasp Luke's purpose in the context of his *Sitz im Leben*. The issue before us today is this: How can one discern the unity of the author's thought and thereby infer what are the central problems of his time and place? (1989: 305).

Talbert sees many problems in arriving at a theology of Luke on the basis of Luke's modifications of Mark. So do I. In the above survey of preliminary questions I have concluded that Luke–Acts is one literary composition. I argued that it sets out to give an accurate account of the movement of the Gospel from within Judaism to embrace all peoples, including, of course, Jews. We see the element of universalism as the most distinctive trait of Luke–Acts, and, as we shall see, it features prominently in the text of the Nazareth scene.

1. *Preliminary Questions*

Gospel Study and the Standpoint of the Reader

One of the major concerns of biblical interpretation—and indeed one might be forgiven for concluding that it was the only one—has been to get at the original historical context of the writings. This involves a search for the intention of the author. The so-called historic-critical method has dominated biblical studies for some time. Of course, even in its own terms, the search has been only partially successful.

But even if it had been completely successful the curiosity of the human mind and heart would not have been satisfied. The Bible is the book of the Church, and church people desire more than an unearthing of the past. Even if they had a desire to do so, they could not live in the past of the biblical period. Church people not unreasonably expect their religious tradition to illuminate the context of their present and future lives. The past has some wisdom to offer, and it is appropriate to let it have its say. But each new engagement of the believer with the text of the Bible unleashes a new encounter. The reality is that each generation of readers, and, more realistically, hearers of the Bible desires to make sense of its world. In theological terms, it is not sufficient to discover how the person and teaching of Jesus Christ was significant in first century Capernaum, or Jerusalem, but how it is consequential today in Jerusalem, Strawberry Hill, Rwanda, or the Appalachian Mountains.

Investigation of the biblical text reflects all the methods which are applied in contemporary literary criticism. It should be borne in mind that most of these are derived from an examination of literature which is very different in origin and purpose from the biblical text. Much of contemporary literature is composed by people who write in an individualistic way, although no writing is purely private, if only because the act of publishing requires a sensitivity to others. The biblical texts have survived and been preserved within communities precisely because these communities recognized in them a lasting significance.

A major difference between the Bible and any example of modern literature is the fact that most of the former was written with the intention of being read aloud, while most of the latter is for private reading. In the case of the Gospels, moreover, the original context of reading was probably public, and in the company of people who were for the most part familiar with at least some of the contents, and were well disposed towards its hero. Since any contemporary comment on a biblical text must respect the realities of life, it must not be forgotten that for most people the Bible is heard in snippets, and in a context of shared values and, very likely, common worship.

The encounter between the reader and the text is an experience that can be highly particularized. A third person may suggest what can transpire, but can never dictate the character of the event. In most narrative literature there are elements which promote the engagement of the reader. These include questions asked by the actors in the narrative, pauses within the text, and editorial comments and asides which may be more or less evocative. These invite the readers to embellish the story with the fruits of their own imaginations.

The perspective of the author is a significant element in the content of a narrative, and therefore in the encounter of the reader with the text. When we come to much of the biblical material, however, we simply do not know the identity of the author, not to mention her or his point of view. In the case of most modern literature access to the outlook of the author is readily available, although the frame of mind of the author in fiction is often submerged in the morass of attitudes of the fictional characters. In the case of each of the gospels we cannot go much further than to guess the identity type of the author, and his less unlikely geographical and cultural milieu. Suggestions as to the identities of the authors of the Gospels and their locations should be advanced with appropriate tentativeness.

In the case of the two volumes of Luke–Acts the author presents himself (I use the masculine only for convenience) as a writer who has examined and selected his sources and arranged them in a way which seemed fit to him (Lk. 1.1-4). After the prologue, however, the individuality of the author recedes into the background, and is reflected only obliquely in the remainder of the work. The literary style changes very abruptly from the elegant Greek of the prologue (1.1-4), with its intricate subordinate clauses, to the typically Semitic style of the Infancy account, with its co-ordinate clauses joined by 'and' and 'and'. Luke's style is in between the classical and the everyday, vulgar one, a *Zwischenprosa*, by no means vulgar, but distinct from the literary Greek of the period. It is like the language of official documents and technical prose. Alexander argues that the author was 'thoroughly at home in Greek technical literature, so much so that he naturally falls into its style and adopts its preface-conventions when he finds himself at the beginning of a major literary undertaking' (L. Alexander 1993: 173). Such a transition is often the case in scientific prefaces (p. 93). The style gives an indication of the dispositions of the author, who in the vocabulary of literary criticism is called *the implied author*. Such qualities also give hints about the nature of the audience/reader the author has in mind (the so-called *implied reader*). Alexander concludes, on the basis of the preface alone, that there are no grounds for saying that with Luke the Gospel has left the milieu of ordinary people, and entered the cultural world of antiquity (*pace* Haenchen 1971: 136). When he moves beyond the preface his style derives from that of the Greek Bible and the synoptic tradition, rather than from that of Greek rhetorical literature. Similarly, the style in Acts is far less rhetorical than that of much hellenistic Jewish literature (L. Alexander 1993: 175).

A narrative generally has a beginning, a middle and an end. The prologue of *the implied author* of Luke–Acts, commonly called Luke, promises that the plot about to enfold contains information about what was accomplished 'among us'. He clearly sees himself within a tradition which preserved eyewitness and 'preached' accounts of what happened from the beginning. He, as an individual author, now proposes to write a narrative, selecting material from his sources, and presenting them in an orderly fashion, so that Theophilus may know the truth concerning the things of which he had been informed (Lk. 1.1-4). He appears to present himself as some kind of historian, whose accounts can be subjected to verification tests, rather than as a writer of fiction who has no such pretensions. His sources include other narratives (oral and/or written), and eyewitness reports and 'preachings' which may very well have been oral rather than penned.

Intriguing questions arise about the identity of Theophilus and the 'us'. The dedication to Theophilus does not preclude other people from his intended readership, in which case they, too, presumably, are included in the 'us'. What is clear from the Prologue is that the readers who constitute the 'us' are already informed, and are desirous of more information leading to the truth. By his own admission, then, the author is within a literary and believing tradition, and is writing with a view to embellishing it. He is no 'lone' artist indulging himself in self-expression, but one who from the beginning is involved in an act of communication with the implied readership. Even when one is writing for a person with whom one is intimate there is always an element of the unknown in the communication. The author to a certain extent creates the implied reader, by estimating readers' needs and imagining their probable level of comprehension. On the assumption that the author had in mind more than one reader, Theophilus, he would have had to have a complex *intended readership*, although he would have considered himself justified in assuming a commonality of some knowledge and shared values.

It is widely conceded nowadays that the horizon of the reader of a text as well as that of the author must be brought into the discussion, and a certain interaction, and perhaps even fusion, take place. The interpretative process involves not only some relationship between the author and the modern reader, but should also engage with the tradition of investigation. On literary grounds alone, there is a tradition of investigation and a community of exegetes. In addition there are theological factors. People within a religious tradition will regard the original biblical text to have come under the influence of the Holy Spirit. The same Spirit may be considered to have been active among the generations which have engaged in the interpretation. Such activity, of course, does not protect the text from interpretations which are adjudged to be false.

Until recently the exegetical discipline in the West has been dominated by the preoccupations of one region and one period, nineteenth-century Germany. It has been in captivity to its dogmatic and academic presuppositions as any previous generation was to its own ones. Although much recent scholarship shows a welcome and much needed sensitivity to the role of the reader in the art of interpretation (the so-called *reader-response* approaches), the prehistory of a text, and an understanding of it in its original context, still tend to be the *foci* of exegetical interest. The post history of a text, if represented at all, is relegated to footnotes, while the issue of contemporary meaning is shifted conveniently from the centre of exegetical concern to seek out a place in the domain of spirituality. The present work argues for a contemporary reading of the text, illuminated by a variety of exegetical methods, beginning with the historical-critical and ending with a current reading which respects the original proclamation of liberation.

The historical understanding of a text can never be exhausted by enquiring only into the prehistory of the text, the circumstances obtaining at the time of composition, and the intention of the author. Just as texts may have histories before their final form of composition, they also have histories within the experience of different generations of interpreters after the time of composition. The Scripture has remained a living voice in each era of the two millenia of interpretation.

Sensitivity to the fact that the Gospels have traditions of interpretation for each of the two thousand years since their composition guarantees a much needed corrective to the academic arrogance of any one age or place. Exegesis within a community and tradition of interpretation ought not to be satisfied with a mere unearthing of the past, and an almost idolatrous veneration of the original historical context.

We must also be aware of the influence our own social circumstances impose on our understanding of any text, and this applies no less to the Gospels than to any other literature, old or new. Any reader of any text, but particularly of one which is likely to provoke a moral response, will do well to enquire into her or his dispositions *prior* to engaging the text. Contact with any literature has the possibility of correcting, reshaping and enlarging the individual reader's standpoint, and readers would do well to enquire whether they are embarking on the examination of a text in the hope of having their own prior expectations confirmed, or whether they are prepared to place themselves under the power of the word of the text even if it should invite a radical change of values and lifestyle. To be sensitive to one's own pre-understanding and predisposition may turn out to be more fundamental to 'understanding' a text than any enquiry into its putative meaning.

Suppose our enquiry into the meaning of 'the poor' in Luke concludes that 'the poor' are to be identified with the destitute and the beggars of society. Is one required, or at least invited, to align her or his energies to the evangelization of the destitute and the beggars of our society? Suppose, on the other hand, that our enquiry concludes that 'the poor' are those who because they are so deficient in material possessions put all their trust in God. Is a reader to let go of all material possessions in order to share the blessedness of the poor?

Conclusion

The major achievement of the author of Luke–Acts is that he composed a two-volume work. The first, like other examples before him, dealt with what transpired in the ministry of Jesus. The second gave a sustained account of aspects of the Christian beginnings, in a manner which showed how they developed not only after, but from the period of Jesus. The genius of the author resides partially in his success in illustrating how the power and Spirit of God, active in the life of Jesus, was manifest subsequently in the life of Christian believers. Where he can be checked against other information, the author is found to be impressively reliable. His work, of course, does not even pretend to be objective, in the sense in which we imagine much modern history to be. It is an Apologia for the faith of Christian believers, constructed in the form of a historical narrative. At many points, he integrates the Christian Way into the wider history of the Roman Empire, and the affairs of its people. If the hero of his Apologia came from within the bosom of first-century Palestinian Judaism, he traces his roots to the first human being, Adam, and brings the story to a successful end in Rome, the capital of the empire.

***

We shall now examine the Nazareth Synagogue Scene (Lk. 4.16-30) against the background of the much wider question of the relationships between the Synoptic Gospels. We shall introduce the complex question of the possible literary relationships between the Gospels of Matthew, Mark and Luke. We shall then examine the text of Lk. 4.16-30, together with those with which it is frequently associated, Mk 6.1-6 and Mt. 13.53–14.1. We shall then enquire into the problem of relationships between the accounts in the three Gospels of the rejection of Jesus in his own town.

Part II

FIRST-CENTURY SETTING

Chapter 2

THE SOURCE QUESTION

The Synoptic Gospels in General

Any theory which purports to explain the origins of the different accounts of the beginning of the Galilean ministry of Jesus must reckon with the much more complex question of the relationships between the Gospels in their entirety. When in 1774 J.J. Griesbach published his famous 'synopsis' of the gospels, giving in parallel columns the full text of Matthew, Mark and Luke, and some passages of John, the first three gospels could be seen to share much in common, and were given the title, the *Synoptic Gospels*. The three gospels of Matthew, Mark and Luke have a range of both similarities and differences in their content, in their order, and in the terminology and language they employ, while John's gospel is significantly different from all of them. How to account simultaneously for both the similarities and the differences between these three synoptic gospels is called *the synoptic problem*, and it has proved to be one of the most intractable of all problems of literary relationship.

The Synoptic Problem

From the perspective of content, Mark, the shortest of the three, has 661 verses, of which some 80 per cent are closely paralleled in Matthew and some 65 per cent in Luke—only a very few of Mark's sections do not have a parallel in either Matthew or Luke, and most are paralleled in both (the *triple tradition*). Moreover, Matthew and Luke have some 220 verses of material in common which are not in Mark (the *double tradition*). In addition, the much longer Matthew (1068 verses) and Luke (1149 verses) have materials unique to each, to the extent of about one third and one half, respectively.

The major sections of the synoptic gospels, in their canonical order, may be represented as follows:

2. The Source Question

	Matthew	Mark	Luke
Infancy gospel	1–2		1–2
Preliminaries	3.1–4.11	1.1-13	3.1–4.13
Galilean ministry	4.12–18.35	1.14–9.50	4.14–9.50
Journey to Jerusalem	19–20	10	9.51–19.28
Ministry in Jerusalem	21–25	11–13	19.29–21.38
Passion	26–27	14–15	22–23
Resurrection	28	16	24

This broadly similar order, which hides considerable differences in the order of sections within the major divisions, is understandable in terms of the stages in Jesus' ministry. The similarities in the more detailed arrangement of material call for an explanation. Since our major concern is the Gospel of Luke let us enquire into the order from its perspective. The order of the material in Lk. 3.1–6.19 is strikingly similar to that of Mk 1.1–3.12, although there are some notable exceptions. The material in Lk. 6.20–8.3 is virtually absent from Mark. Luke's order of material from 8.4–9.50 is strikingly similar to that of Mk 4.1–9.41, while the order of the corresponding material in Matthew is less marked. However, nothing in Luke corresponds to the material in Mk 6.45–8.26. The major section of Luke's so-called Journey to Jerusalem (9.51–18.14—Jesus enters the Temple in Jerusalem at Lk. 19.45) has very few parallel passages in Mark. As we approach the account of the last days of Jesus' life the order of material in all three is similar: that of Lk. 18.15–24.12 is strikingly similar to that of Mk 10.13–16.1-8, as is that of Mt. 19.13–28.10.

With respect to Matthew, in broad terms the order of material in Mt. 3.1–4.25 is that of Mk 1.1–39. Most of Jesus' Teaching on the Mount (Mt. 5–7) is not in Mark. The order of material in Mt. 8.1–9.34 is not quite that of Mk 1.40–2.22, since we have material from Mark 4–5 also. Most of Jesus' Discourse on Mission (Mt. 9.35–11.1) is not in Mark, but has correspondences in Luke, chs. 9, 10, 12 and 14. From 12.1–13.35 Matthew's order is that of the corresponding sections in Mk 2.23–4.34, and the order of Mt. 13.53–28.8 is almost identical to that of Mk 6.1–16.8.

The discussion of order alone suggests some literary dependence between the three gospels, and this dependence is more likely when one considers also the vocabulary and language of the three gospels. Further examination shows that where the order of Matthew is different from that of Mark, that of Luke is similar to Mark's order. Moreover, where the order of Luke is different from that of Mark, that of Matthew is similar to Mark's order. The argument from order, then, appears to reflect Mark's special relationship with both Matthew and Luke. The evidence from order could be accounted for by suggesting any of the following: Mark is original, and was used by the other two; Matthew is original, and was used by Mark, and subsequently Mark was used by Luke; Luke is original, and was used by Mark, and subsequently Mark was used by Matthew; Mark used both Matthew and Luke. Each of these views, as well as suggestions of dependence on lost sources, has been proposed in the history of the investigation of the problem.

Clement of Alexandria held that those gospels with genealogies (Matthew and Luke) were earlier than those without them (Mark and John) (Eusebius, *Hist. Eccl.* 6.14.5). St Augustine proposed the order of composition to be Matthew, Mark, Luke and John, and claimed that each evangelist was aware of his predecessor (*De Consensu Evangelistarum* 1.2-3). Papias stated that Mark was the interpreter of Peter (but, of course, not necessarily our Gospel of Mark), but did not give an order of composition (Eusebius, *Hist. Eccl.* 3.39.15). In the modern period, J.J. Griesbach propounded his hypothesis that Mark was written later than Luke and was dependent on both Matthew and Luke (1783). His theory had the advantage of simplicity, in not postulating any unknown sources, and was the most widely accepted hypothesis in the first half of the nineteenth century.

Farmer (1976) surveys the contribution of the major figures in the modern debate: Lessing (1784); Storr (1786), who argued that Mark is the earliest of the extant gospels; Eichhorn (1794); Herder (1797), who proposed that Mark's gospel was close to the earliest preaching of the primitive church, thus giving it an implicit priority which it never had in the known history of the church; Marsh (1798); Schleiermacher (1832), who proposed a modification of the Griesbach hypothesis; Lachmann (1835); Weisse (1838), whose proposals laid the basis for the two-document solution to the synoptic problem which was advanced by Holtzmann (1863).

The hypothesis which has widest support among scholars today derives from B.H. Streeter (1924): Mark was written first, and was used by both Matthew and Luke, but independently of each other. The material common to Matthew and Luke, but not in Mark, which consists of about 220 verses, mainly of sayings of Jesus, is ascribed to a different source called *Q*, from the German *Quelle* (source). In addition, the one half of Luke, and one third of Matthew which consists of material unique to each of them, is called the special Lukan, and the special Matthean material, respectively. This attempted solution to the problem is referred to as the Two Source (or Two-Document) Hypothesis.

Over the past thirty years or so there have been several challenges to this hypothesis. Both the priority of Mark's Gospel, and the hypothesis of the *Q* document have been attacked. Determined efforts have been made to revive the Griesbach Hypothesis, that is, the view that Matthew was the first gospel, and was used by Luke, and that Mark was the third in the order of composition, and was a conflation of the other two (by W.R. Farmer, J.B. Orchard, D.L. Dungan, *et al.*; see Tuckett 1983 and Bellinzoni 1985). There are several other attempts at a solution. Some (e.g. Farrer, Goulder) dispense with the hypothesis of the *Q* document, and suggest that Luke was aware of Matthew's material. Predictably, there is also a suggestion that Luke was the first gospel, and was used by the other two (Lindsey 1963), but this view has very little support. For other scholars the synoptic problem is so complex that only a more intricate, multi-Document theory can account for it. M.-E. Boismard suggests that there were four documents (A, B, C and *Q*), followed by intermediate states of our Matthew, Mark and Luke, prior to our gospels. Already in the nineteenth century G. Ewald proposed a nine-document hypothesis which was dismissed by his contemporaries because of its perplexity (see Prior 1986: 19 n. 24). Neirynck surveys the synoptic problem, and outlines some of the proposed solutions, concentrating on the arguments from order (1989), and Fitzmyer provides a detailed discussion of the sources of Luke's gospel (1981: 63-106).

In accepting the hypothesis of Markan priority there is a tendency to regard it as a more straightforward account, which is closer to the bedrock of the events in the life of Jesus than is the case for Matthew or Luke. Gospel material not in Mark, then, is accorded more dubious historical credentials, and, not infrequently, is regarded as deriving from the literary creation and rhetorical flourishes of the evangelist, rather than from the words and deeds of Jesus himself. Followers of the two-source hypothesis use language like, 'Luke (or Matthew) derived this material from Mark, or the *Q* source, and modified it in such and such a way, reflecting his own theological and pastoral perspectives'.

Almost every theological book which uses the results of gospel scholarship works on the assumption that Mark was the first gospel, that

Matthew and Luke used it and *Q*, and that each used additional material peculiar to itself. A crude application of this perspective to Lk. 4.16-30 would look to Luke's literary creativity for its explanation of the material, rather than to any reliable contact with what actually happened during Jesus' ministry. Because of the lack of agreement on the matter, I operate by reserving judgment on the solution to the synoptic problem. Rather than use language such as, 'Luke modified Mark at this point, etc.', I prefer to note that Luke's version is different from that of Mark/Matthew. This approach prevents me erecting large redactional edifices on the shaky sands of source 'certainties'.

The Source Question and Luke 4.16-30

Rather than impose on Lk. 4.16-30 a source hypothesis which attempts a solution to the wider synoptic problem, it is wise to examine the text in its own right first. But before doing so it is instructive to see how the three gospels deal with the material. The chart which follows gives the sequence of events, from the preliminaries to Jesus' public ministry to the end of the Galilean ministry. It follows Luke's order, and places Mark between Luke and Matthew.

	Luke	Mark	Matthew
Preliminaries			
1. The Beginning of John' Ministry	3.1-6	1.1-6	3.1-6
2. Preaching of John	3.7-9		3.7-10
3. Ethical Teaching of John	3.10-14		
4. Coming of the Stronger One	3.15-17	1.7-8	3.11-12
5. John's Imprisonment	3.18-20	6.7-8	14.3-4
6. The Baptism of Jesus	3.21-22	1.9-11	3.13-17
7. The Genealogy of Jesus	3.23-38		1.1-16
8. The Temptation of Jesus	4.1-13	1.12-13	4.1-11

Since the material deals with John (sections 1–5), and two events prior to Jesus' ministry in Galilee (6 and 8), it is not surprising that the order of events is similar in all three synoptics.

	Luke	Mark	Matthew
Preliminaries			
9. Introductory Summary	4.14-15	1.14a	4.12
10. Visit to Nazareth	**4.16-30**	**6.1-6a**	**13.53-58**
11. Capernaum Synagogue Teaching	4.31-32	1.21-22	7.28b-29
12. Exorcism of Demoniac	4.33-37	1.23-28	

2. The Source Question

	Luke	Mark	Matthew
13. Healing of Peter's Mother-in-Law	4.38-39	1.29-31	8.14-15
14. Healings in the Evening	4.40-41	1.32-34	8.16-17
15. Leaving Capernaum	4.42-43	1.35-38	
16. First Preaching Tour	4.44	1.39	4.23
17. The Miraculous Catch of Fish	5.1-10a		
18. The Catch of Disciples	**5.10b-11**	**1.16-20**	
19. Healing of a Leper	5.12-16	1.40-45	8.1-4
20. Healing of Paralytic	5.17-26	2.1-12	9.1-8
21. Call of Levi	5.27-32	2.13-17	9.9-13
22. Question about Fasting	5.33-39	2.18-22	9.14-17
23. Plucking Corn on the Sabbath	6.1-5	2.23-28	12.1-8
24. Man with a Withered Hand	6.6-11	3.1-7a	12.9-15a
25. Call of the Twelve	**6.12-16**	**3.13-19**	**10.2-4**
26. Great Crowds Come to Jesus	6.17-19	3.7b-12	4.24-25
27. Two Kinds of People	6.20-26		5.3-6, 11-12
28. Love and Mercy	6.27-38		5.39-42, 42-46
29. Inward Character of Disciples	6.39-49		
30. Healing of Centurion's Servant	7.1-10		8.5-13
31. Raising of Widow's Son	7.11-17		
32. Jesus' Answer to John	7.18-23		11.2-6
33. Jesus' Witness about John	7.24-28		11.7-11
34. Rejection of John and Jesus	7.29-35		11.12-19
35. Woman who was a Sinner	**7.36-50**	**14.3-9**	**26.6-13**
36. The Ministering Woman	8.1-3		
37. Preaching in Parables	8.4	4.1-2	13.1-3a
38. Parable of the Sower	8.5-8	4.3-9	13.3b-9
39. Reason for Parables	8.9-10	4.10-12	13.10-13
40. Meaning of the Sower	8.11-15	4.13-20	13.18-23
41. Parable of the Lamp	8.16-18	4.21-25	var.
42. Jesus' True Relatives	**8.19-21**	**3.31-35**	**12.46-50**
43. Stilling of the Storm	8.22-25	4.36-41	8.23-27
44. The Gerasene Demoniac	8.26-39	5.1-20	9.1-8
45. Jairus' Daughter— Woman with Haemorrhage	8.40-56	5.21-43	9.18-26
46. The Mission of the Twelve	9.1-6	6.8-11	10.5-15
47. Herod's Question about Jesus	9.7-9	6.14-16	14.1-2
48. Feeding of 5000	9.10-17	6.30-44	14.13-21
49. Peter's Confession	9.18-20	8.27-29	16.13-16
50. Reply of Jesus	9.21-22	8.30-31	16.20-21
51. Implications for the Disciples	9.23-27	8.34-9.1	16.24-28
52. Transfiguration of Jesus	9.28-36	9.2-8	17.1-8

	Luke	Mark	Matthew
53. Healing of Boy—Unclean Spirit	9.37-43a	9.14-28	17.14-19
54. Jesus Announces his Betrayal	9.43b-45	9.30-32	17.22-23
55. Strife among the Disciples	9.46-48	9.33-37	18.1-5
56. The Strange Exorcist	9.49-50	9.38-41	

From the perspective of Luke's gospel, the order of the material from 4.31-44 (sections 11–16), from 5.12–6.11 (sections 19–24), from 8.4-18 (sections 37–41), and from 8.22–9.50 (sections 43–56) is in sequence with the corresponding sections of Mark. The major differences in order are emboldened. The visit to the Nazareth synagogue (Lk. 4.16-30, section 10) precedes the material in sections 11–45, whereas Jesus' visit to a synagogue in his own country does not occur in Mark until 6.1-6a. Secondly, the calling of disciples occurs later in Luke (5.10b-11, section 25) than in Mark (1.16-20). The content of sections 25 (Call of the Twelve) and 26 (Great Crowds Come to Jesus) is in the reverse order in Mark. The account of the Woman who anointed Jesus (section 35) occurs much earlier in Luke (7.36-50) than in Mark (14.3-9), and is given quite a different emphasis, since it concentrates on the fact that she was a sinner. The account of Jesus' True Relatives (Lk. 8.19-21, section 42) occurs earlier in Mark (3.31-35).

From the perspective of content, Lk. 6.20–8.3 (sections 27–36—with the exception of section 35) does not occur in Mark, while Mk 6.45–8.26 is absent from Luke.

The chart which follows shows the sequence of events in Mark, beginning with his opening of the Galilean ministry, and ending with the scene in the synagogue in his own country. Luke is positioned between Mark and Matthew.

	Mark	Luke	Matt
1. Call of the Four Fishermen	**1.16-20**	**5.10b**	**4.18-22**
2. Teaching with Authority	1.21-22	4.31-32	7.28b-29
3. Expulsion of the Unclean Spirit	1.23-28	4.33-37	
4. Healing of Peter's M.-in-law	1.29-31	4.38-39	8.14-15
5. Healings in the Evening	1.32-34	4.40-41	8.16-17
6. Leaving Capernaum	1.35-38	4.42-43	
7. First Preaching Tour	1.39	4.44	4.23
8. Cleansing of a Leper	1.40-45	5.12-16	8.1-4
9. Healing of Paralytic	2.1-12	5.17-26	9.1-8
10. Call of Levi	2.13-17	5.27-32	9.9-13
11. Question about Fasting	2.18-22	5.33-39	9.14-17
12. 'Working' on the Sabbath	2.23-28	6.1-5	12.1-8

2. The Source Question

	Mark	Luke	Matt
13. Man with a Withered Hand	3.1-7a	6.6-11	12.9-15a
14. Great Crowds come to Jesus	**3.7b-12**	**6.17-19**	**4.24-25**
15. Choice of the Twelve	**3.13-19**	**6.12-16**	**10.2-4**
16. Jesus' Entourage Upset	3.20-21		
17. Blasphemy against the Spirit	**3.22-30**	**11.15-17**	**9.34;**
			12.24-26
18. Jesus' Mother and Brothers	**3.31-35**	**8.19-21**	**12.46-50**
19. Preaching in Parables	4.1-2	8.4	13.1-3a
20. Parable of the Sower	4.3-9	8.5-8	13.3b-9
21. Reason for Parables	4.10-12	8.9-10	13.10-13
22. Meaning of the Sower	4.13-20	8.11-15	13.18-23
23. Moral of the Sower	4.21-25	8.16-18	var.
24. The Self-Developing Seed	**4.26-29**		
25. The Mustard Seed	**4.30-32**	**13.18-19**	**13.31-32**
26. Jesus' Use of Parables	**4.33-34**		**13.34-35**
27. On Following Jesus	**4.35**	**9.57-60**	**8.18-22**
28. Stilling of the Storm	4.36-41	8.22-25	8.23-27
29. Possessed at Gadara	5.1-20	8.26-39	9.1-8
30. Raising of Jairus' Daughter	5.21-43	8.40-56	9.18-26
31. Visit to Home Country	6.1-6a	4.16-30	13.53-58

It will be seen immediately that the sequence in Luke is the same as Mark in sections 2–7, and after the special material, the Miraculous Catch (Lk. 5.1-11), the Lukan sequence is that of Mark for sections 8–13 also. Luke's order for sections 14 and 15 is the reverse of Mark's order. Section 16 is unique to Mark, and section 17 occurs in an altogether different place in Luke (ch. 11). Although there is a number of exceptions—Lk. 8.19-21 (section 18) is outside Mark's order; section 24 is unique to Mark; Lk. 13.18-19 (section 25) is outside Mark's order; section 26 is not in Luke; Lk. 9.57-60 (section 27) is outside Mark's order—Mark's order for sections 18–30 is very close to that of Luke's.

In brief, then, almost all the Markan material preceding the scene in Jesus' home country (6.1-6a) is also in Luke, but after the Nazareth scene of Lk. 4.16-30. In Luke it includes all of Luke 5, some of Luke 6, nothing of Luke 7, and much of Luke 8. While there are similarities with the order in Matthew also it is not at all as striking. Probability alone suggests that such a similarity of sequence between Mark and Luke is hardly a coincidence. Some form of literary or oral dependence must be invoked. It can be explained by suggesting that one used the sequence of the other, or that each depended on a common source, or on sources which had much in common. On the basis of order alone, however, there is no need to presume that the dependence must have been literary.

It is plausible to suggest that either Luke followed Mark's order, and brought the Nazareth scene to the beginning, or that Mark followed Luke and put his home-country scene at the end. The former view is the most favoured, but the fact that other scholars do not accept such a simple solution to the Synoptic Problem, and propound alternative ones, cautions the reader against regarding the favoured hypothetical solution as a fact.

It is appropriate at this stage to look more closely at Lk. 4.16-30 itself, from the perspective of source criticism. An examination of the texts shows that there are both similarities and differences between Luke 4.16-30, Mk 6.1-6, and Mt. 13.53–14.1. Let us consider the extent of this by examining the texts of Luke, Mark and Matthew separately at first, in order to allow each text to be seen in its own right, and then together, with a view to detecting the patterns of agreement and disagreement.

The Text of Luke 4.16-30

Setting the Scene (Luke 4.14-15)
[14] And Jesus returned in the power of the Spirit into Galilee, and a report concerning him went out through all the surrounding country. [15] And he taught in their synagogues, being glorified by all.

Synagogue Reading and Teaching
[16] And he came to Nazareth where he had been brought up; and he went to the synagogue as his custom was, on the sabbath day. And he stood up to read; [17] and there was given to him the book of the prophet Isaiah. He opened the book and found the place where it was written, [18] 'The Spirit of the Lord is upon me, because he has anointed me to preach good news to the poor. He has sent me to proclaim release to the captives and recovering of sight to the blind, to set at liberty those who are oppressed, [19] to proclaim the acceptable year of the Lord.' [20] And he closed the book, and gave it back to the attendant, and sat down; and the eyes of all in the synagogue were fixed on him. [21] And he began to say to them, 'Today this scripture has been fulfilled in your hearing'.

Congregation Reaction
[22] And all spoke well of him, and wondered at the gracious words which proceeded out of his mouth; and they said, 'Is not this Joseph's son?' [23] And he said to them, 'Doubtless you will quote to me this proverb, "Physician, heal yourself; what we have heard you did at Capernaum, do here also in your own country"'. [24] And he said, 'Truly I say to you, no prophet is acceptable in his own country. [25] But in truth, I tell you, there were many widows in Israel in the days of Elijah, when the heaven was

shut up three years and six months, when there came a great famine over all the land; ²⁶And Elijah was sent to none of them but only to Zarephath, in the land of Sidon, to a woman who was a widow. ²⁷And there were many lepers in Israel in the time of the prophet Elisha; and none of them was cleansed but only Naaman the Syrian.' ²⁸When they heard this, all in the synagogue were filled with wrath. ²⁹And they rose up and put him out of the city, and led him to the brow of the hill on which their city was built, that they might throw him down headlong. ³⁰But passing through the midst of them he went away.

The Next Pericope
³¹And he went down to Capernaum, a city of Galilee. And he was teaching them on the sabbath; ³²and they were astonished at his teaching, for his word was with authority. ³³And in the synagogue there was a man who had the spirit of an unclean demon; and he cried out with a loud voice.

The Text of Mark 1.14a-15; 6.1-6

¹·¹⁴ᵃNow after John was arrested, Jesus went into Galilee, preaching the gospel of God, ¹⁵and saying, 'The time is fulfilled, and the kingdom of God is at hand; repent and believe in the gospel'.

Setting the Scene
⁶·¹He went away from there and came to his own country; and his disciples followed him.

Synagogue Teaching
²And on the sabbath he began to teach in the synagogue;

Congregation Reaction
²and many who heard him were astonished, saying, 'Where did this man get all this? What is the wisdom given to him? What mighty works are wrought by his hands! ³Is not this the carpenter, the son of Mary and brother of James and Joses and Judas and Simon, and are not his sisters here with us?' And they took offence at him. ⁴And Jesus said to them, 'A prophet is not without honour except in his own country, and among his own kin, and in his own house'. ⁵And he was not able to do any mighty work there, except that he laid his hands upon a few sick people and healed them. ⁶ᵃAnd he marvelled because of their unbelief.

The Next Pericope
⁶ᵇAnd he went among the villages teaching. ⁷And he called to him the twelve, and began to send them out two by two...

The Text of Matthew 4.12-13, 17; 13.53–14.1

⁴·¹²Now when he heard that John had been arrested, he withdrew into Galilee, ¹³and leaving Nazareth he went and dwelt in Capernaum by the sea...¹⁷From that time Jesus began to preach, and to say, 'Repent, for the kingdom of heaven is at hand'.

Setting the Scene—Synagogue Teaching
[13.53]And when Jesus had finished these parables, he went away from there, [54]and coming to his own country he taught them in their synagogue,

Congregation Reaction
[54]so that they were astonished, and said, 'Where did this man get this wisdom and these mighty works? [55]Is not this the carpenter's son? Is not his mother called Mary? And are not his brothers James and Joseph and Simon and Judas? [56]And are not all his sisters with us? Where then did this man get all this?' [57]And they took offence at him. But Jesus said to them, 'A prophet is not without honour except in his own country, and in his own house'. [58]And he did not do many mighty works there because of their unbelief.

The Next Pericope
[14.1]At that time Herod the tetrarch heard about the fame of Jesus; and he said to his servants,...

It is clear that the following elements are common to Luke 4, Mark 6 and Matthew 13:

> Jesus' visit to his home town (Lk. 4.16; 4.23; 'his own country' Mk 6.1; Mt. 13.53)
> Teaching/speaking in the synagogue on the Sabbath (Lk. 4.16; Mk 6.2; Mt. 13.53)
> The synagogue audience's reaction of astonishment/wonderment (Lk. 4.22; Mk 6.2; Mt. 13.54)
> The question about Jesus' origins (Lk. 4.22; Mk 6.3; Mt.13.54)
> Jesus' response: the saying about the prophet (Lk. 4.24; Mk 6.4; Mt. 13.57)
> The impossibility/refusal to work (many) miracles in Nazareth (Lk. 4.23ff; Mk 6.5; Mt.13.58)
> Rejection (Lk. 4.28-29; cf. Mk 6.3; Mt. 13.57).

It is instructive to examine the texts together. In order to see more clearly the points of similarity and dissimilarity, it is illuminating to examine the texts using a horizontal line synopsis (Swanson), rather than the more usual vertical ones (Huck, Aland, Sparks, Orchard, *et al.*—see the discussion of the relative merits of synopses in Prior 1986). I include *in italics* verses from the Fourth Gospel which resonate with those in the synoptics. The verses in John, it is to be noted, do not occur in the synagogue in Nazareth, but in quite different settings in his Gospel.

Setting the Scene

Luke 4.14	And				Jesus
Matt 4.12	Now when he heard that	John had been arrested,			he
Mark 1.14a	Now		after	John was	arrested,	Jesus

2. The Source Question

Luke 4.14	returned in the power of the Spirit into Galilee,
Matt 4.12	withdrew into Galilee,
Mark 1.14a	came into Galilee,
Matt 4.13	and leaving Nazareth he went and dwelt in Capernaum by the sea...
Luke 4.14	and a report concerning him went out through all the surrounding country.
Matt 4.24	So his fame spread throughout all Syria...
Luke 4.15	And he taught in their synagogues,
Matt 4.17	From that time Jesus began to preach,
Mark 1.14a	preaching the gospel of God,
Luke 4.15	being glorified by all.
Matt 4.17	and to say, 'Repent, for the kingdom of heaven is at hand'.
Mark 1.15	and saying, 'The time is fulfilled, and the kingdom of God is at hand; repent and believe in the gospel'.
Matt 13.53	And when Jesus had finished these parables, he went away from there,
Mark 6.1	He went away from there

The Nazareth Scene

Luke 4.16	And he came to Nazareth where he had been brought up;
Matt 13.54	and coming to his own country
Mark 6.1	and came to his own country; and his disciples followed him.

Synagogue Teaching

Luke 4.16	and he went to the synagogue as his custom was, on the sabbath day.
Matt 13.54	he taught them in their synagogue,
Mark 6.2	And on the sabbath he began to teach in the synagogue;

The Reading

Luke 4.16 And he stood up to read; [17]and there was given to him the book of the prophet Isaiah. He opened the book and found the place where it was written, [18]'The Spirit of the Lord is upon me, because he has anointed me to preach good news to the poor. He has sent me to proclaim release to the captives and recovering of sight to the blind, to set at liberty those who are oppressed, [19]to proclaim the acceptable year of the Lord.'

[20]And he closed the book, and gave it back to the attendant, and sat down; and the eyes of all in the synagogue were fixed on him. [21]And he began to say to them, 'Today this scripture has been fulfilled in your hearing'.

Congregation Reaction

Luke 4.22	And all spoke well of him, and wondered at the gracious words which proceeded out of his mouth;
Matt 13.54	so that they were astonished,
Mark 6.2	and many who heard him were astonished,
John 7.15	The Jews marvelled at it,
Luke 4.22	and they said,
Matt 13.54	and said,
Mark 6.2	saying,
John 7.15	*saying,*
Luke	
Matt 13.54	'Where did this man get this wisdom
Mark 6.2	'Where did this man get all this? What is the wisdom given to him?
John 7.15	*'How is it that this man has learning, when he has never studied?'*
Luke	
Matt 13.54	and these mighty works?
Mark 6.2	What mighty works are wrought by his hands!
Luke 4.22	'Is not this Joseph's son?'
Matt 13.55	Is not this the carpenter's son?
Mark 6.3	Is not this the carpenter,
John 6.42	*'Is not this Jesus, Joseph's son?'*
Luke	
Matt 13.55	Is not his mother called Mary?
Mark 6.3	the son of Mary
John 6.42	*whose father and mother we know?*
Luke	
Matt 13.55	And are not his brothers
Mark 6.3	and brother
Luke	
Matt 13.55	James and Joseph and Simon and Judas
Mark 6.3	of James and Joses and Judas and Simon,
Luke	
Matt 13.56	And are not all his sisters with us?'
Mark 6.3	and are not his sisters here with us?'
Luke	
Matt 13.57	And they took offence at him.
Mark 6.3	And they took offence at him.

2. The Source Question

Luke 4.23 And he said to them, 'Doubtless you will quote to me this proverb, "Physician, heal yourself; what we have heard you did at Capernaum, do here also in your own country"'.

Luke 4.24	And he said,	'Truly I say to you,
Matt 13.57	But Jesus said to them,	
Mark 6.4:	And Jesus said to them,	
John 4.44:	For Jesus himself testified (emarturēsen) that	

Luke 4.24	no prophet is acceptable	in his own country.
Matt 13.57	'A prophet is not without honour except in his own country, and in his own house'.	
Mark 6.4	'A prophet is not without honour except in his own country, and among his own kin, and in his own house'.	
John 4.44	a prophet has no honour	in his own country

Luke 4.25 But in truth, I tell you, there were many widows in Israel in the days of Elijah, when the heaven was shut up three years and six months, when there came a great famine over all the land; [26]And Elijah was sent to none of them but only to Zarephath, in the land of Sidon, to a woman who was a widow. [27]And there were many lepers in Israel in the time of the prophet Elisha; and none of them was cleansed but only Naaman the Syrian.'

[28]When they heard this, all in the synagogue were filled with wrath. [29]And they rose up and put him out of the city, and led him to the brow of the hill on which their city was built, that they might throw him down headlong. [30]But passing through the midst of them he went away.

Luke	
Matt 13.58	And he did not do many mighty works there
Mark 6.5	And he was not able to do any mighty work there, except that he laid his hands upon a few sick people and healed them.
Matt 13.58	because of their unbelief.
Mark 6.6a	And he marvelled because of their unbelief.

Next Pericope

Luke 4.31 And he went down to Capernaum, a city of Galilee. And he was teaching them on the sabbath; [32]and they were astonished at his teaching, for his word was with authority. [33]And in the synagogue there was a man who had the spirit of an unclean demon; and he cried out with a loud voice.

Matt 14.1 At that time Herod the tetrarch heard about the fame of Jesus; and he said to his servants...(cf. Mk 6.14-16; Lk. 9.7-9)

Mark 6.6b And he went among the villages teaching. [7]And he called to him the twelve, and began to send them out two by two...

Having noted earlier the points in common between the synoptic accounts of the scene, it is appropriate now to draw attention to the unique features of the Lukan account. These include:

> The dramatic character of the scene
> The ritual of the synagogue service
> The fact of the reading from Isaiah
> The detail of the reading from Isaiah
> The detail of the teaching
> The detail of the reaction of the audience
> The detail of the reaction of Jesus
> The absence of the phrase, 'Where did this man get all this? What is the wisdom given to him? (Mk 6.2)
> The absence of the phrase, What mighty works are wrought by his hands! (Mk 6.2).
> The mention of Joseph's, rather than the carpenter's son
> The absence of reference to Mary and brothers
> The reference to 'Physician, heal yourself'.
> The reference to 'what we have heard you did at Capernaum, do here also in your own country'
> The reference to Elijah and Elisha
> The anger of the audience
> The attempt to kill Jesus
> The mode of Jesus' escape.

Clearly there are elements of similarity between the texts, and some very substantial differences. How does one account for both the similarities and the differences? A number of explanations suggest themselves: that Lk. 4.16-30 is dependent upon Mk 6.1-6; that Luke embellished Mark's account of the event, with, or without the aid of sources; that Luke owes nothing to Mark's account; that there were two distinct visits, one recorded by Mark and Matthew, and a quite different one by Luke; that there was only one visit, but recorded differently in the sources of the gospels.

Is Luke 4.16-30 Dependent upon Mark 6.1-6?

Is there a literary dependence of one version on another? In particular, in line with the majority hypothetical solution to the synoptic problem, to what extent, if at all, is Lk. 4.16-30 dependent upon Mk 6.1-6?

Modern commentators vary in their assessment of the arguments. The majority opinion is that Luke does depend upon Mark, and the longer Lukan account is explained by postulating that Luke expanded Mark's version, with or without the use of another source. In addition to expanding Mark's version many scholars conclude that Luke removed it from its place in Mark's sequence, and transferred it to the beginning of his account of Jesus' public ministry. He made this transposition for his own theological reasons.

Fitzmyer's conclusion is that the Lukan form of the Nazareth visit owes its inspiration to Mk 6.1-6a, but that the additional material may come from Luke's private source, or may be entirely his own composition. He rejects the view of some scholars that the Lukan episode came to the evangelist from a non-Markan source. He postulates literary creativity on the part of Luke or his sources, noting the artistic quality of Luke's account in its build-up of the reactions to Jesus. He sees the episode to have been transposed from a different context in its source, Mark's gospel, and to have been inserted into the beginning of the public ministry of Jesus in Luke, to show from the beginning of the gospel that Jesus' ministry would be met with success, but more especially with rejection (1981: 526-29).

The recent commentary of Evans follows a broadly similar line. Luke took his cue from Mark, and made good Mark's deficiency in not anywhere giving an account of what Jesus actually said in any of the synagogue visits: 'Luke's opening is far more artistic and impressive, being perhaps the most dramatically elaborated story in his Gospel'. It draws attention to the similarities in form and content between this sermon of the spirit-filled Jesus, and those of the spirit-filled preachers in Acts (e.g. Acts 10.34-39; 13.17-19; 17.2-4) (Evans 1990: 266). This interpretation pays particular attention to the quality of Luke as a writer, and to the unity of Luke–Acts as the two-volume work of the same author.

On the other hand, Marshall sums up his discussion as follows: 'It is difficult to see why anyone should have invented the conclusion of Luke's story, and it is more probable that Mark's tradition has abbreviated the story' (1978: 180). Those who do not regard the similarity of elements as suggestive of Luke's dependence on Mark are driven to suggest other sources, perhaps some undefined Lukan special material, or the sayings source, *Q*.

Lukan Redaction and Luke's Sources

On the hypothesis that Luke was dependent upon Mark, one must enquire into how much of Luke's additional material comes from another source available to him, and how much comes from his own editorial creativity. The resolution of the problem is difficult in the extreme, as the variety of scholarly conclusions reflects. One is left wrestling with the question of how one can differentiate between Luke's own literary style, including his possible penchant for creative writing, and his employment and redaction of some hypothetical source(s) of which one is of necessity ignorant.

Among those who identify a second source for Luke, Busse argues that Luke composed his account of the Nazareth scene, influenced by Mk 1.14-15 and 6.1-6, but with the freedom befitting an author. While he did use an additional source, *Q*, he did so in a way which expanded on ideas found in Mark and *Q*. The Isaian citation was taken from Lk. 7.22-23/Mt. 11.5-6 (1978: 62-67). Christopher Tuckett, on the other hand, argues that most of the material comprising Lk. 4.16-30, namely vv. 16-21, 23, 25-27, forms a unit and comes from a source used by Luke, namely *Q* (1982: 354).

On the opposite side, and in line with his rejection of the hypothesis of *Q*, Michael Goulder proposes that in composing 4.16-30 Luke had before him no source other than Mark and Matthew. A novel feature of his argument is the suggestion that the account of the attempt to throw Jesus from the mountain on which the city is built draws on the report of the fate of the herd of pigs, who rushed down the steep bank into the sea, and were drowned in the sea (Mk 5.13). There are so many disjunctures in the two accounts that one cannot avoid the conclusion that in this instance Goulder's imagination has run wild (Goulder 1989: 305).

The confused state of scholarship on the subject is reflected in the comments of Fitzmyer. While he acknowledges that there is little similarity in the wording of the Lukan and Markan accounts of the visit, he concludes that the substance of the two accounts is the same! He explains himself as follows: 'The Lucan form of the story of the Nazareth visit owes its inspiration to Mk 6.1-6a; in vv. 16, 22, 24 the wording probably comes from "Mk". As for the rest, vv. 17-21, 23, 25-30, one may debate whether they are derived from Luke's primitive source ('L') or are to be ascribed to Lukan composition' (1981: 526).

Do Luke 4.16-30 and Mark 6.1-6 Record Two Distinct Visits?

It is possible to argue that Lk. 4.16-30 is a literary account combining the reports of two separate visits of Jesus to the Nazareth synagogue, only one of which is recorded in Mk 6.1-6, while the account of the second visit comes from an independent source. The justification for this

2. The Source Question

conclusion is that the parallel between the two accounts is very slight, and depends primarily on the not uncommon aphorism, 'a prophet is not accepted in his own country':

Matt 13.57	A prophet is not without honour except	in his own country, and in his own house.
Mark 6.4	A prophet is not without honour except among his own kin, and in his own house.	in his own country, and
Luke 4.24	No prophet is acceptable	in his own country
John 4.44	*A prophet has no honour*	*in his own country*

The sentence occurs on the lips of Jesus also in *The Gospel of Thomas*: 'Jesus said, "No prophet is accepted in his own village; no physician heals those who know him"' (Logion 31), and in the Oxyrhynchus papyrus of the Sayings of Jesus: 'Jesus says, "A prophet is not acceptable in his own country, neither does a physician work cures upon them that know him"' (*P. Oxy.* 1, Logion 6). Jn 4.43-45 reads,

> After the two days he departed to Galilee. ⁴⁴For Jesus himself testified that a prophet has no honour in his own country. ⁴⁵So when he came to Galilee, the Galileans welcomed him, having seen all that he had done in Jerusalem at the feast, for they too had gone to the feast.

The wording in Jn 4.44 is not identical with either Mt. 13.57 // Mk 6.4 or Lk. 4.24. One can ask with Rudolf Schnackenburg (1968: 463) whether Jn 4.44 contains a rudimentary trait of the tradition of rejection in Nazareth, which is also alluded to in Jn 6.42 ('They said, "Is not this Jesus, the son of Joseph, whose father and mother we know? How does he now say, 'I have come down from heaven'"?'). It must be noted, however, that in the Johannine account the scene is in the synagogue in Capernaum (6.59), rather than in that at Nazareth.

Another possibility is that while there may have been only one visit behind two different accounts of it, Luke has used both Mk 6.1-6 and another hypothetical source describing the same visit.

Conclusion

The prolonged assault on the widely accepted Two-Document/Two-Source hypothesis (Mark and *Q* as the main sources of Matthew and Luke) over the last thirty years makes one less secure in accepting it as a solution to the wider synoptic problem. Although no alternative hypothesis has gained general consensus, there has been a steady attack on the priority of Mark, and on the very existence of *Q*, sufficient to make theories based on it less than secure. As far as possible, I prefer to assume neither the two-source theory, nor any other hypothesis as a basis for making judgments on the redactional techniques of Luke. In general, I consider it more prudent to retain a working scepticism on any source theory, and to concentrate on the finished product of each evangelist. However, one cannot suspend one's pragmatic judgment *sine die* simply on the basis that even the most likely hypothesis does not enjoy the status of a fact.

On the specific question of Lk. 4.16-30, the existence of somewhat similar material in Mk 6.1-6 and Mt. 13.53-58 suggests that Luke may have given a new context to the scene as recorded in Mark and Matthew, and elaborated it after his own fashion, with or without the use of other material from the tradition. This is the general hypothesis of scholars who subscribe to the Two-Source Theory of gospel origins. Of course it begs the wider source question of the dependence of Luke on either Mark or Matthew. The dependence may have been in the other direction, if only in the sense that Mark or Matthew may have been aware of the tradition of rejection at Nazareth from the source behind Luke's gospel. While it is true that the accounts have elements in common, there are many differences. That the two gospels record two separate incidents is not an impossible solution.

Whether or not the link between Lk. 4.16-30 and Mk 6.1-6a is too tenuous to propose a literary dependence of Lk. 4.16-30 on Mk 6.1-6a, it is clear that the most distinctive material in Luke's account does not derive from Mark. To account for the presence of so much material in Lk. 4.16-30 that is not contained in Mark, material of such theological significance, one must conclude either that Luke had access to a source other than or additional to Mark, or that he exercised great dramatic and literary imagination in embellishing the Markan material. Scholarship is divided as to whether the text can be explained as a free Lukan expansion/reworking of Mk 6.1-6, or whether Luke had an additional source (Q, or some other special one), in addition to Mk 6.1-6a. However, the suggestion that the material came in the main from Q is not altogether satisfactory, since it is a rather loosely defined hypothetical source, whose existence is guaranteed only by the persistence of scholars whose hypotheses demand it. Another problem arises by virtue of the fact that since it is by definition a sayings source available also to Matthew, some explanation for the absence from Matthew of such details as the Isaiah reading and its aftermath is required. The question

2. *The Source Question*   87

fundamentally is a methodological one: by what criteria does one decide whether Luke is redacting Mark by some combination of creative interpolation and extrapolation, and/or is using another source? The lack of certainty in the matter leaves the innocent reader somewhat at a loss

I am of the view that all three synoptic gospels represent a scene in which Jesus encountered opposition among his own. Luke's account is significantly different from that of the other two, and I incline to the view that his account represents a fuller tradition of such opposition which was not available to the other two synoptists, but which was available to him from one or more of the *many* sources referred to in his preface (Lk. 1.1). Luke's use of *many* raises the question of how many. Is the *many* to be restricted to the two documentary ones appealed to by the scholarly consensus, Mark and *Q*, and the convenient catch-all term, the Special Lukan source? Is it not more likely that there were many other sources, not necessarily all written, than that the *many* is an exaggeration for *two*, or *three*? If there were several other sources, what happened to them?

I agree with Alexander, who, on the basis of her investigation of prefaces in antiquity, concludes that,

> There was no convention which could *compel* Luke to mention 'many' predecessors unless he wanted to do so. It is simplest, then, to conclude, short of positive indication to the contrary, that Luke meant what he said. If this causes problems for our views on Gospel sources or chronology, perhaps we need to look more closely at those views and their assumptions. Part of the problem, I suspect, is the tendency of critics to think exclusively in terms of the documents we know: Mark and Matthew/Q are two, not 'many', and it seems unwarranted to hypothesize a number of other written Gospels, now lost without trace. But Luke never says that his predecessors had produced *written* documents: using the conventional language of any school treatise, he says merely that they had tried to 'put together an account'—a splendidly ambiguous phrase which could be interpreted in a number of historically plausible ways (Alexander 1993: 115).

I find little persuasion in the view that Luke derived the core of his material in 4.16-30 from our Mark, and added to it. Neither am I convinced by the argument that the present text of Luke combines two distinct narratives, with the joining coming at v. 22. Mark's account looks more like a general summary of the opposition to Jesus after he had spoken in a synagogue near his home-town. I propose that Luke transmits responsibly a summary of the account, or the summarized account itself, of an incident which happened in Nazareth on a Sabbath, which was available to him from his several sources, oral and/or written.

However, several arguments seem to me to be decisive concerning Luke's positioning of the material so early in Jesus' Galilean ministry. The prominent place given to the universalistic character of the preaching of Jesus in the stories of the Zarephath widow and Naaman the Syrian may be out of place so early in the public ministry of Jesus. But that objection is not decisive, since it is quite natural to invoke a precedent from within the Israelite traditions. However, internal evidence suggests that the placing of the section virtually at the beginning of Jesus' public ministry is the work of the author. In addition to the argument deriving from Mark's presentation later in the Galilean ministry, there is the reference to previous success in Capernaum in Lk. 4.23. This makes it clear that the Nazareth incident came after some activity in Capernaum, rather than where Luke places it. The reference could be explained as being implied by the general reference to Jesus' Galilean activity in Lk. 4.14-15, but v. 31 clearly implies that he had not been there before. The difficulty would disappear if the events in the Capernaum synagogue (Lk. 4.31-37) preceded the Nazareth scene in Luke, but, of course this is not the case. What was the motive for Luke's placing the material in this place?

Marshall takes the view that the author has placed the narrative in this place 'for its programmatic significance', and he notes that it contains many of the main features of Luke–Acts in a nutshell (1978: 178). Similarly, Fitzmyer claims that

> Luke has deliberately put this story at the beginning of the public ministry to encapsulate the entire ministry of Jesus and the reaction to it. The fulfilment-story stresses the success of his teaching under the guidance of the Spirit, but the rejection story symbolizes the opposition that his ministry will evoke among his own. The rejection of him by the people of his hometown is a miniature of the rejection of him by the people of his own patris in the larger sense (1981: 529).

I consider that it is possible to respect both the substantial historicity of the Lukan account, and the literary artistry of the author, by concluding that in 4.16-30 Luke gives a sketch of a real event in the synagogue at Nazareth, which was critical for the public ministry of Jesus, and which he places almost (but not quite, cf. 4.14-15) at the inauguration of that ministry in Galilee. It is possible, but unprovable, that Luke saw in the incident a foretaste of what he knew to have happened in the rest of the ministry of Jesus, and in that of the disciples who carried on evangelizing the poor after he had ascended. The story emphasizes that the ministry of Jesus, which is about to take place, is in fulfilment of Old Testament passages, directly in the quotation from Isaiah 61, and indirectly in presenting Jesus as a counterpart of Elijah and Elisha. The eschatological era has begun in the person of Jesus, in that the Spirit, long dormant, has come upon him, anointing him to evangelize poor people, to proclaim liberty to captives, to give sight to the blind, to set free the oppressed, and to proclaim the acceptable year of the Lord.

***

Having considered how far the discussion about sources can bring us, it is now apposite to consider the scene from a different perspective, namely, that of the coherence of the account.

Chapter 3

THE COHERENCE OF LUKE'S ACCOUNT

I have argued that Lk. 4.16-30 gives the sketch of a real event in the synagogue at Nazareth, which the author brings virtually to the beginning of the public ministry of Jesus. I consider it likely that the information was somewhere in the several sources which the author had available to him (Lk. 1.1-2). There are, however, several elements in the account which call into question the historical reliability of the event Luke summarizes, and it is to these that we now turn our attention.

From the Gospels to Jesus

Several questions may suggest themselves to the reader. As someone within the tradition of nineteenth-century historiography, you may consider, 'What really happened?' to be the most important one to deal with. On the other hand, you may be sensitive to the power of story, and of other powerful forms of literary communication, and may recognize in Luke's account aspects of his perception which are not exhausted by answering the rather mechanical question, 'What really happened?' In any event one should seek a satisfactory answer to one's own questions. It may be the case that they are more important than those which have dominated scholarly investigation in the wealthier parts of the world this century.

Whence did the setting, content and teaching of Lk. 4.16-30 come to Luke? Is Luke's account of the opening of the public ministry of Jesus in Galilee closer to what actually happened, than that of Matthew and/or Mark? Or is it the case that Luke, or his source, has dramatized a scene hinted at in (the tradition behind) the other two gospels, and given it a place in the opening of the public ministry in Galilee? Such questions are not without importance. Our estimate of the authority of the passage will take into account whether we are dealing with the very words of Jesus,

3. *The Coherence of Luke's Account* 91

or with some Lukan (or pre-Lukan) redaction of them, or whether we are dealing with a mainly Lukan composition.

What we have before us is the finished account of Lk. 4.16-30. In the language of mainstream modern gospel scholarship we are at the final (third) stage of gospel composition, that of *the context of the author*. The earlier second stage, containing *the record of the event as kept alive* in a community, or some communities of the early Church, is embedded in the text. Behind these two stages lies *the event in the life of Jesus himself* (the first stage).

Our situation is not unlike that of an archaeologist investigating a new site. What one may see in the first instance is a mound in its finished state. As soon as the excavator probes what lies below, it will be clear that the different layers reflect different stages. Most of us would love to move from the present text to the bedrock of the event as it happened in the ministry of Jesus (the first stage). Were it possible to know that for sure, we would then have arrived at an account of the event in the life of Jesus, which was free of the kind of literary evolution that took place later (in the second stage), culminating in the finished account of Luke's gospel (the third stage of gospel composition). However, even in that situation we could never say that 'this is exactly what happened', but only that this is how somebody reported what had happened, since all accounts of events involve selections and interpretations.

We will be able to make some assessment of the historicity question, however, and this will grow out of our conclusions concerning the sources, and other factors, such as the internal coherence of Luke's account. To the examination of these issues we now turn.

What Really Happened in Nazareth?

What is it in Luke's account that makes us suspicious about whether it represents what really happened at the beginning of the public ministry of Jesus? Had we only his description to go by, we might have no such suspicion, although we still would have to contend with the question of the coherence of Luke's description. The fact that Jesus' Galilean ministry opens differently in Matthew and Mark poses the problem for us.

Several features in Luke's account make us wonder if in fact it reflects the situation in the ministry of Jesus:

The account in 4.16-30 seriously conflicts with what one might expect to find after 4.15: 'And he taught in their synagogues, being glorified by all'. Is it likely that his own people should have turned on him in such a violent fashion? However, given the general opposition to the acknowledgment of a prophet in his home base, it is not impossible, to say the least. The placing of the two reactions, enthusiastic acceptance and total rejection, side by side highlights Luke's presentation of the ambivalence of the response to Jesus.

There is the additional problem posed by the very material in the account of Luke. We might well wonder about the likelihood of the crowd in the synagogue turning on Jesus to the extent of wishing to throw him from the brow of the hill 'on which Nazareth is built'.

There are two mood changes to account for. How can one understand the abrupt transition in the congregation's mood from what appears to be a positive reaction (v. 22), to one approaching the anger and fervour of a lynch-mob (vv. 28-29)? There also appears to be a change of attitude on the part of Jesus, who goes from hearing what can be understood to be the favourable response of the congregation, to one of turning the tables on them, and addressing them in a combative fashion. How does one explain the movement from v. 22, 'And all spoke well of him, and wondered at the gracious words which proceeded out of his mouth; and they said, "Is not this Joseph's son?"', to v. 23, 'And he said to them, "Doubtless you will quote to me this proverb, 'Physician, heal yourself; what we have heard you did at Capernaum, do here also in your own country'"'.

For many scholars the abrupt changes in attitude are the result of putting together different sources in a rather rough fashion. Leaney, for one, protests that 'Luke has given us an impossible story', in his desire to combine the narrative of a triumphant visit with a rejection. Luke's motive in giving us such an unlikely story was to show that even the beginning of Jesus' ministry conformed to what happened later: 'The author of Acts believed that the Gospel was sent to the Jews and on their rejection of it to the Gentiles' (1966: 52).

Was the Crowd Enraged, or Merely Amazed? Enraged!
Another strand of interpretation has rather more regard for the literary skills of the author, and seeks a solution other than one of conflating sources which reflect different moods. Bornhaüser reads the Nazareth scene very differently. For him the mood does not change from admiration to disenchantment. The problem was already established in Jesus' form of the citation from Isaiah. A particular irritant was that Jesus

stopped short at, 'to proclaim the acceptable day of the Lord', and omitted the second half of that sentence, 'and a day of vengeance of our God' (Isa. 61.2). In his presentation of God's good news through Isaiah, then, Jesus had removed the promise of vengeance on the Gentiles from his prediction of the future. Israel anxiously awaited the day of vindication, when its enemies would be overthrown, and it would be free. The audience waited to see if Jesus would redress the balance in his exegesis of the text in his sermon, but in vain, since Jesus was interested in words of God's grace only, and not at all in vengeance. Hence they all witnessed (i.e., in this case, brought a charge) against him (1924: 59).

The view that the Nazareth audience was enraged, and not merely astonished, has been taken up by others. Violet argues from the context that the audience was astounded (*thaumazō*), in the negative sense of being deeply shocked and very perturbed, rather than in the positive one of being thrilled and elated. They could not accept Jesus' claims to represent God's will in that way, nor his claims to be a prophet and Messiah (Violet 1938: 268-70). Against the argument that the verb *martureō* with the dative case (to bear witness) should be understood positively (to bear positive witness), he argues that it can have a negative connotation also (to bear negative witness), and claims this latter to be the meaning in Jn 7.7; 18.23 (p. 257).

Jeremias, too, did not regard Lk. 4.22 as registering a break between an initial attitude of acceptance, and a subsequent one of hostility. It merely carries on the outrage which the congregation registered against him. Jeremias claimed that the phrase, *pantes emarturoun autō* itself, being a translation from a Semitic source, can be either positive (the dative of advantage), or negative (the dative of disadvantage), that is, meaning either 'they bore witness for him', or 'they bore witness against him'. Only the context will decide, and the remainder of v. 22 is such that the meaning has to be, 'all bore negative witness to him', rather than positively in the usual reading (e.g. the RSV: 'All spoke well of him'). Jeremias, too, argues that the verb, 'all...wondered' means here, 'all were astonished' at the strangeness of what he was claiming. Not only did Jesus interfere with the text of Isaiah by omitting reference to the day of vengeance, but he claimed to inaugurate the beginning of the time of salvation (Jeremias 1956: 39). The people were astounded that Jesus spoke in that way. This contradicts the usual understanding of the text, that they were very impressed by the gracious words which he spoke.

In support of his view that it was the omission of the reference to the day of vengeance that brought on the disapproval of the audience, Jeremias drew attention to another text in Luke 7.22-23, in which many elements of Lk. 4.18-19 occur. John the Baptist sent two disciples to Jesus, to enquire if he was 'the one who is to come' (7.18-19). In Luke's account, Jesus answers in two ways, by actions, and then words: 'In that hour he cured many of diseases and plagues and evil spirits, and on many that were blind he bestowed sight' (v. 21). The text continues, 'Go and tell John what you have seen and heard: the blind receive their sight, the lame walk, lepers are cleansed, and the deaf hear, the dead are raised up, poor people are evangelized. *And blessed is he who takes no offence at me*' (Lk. 7.22).

Jeremias regards Jesus' verbal response as a mixed quotation from the following texts of Isaiah:

> 35.5-6 Then *the eyes of the blind shall be opened*, and *the ears of the deaf unstopped*;
> then shall *the lame man leap* like a hart, and the tongue of the dumb sing for joy
>
> 29.18-19 In that day *the deaf shall hear* the words of a book,
> and out of their gloom and darkness *the eyes of the blind shall see*.
> The meek shall obtain fresh joy in the Lord,
> and *the poor* among men shall exult in the Holy One of Israel.
>
> 61.1 The Spirit of the Lord God is upon me, because the Lord has anointed me
> *to bring good tidings to the poor*; he has sent me to bind up the brokenhearted,
> to proclaim release to the captives and *recovering of sight to the blind*,
> to set at liberty those who are oppressed...

Jeremias notes that the context of these Isaian texts is the coming of the eschatological Day of Vengeance (*Rachetag Gottes*), as can be seen clearly in the immediate context of each one: 'Say to those who are of a fearful heart, 'Be strong, fear not! Behold, your God will come with vengeance, with the recompense of God. He will come and save you' (Isa. 35.4); 'For the ruthless shall come to naught and the scoffer cease, and all who watch to do evil shall be cut off...' (Isa. 29.20); 'To proclaim the year of the Lord's favour, and the day of vengeance of our God...' (Isa. 61.2). The total omission in the preaching of Jesus of any reference to the vengeance of God as an element in the time of the Messiah is the core reason for the offence which people took.

3. *The Coherence of Luke's Account*　　　　　　　　　95

The emphasis of Bornhaüser, Violet and Jeremias is not without support: for example, for Luke, the Messiah is the bringer of salvation, and not of judgment (Grundmann 1981: 118-23); Luke 'avoids the reference to "the day of recompense" which follows, which...would disturb the emphasis which Luke wished to make. For Luke the ministry of Jesus means the coming of the time of salvation' (Tannehill 1972: 71).

Baarlink offers two further arguments in support of the Bornhaüser, Violet and Jeremias position, one from the theological structure of Luke's gospel, and the second from the presence of the proclamation of judgment in Lk. 21.22, that very element which is omitted in Lk. 4.19 (Baarlink 1982).

Was the Crowd Enraged, or Merely Amazed? Amazed!
The major objection to the solution of Bornhaüser, Violet and Jeremias is that support for understanding the verb *martureo autō* (with the dative case of *autos*) in v. 22 to mean 'to bear *negative* witness' is lacking. Non-biblical use, including that of Philo, Josephus and inscriptions, does not attest the negative meaning (see O'Fearghail 1984: 63 for references). The two New Testament examples advanced by Violet (Jn 7.7; 18.23) employ a preposition (*peri*), and do not in any case refer to a person.

The majority view among scholars, then, is that the congregation's first reaction to Jesus (v. 22) was positive. In that case, however, a major question arises: What was the reason for the rejection of Jesus? Why did the initial positive reaction to Jesus go sour? What element caused the abrupt shift in the congregation's mood? Was it that they liked the message, but did not like the messenger? Or, was it that they rejected the notion that the brash Jesus, who had no formal training as a rabbi, was a prophet? Or, was it the content of what he went on to say that caused the change?

Anderson solves the problem by recourse to what he regards as the theological perspective of Luke. He rejects Jeremias's bold view that rejection is apparent in v. 22. His reasons include the astute observation that the phrase, 'and the eyes of all in the synagogue were fixed on him' (v. 20) implies a positive reception for what he read (1964: 268-69). It must be added, however, that that was before he said, 'Today this scripture has been fulfilled in your hearing' (v. 21). Anderson's explanation is that, for Luke, the Jesus story is ultimately one of success. The conclusion of the Nazareth section, 'But passing through the midst of them he went away' (v. 30), anticipates this, and converts the whole situation into a success story (1964: 271). Luke, in his view, has superimposed the motif of success upon a tradition which told only of failure. He suggests that the account shows Jesus' rejection of the people as much as their rejection of him, thereby anticipating what, in Anderson's view, is the final Jewish rejection of Jesus, and the turning of the gospel to the Gentiles. In this explanation the presence of Luke's putative motive is sufficient to explain the difficulties in the narrative.

Many scholars see in the remark 'Is not this Joseph's son?' (v. 22c) a negative connotation, which provoked Jesus' harsh words, 'Doubtless you will quote to me this proverb, "Physician, heal yourself; what we have heard you did at Capernaum, do here also in your own country"' (Lk. 4.23). The difficulty with this view of v. 22 is how to account for the abrupt change from the positive reaction reflected in the first two elements ('And all spoke well of him, and wondered at the gracious words which proceeded out of his mouth') to the negative one in the third ('And they said, "Is not this Joseph's son?"').

O'Fearghail attempts a solution to the problem which does not involve such a quantum leap from acceptance of his person and words ('All spoke well of him', v. 22a) to an almost immediate rejection of them ('Is not this Joseph's son?', understood with a negative connotation, v. 22c). He agrees that the verb *martureō* (to bear witness to) does not have a negative connotation. But he argues that the good reputation of Jesus does not derive from what he has just said, but comes from the knowledge the people already had of him from much experience. O'Fearghail finds the key in the opening sentence, 'And he came to Nazareth where he had been brought up; and he went to the synagogue as his custom was, on the sabbath day' (v. 16). The people in Nazareth had known him well for many years, both outside and inside the synagogue, and that knowledge was the basis of their esteem for him (O'Fearghail 1984: 65-67). O'Fearghail then draws attention to the ambiguous meaning of *thaumazō*—to wonder, be puzzled, be astonished. Since the verb can carry either a positive or negative sense, the choice of meaning should be determined by the object of the verb (the gracious words), and by the context.

O'Fearghail argues that the phrase *logoi tēs charitos* (the gracious words) of v. 22 conveys much more than mere 'winsome, or attractive words'. The words, in fact, are no less than the word of God, the message of salvation. The phrase, 'which proceeded out of his mouth', suggests to O'Fearghail the nourishing power of the word of God in Deut. 8.3 ('Man does not live on bread alone, but on every word *which proceeds from the mouth of* God man lives'). However, O'Fearghail's argument at this point would be stronger if the Greek Deuteronomy text had used either *logos* or *charis*. Nevertheless, other elements of his argument strengthen his case. Clearly the text of Isaiah 61, and Jesus' insistence on 'today', evokes the atmosphere of salvation. He clinches his argument by referring to v. 43, in which Jesus, in response to people who wanted to detain him, insisted that he must preach the kingdom of God *in other cities also*, thereby implying that that was precisely what he was doing in Nazareth. O'Fearghail adduces texts in which the word *charis* has this salvific connotation (Acts 14.3; especially 20.24; and 20.32).

This brings us back to the appropriate meaning of *thaumazō*. The reaction of the congregation is one of astonishment tainted with criticism, rather than one of admiring surprise. While appreciating the quality of his character (*martureō*), they are astonished at, and critical of (*thaumazō*) his message (*logoi tēs charitos*, the saving words). It was just too much for them to accept that one of their own, no matter how gifted, could be the eschatological prophet of Isaiah 61, who in his own person brought God's salvation. No wonder they protested, 'Is not this Joseph's son?' (v. 22c).

O'Fearghail directs attention to a corresponding use of the verb, 'to be astonished'. The context also has much by way of comparison. Lk. 11.37-52 situates Jesus as a guest at a meal in a Pharisee's house. The Pharisee was *astonished* to see that Jesus did not wash his hands before dinner (v. 38). Jesus' reaction was not to explain his behaviour, or attempt to win approval, but to launch into a series of criticisms (*woes*), first of the Pharisees (vv. 39-44), and then of one of the lawyers (vv. 45-52). The narrative concludes, 'As he went away from there, the scribes and the Pharisees began to press him hard, and to provoke him to speak of many things, lying in wait for him, to catch at something he might say' (vv. 53-54). In a corresponding way, Jesus does not proffer an explanation to the audience in Nazareth in the hope of winning their approval, but instead launches into an attack from v. 23 onwards.

O'Fearghail's understanding of the text can be summed up in his translation of v. 22, 'And they all witnessed to him, but were astonished at the words of grace (i.e. salvation) that came from his mouth; and (i.e. for) they said, "Is not this Joseph's son?"' (1984: 72). In this interpretation, then, there was resentment at what Jesus said from the very beginning, and the opposition to his teaching mounted, culminating in an act of total rejection of the teacher: 'There is...a linear movement of rejection that begins in v. 22, as a result of Jesus' initial message (vv. 18-19, 21), and reaches a climax in v. 29, under the lash of Jesus' tongue (vv. 23-27). The climax is represented by an act expressive of total rejection' (O'Fearghail 1984: 72).

There is much to commend in O'Fearghail's powerful argument. I agree that the opposition to Jesus is reflected both in the verb *thaumazō*, and in the question, 'Is not this Joseph's son?' Understanding the text this way removes the very substantial problem of accounting for Jesus' attack on the audience in the wake of their approval of him. His understanding of, 'They all witnessed to him', however, is not as convincing. I am less inclined than he to dismiss the possibility that this phrase, too, implies a negative connotation, or at least a neutral one.

Conclusion

Unfortunately, one can never be certain when it comes to reconstructing a scene from the past on the basis of the slender evidence we possess. I share with Bornhäuser, Violet, Jeremias and O'Fearghail the view that opposition to Jesus is reflected already in v. 22, and that it is this opposition which provokes Jesus' aggressive attitude to the audience. This will become clearer once we concede that the text of Isaiah 61 and 58.6 does not constitute the totality of a Sabbath reading from the prophets. I contend that Jesus' presentation of the text itself, or, at least, Luke's portrayal of it, was enough to introduce unease in the audience, and that Jesus' claim that the prophecy was being fulfilled in their hearing would have exacerbated the problem. But whether the opposition to Jesus was there already from his choice of text or not, it is indisputable that matters got nasty very quickly.

In rejecting the view of Jeremias *et al.* that opposition is already apparent in v. 22, most scholars interpret Luke's account as one in which the congregation went from accepting Jesus almost totally up to v. 22, to a total rejection of him beginning at v. 23. In that view, Jesus himself brought on the negative reaction by his statement, 'Doubtless you will quote to me this proverb, "Physician, heal yourself"' (v. 23), and by his affirmation, 'Truly I say to you, no prophet is acceptable in his own country' (v. 24). While such a scenario is not impossible, it seems less credible to me than the one that suggests that his treatment of the Isaiah text, and his claim to being the eschatological prophet, already evoked the greatest resentment.

Proponents of the common view have to account for two changes in attitude, that of Jesus first, and then that of the audience. With regard to the first problem, I judge the suggestion that we are dealing with a conflation of sources to be a recourse of desperation, and to be dismissive of the literary skills of the author. With regard to the second problem, the reversal in the mood of the congregation, such a *volte face* is possible, although in my view the situation is explained better by positing opposition at an earlier point, as discussed above.

Obviously, Jesus' statement that God could embrace a preferential option for Gentiles, as exhibited in the ministry of Elijah and Elisha to which he refers, and which he develops, would cause great resentment. Religious people, in general, find it difficult to allow God to act with a generosity that extends his salvation beyond the narrow confines of their tradition.

But even if one accepts it as more likely that there was an abrupt change in the mood of the audience, from one of admiration to growing offence, experience shows that such a change of mood could take place in the course of a session. Smooth words are well received, especially in a religious context, in which, for the most part, people do not expect to be ruffled. It is only when the tables are turned that indignation surfaces. Perhaps there is in Jn 8.59 some reflection of this attitude to Jesus ('So they took up stones to throw at him; but Jesus hid himself, and went out of the temple'), and also in Jn 10.39 ('Again they tried to arrest him, but he escaped from their hands').

A recent example of the rejection of a 'prophet' by his own Jewish people is provided by the account of the address of Professor George Steiner to the packed audience of the World Union of Progressive Judaism Conference at West London Synagogue in May 1990. He claimed that Israel was 'edging towards sheer brute ungovernability, towards a dread isolation among unforgiving enemies, towards political corruption, political cowardice, political mediocrity of the most profound kind...which fill all of us with shame'. *The Jewish Chronicle* laconically adds, 'Some in the audience hissed with anger' (May 11, 1990).

In a less spectacular way, a homily I delivered on *Peace Sunday*, while the Gulf War was in progress, ruffled some feathers. It stimulated Desmond Albrow's 'Opinion' in the *Catholic Herald*, 9 February 1991, and caused Paul Johnson to fulminate in his 'Kindly leave the Pulpit', *The Spectator*, 16 February 1991. Parishioners come to Mass for peace and consolation, Albrow said, and not to have their prejudices polished or their antipathies aroused. Quite right, said Johnson, who proposed that organized mobs should take over such pulpits, and bring any political harangue to an abrupt end. My crime was to have directed the attention of the congregation to the absurd situation that protagonists on both sides of the conflict claimed to have God on their side. More significantly for a Catholic audience, I had drawn attention to what the Pope had said on the outbreak of the war, which he had predicted would be a 'reckless adventure': 'We pray that God may show those responsible that they should abandon immediately this war which is so unworthy of humanity'.

In my subsequent letters to the Editor of the *Catholic Herald* and the *Spectator*, I confessed that I presumed that people come to Mass also to confess their sins, and to allow the light of the Gospel to challenge their values. I suggested that Christians who did not protest against the obscenity of that war, and call for a halt to it, have reason to question whether their values derive from the universalism which characterizes the Christian vision, or from the multiple forms of militaristic and xenophobic nationalism which corrupt it. I trusted that I would escape the fate of the preacher who disturbed the peace in his synagogue in Nazareth, claiming that God cannot be contained within the closed system of one religious nationalism, and expressed relief that that there were no hills around where I live!

Chapter 4

THE HISTORICITY OF THE NAZARETH SYNAGOGUE SCENE

Christian visitors to the Holy Land in search of the places associated with the ministry of Jesus might wish to visit the synagogue in Nazareth, if they are prepared to do more than spend the thirty minutes or so that it takes to get some photos of the Basilica of the Annunciation. The sixth-century pilgrim from Piacenza provides one of the earliest references to the site:

> We travelled on to the city of Nazareth, where many miracles take place. In the synagogue there is kept the book in which the Lord wrote his ABC, and in this synagogue is the bench on which he sat with other children. Christians can lift the bench and move it about, but the Jews are completely unable to move it, and cannot drag it outside. The house of Saint Mary is now a basilica, and her clothes are the cause of frequent miracles (v. 161, in Wilkinson 1977: 79).

Unfortunately the extant text of Egeria's travels does not contain accounts of the visits she paid to Galilee in 383. Although Peter the Deacon, the twelfth-century monk of Monte Cassino used her as a source, his statement, 'Inside the city the synagogue where the Lord read the book of Isaiah is now a church', probably relies on twelfth-century sources (Wilkinson 1981: 193-94).

There is currently a vigorous debate about the meaning of the word *sunagōgē* in New Testament times (Kee 1990; Oster 1993), and it is necessary to engage in a discussion of the matter, in order to have a clearer idea of the setting in the synagogue of Nazareth.

The common view that first-century synagogues were purpose-built, and that the pattern of systematic instruction, prayer and worship reflected in the later literature obtained in pre-70 AD has recently been challenged by Kee, who insists that it has no foundation (Kee 1990: 4). According to Kee's revisionist view, then, the synagogues in which Jesus exercised so much of his teaching were either originally private houses, with their limited space, or portions of larger buildings, perhaps set aside for the purposes of the Jewish community (Kee 1990: 8-9). There is no reason to think that such buildings would accommodate hundreds of people. Moreover, the indications in Luke–Acts that there was some institutional organization, formal programmes or patterns of instruction, and liturgical formulae are Lukan anachronisms (Kee 1990: 13). The synagogal formalization of Lk. 4.16-30 is a greatly expanded version of the brief account of Jesus teaching in the synagogue in Nazareth found in Mk 6.1-6, in the light of later synagogal practice, Kee claims. The absence in either Matthew or Mark of the liturgical details of the Lukan text must be due to 'later forms of synagogal worship read back into the time of Jesus' (Kee 1990: 18). Pre-70 AD Pharisaic piety was more concerned with the piety manifested at home than with the affairs of the synagogal gatherings, which 'seem to be no more than informal gatherings of faithful Jews in homes or available public places, although the reference to weekly meetings may well reflect the early stages of the systematization of synagogal practice that we have seen to be in process in the later first century' (Kee 1990: 19).

The argument concerns whether *sunagōgē* refers merely to an assembly of people, or whether it can also refer to the meeting place. More significantly for our purposes, what is at stake is the reliability of Luke–Acts as an indication of what happened in synagogue incidents he describes, and, more specifically, in the Nazareth synagogue.

The Term sunagōgē

It is instructive to consider the available information on the Jewish synagogue. The first meaning of the Greek term *sunagōgē* is a gathering of persons, whether of individuals, or of a public assembly (e.g. Plato *Theaetetus* 150a; Polybius 4.7.6), or a gathering of things (e.g. Polybius 27.13.2), such as letters (Cicero *Ad Atticum* 9.13.3). The term is widely used of Greek societies which met to worship their heroes and their gods. In general, *sunagōgē* was used predominantly for the festive assembly or meeting, whether cultic or not (Schrage 1971: 800). Horsley discusses three non-Jewish uses of *sunagōgē* (1981: 28-29; 1983: 43; 1987: 202).

The term *sunagōgē* occurs over 200 times in the Septuagint translation of the Hebrew Scriptures (LXX), mostly for *'edâ* (the national, legal and cultic assembly of Israel, some 130 times), and *qāhāl* (some 35 times), terms which are very similar. *sunagōgē* and *ekklēsia* are used almost interchangeably in the LXX.

With the possible exception of Susanna 28, the LXX never uses *sunagōgē* for the house of assembly (Schrage 1971: 805). In Greek-speaking Judaism *sunagōgē* often refers to the local Jewish synagogal community. It is not at all clear that a distinction is made between *sunagōgē*, understood as assembly, and the building, for which other terms are also used (e.g. *proseuchē*, *CIJ* I, 683, 19; or *ho hagios topos*, *CIJ* I, 694, 5; see also the other Greek words used of Second Temple synagogues, collected in Oster 1993: 186).

The archaeological and epigraphic records point to Egypt, rather than Babylon, as the place of origin of the synagogue. There was a Jewish diaspora there already by the sixth century BC (Hengel 1975). The standard term is not *sunagōgē*, but *proseuchē*, a term not in common use among the Greeks of the period (Kee 1990: 5). Hengel thinks that these *proseuchai*, as the name suggests, were primarily places of prayer and worship. Horsley reproduces inscriptions of nine examples of *proseuchē* meaning *sunagōgē*, between mid-third-century and first-century BC Egypt (1987: 201).

Scholars have attempted to account for the existence and usage of the two words, *proseuchē* and *sunagōgē*. Some appeal to a chronological development. Horsley suggests that by I BC/I AD *sunagōgē* was ousting *proseuchē* as the Jewish technical term, and that because *sunagōgē* became *the* term for the Jewish synagogue, the use of the word to refer to non-Jewish associations apparently diminished considerably (1987: 220). Zeitlin suggested that while the synagogue initially was a secular meeting place in post-exilic Judaism, which also served as a locus of worship for Jews, its religious function increased with the fall of Jerusalem in 70 AD (1930–31). Other explanations appeal to regional differences, with *proseuchē* being the preferred term in the Diaspora and *sunagōgē* that in Palestine. A third category of explanation appeals to different architectural styles, with *proseuchē* suggesting a more simple form, and *sunagōgē* a more ornate one.

It is argued that *sunagōgē* began to supersede *proseuchē* in Palestine first, and then only began to spread to the Diaspora during the first century AD (Horsley 1987: 220). The earliest use outside Palestine of *sunagōgē* for a building is in an inscription from Berenice (Benghazi) in Cyrenaica, dated to 55 AD (see Horsley 1987: 202). It reads, 'In the second year of the emperor Nero Claudius Caesar Drusus Germanicus, on the 16th of Chorach. It was resolved by the *sunagōgē* of Jews in Berenice that those who donated to the repairs of the *sunagōgē* be inscribed on a stele of Parian marble.' The fact that the two uses of *sunagōgē* occur in this one inscription warns against the dogmatism which attempts to establish criteria for dating on the basis of some notion of normative vocabulary.

Although Josephus refers to the synagogue at Tiberias as a *proseuchē*, there are other places in which his use of the term *sunagōgē* clearly refers to a building. In fact, the event which, according to Josephus, precipitated the war with the Romans was the failure of Jucundus, the Roman cavalry commander, to quell the riot after a Greek mischief-maker in Caesarea sacrificed birds on an upended pot beside the entrance to the *sunagōgē* on a sabbath (*War* 2.285-91, wherein the word *sunagōgē* meaning 'building' occurs at 285 and 289). Similarly, the use of *sunagōgē* in 7.44 clearly refers to the Jewish building at Antioch. Furthermore, it is indisputable that *sunagōgē* in *Ant.* 19.300 refers to the Jewish shrine/place of worship in the city of Dora, rather than to the assembly of Jews.

Although four of the five uses of *sunagōgē* in Philo (see Mayer 1974) occur only in quotations from Num. 27.16-17 (twice each in *Poster. C.* 67 and *Agr.* 44), his fifth usage refers to the 'sacred places', which are called *sunagogai*, where Essenes meet on the seventh day (*Omn. Prob. Lib.* 81). I agree with Oster (1993: 191) against Kee (1990: 5) that Philo's one clear use of *sunagōgē* to refer to a building is more significant as an indication of contemporary terminology than the four uses which merely follow the vocabulary of the Septuagint.

As we shall see, while in some New Testament texts *sunagōgē* can be understood best as an assembly of Jews, there are places in which it indisputably means the place of meeting.

proseuchē was still in use in the second century AD (Artemidorus 3.53), and it occurs in an inscription in the Bosporan kingdom in 306 AD, and was the term used by the Judaizing Messalian sect for their meeting place. Moreover, papyri from the second and third centuries AD continue to employ it (Noy 1992: 120). Nevertheless, certainty in these matters is elusive, since a Jewish Greek inscription in Amastris, albeit at the time of Diocletian, uses *proseuchē* in reference to community, rather than meeting-place (Oster 1993: 187 n. 36)!

sunagōgē is used in the post-Apostolic period for assemblies, even of Christians: e.g. Ignatius *(Pol.* 4.2 calls for frequent gatherings; see also

Trall. 3). *Herm. Man.* 11, 9, 13, 14 speaks of a synagogue of righteous men gathered for worship. Justin has *sunagōgē* and *ekklēsia* side by side (*Dial.* 63.5). Epiphanius complained of Jewish Christians that they called their *ekklēsia* a *sunagōgē*, rather than an *ekklēsia*. In the *Acts of Philip* the meeting place of the Christian assembly is called the *sunagōgē christianōn* (50).

But, as Oster emphasizes, arguments based on a simplistic dichotomy between *sunagōgē* and *proseuchē*, such as those of Kee, carry little conviction, since pre-70 references to 'synagogues' employ at least eight diverse terms, in addition to *sunagōgē* and *proseuchē* (Oster 1993: 186).

The rabbinic equivalent of *sunagōgē* is *knesset*, or its Aramaic equivalent. In general, these terms denote gathering, and only seldom a building. The building is generally called *bet haknesset*. However, *knesset* can also be used for the building, and *bet haknesset* for the congregation. Neither *knesset* nor *bet haknesset* occurs in the Dead Sea Scrolls. The Qumran community saw itself as the community of Israel of the Last Days (1QSa 1.1), a remnant of the whole congregation of Israel. The community probably used the expression, *bet mō'ed* ('House of Assembly') for their meeting-place (1QM 3.4).

The Origins of the Synagogue

J. Gwyn Griffiths considers that it was the Egyptian school, attached to the Temple, and the place of instruction based on the traditional Egyptian sacred texts, that was the source of the synagogue. Unlike the culture of the Greeks, the Egyptians associated education with the temples. Instruction and worship were united in the *Per Ankh* (the House of Life), an adjunct of the Temple which functioned both as a library and as a centre of worship. Reading of the sacred books was an important element. Griffiths argues that the combination of worship and instruction provides links between the Jewish and the Egyptian practices, one lacking in the Greek school or gymnasium (Griffiths 1987: 12). Having indicated the possible sources of the Jewish synagogue, Griffiths concludes that, 'Whatever influences are detected, however, the synagogue remains a Jewish creation. Institutionally it is the greatest creation of the Jewish genius' (p. 15).

First Century Synagogues: Purpose-Built?
The efforts made to locate the synagogue of Jesus' time have not been successful. Indeed there is no indisputable archaeological evidence for

any synagogue in Palestine in the first century AD. However, there is no scholarly consensus about the interpretation of this fact, since there is no agreement on the criteria by which one may identify a synagogue from the Second Temple period. The major source of archaeological evidence is provided by the six excavated Diaspora synagogues (Ostia, Stobi, Delos, Priene, Sardis and Dura-Europos), but these, with the exception of that at Delos, belong to the late Roman and Byzantine period. Within Palestine there are only three possible first-century synagogues, at Masada, Herodium and Gamala.

The lively debate about the nature of the *sunagōgē* in the New Testament period is complicated by the consistent English transliteration ('synagogue') of the original Greek *sunagōgē*, which creates the impression that the word *synagogue* connotes a single, consistent structure with clearly-defined identical functions (Oster 1993: 183). Oster quotes Cohen in support: 'There was no United Synagogue of Antiquity that enforced standards on all the member congregations. The word "synagogue" covers a wide variety of phenomena, and a definition that fits one place and time may not be appropriate for another' (Cohen 1989: 114).

On the one side, Schrage claims, 'In the overwhelming majority of instances *sunagōgē* in the NT means the Jewish building. At most one could only ask whether sometimes the gathering or congregation might not be implied too' (1971: 830). On the otherside, Kee bemoans the fact that any mention in Acts of a synagogue is assumed to be a building where a fixed pattern of study and worship was being carried out, even though only one such passage (Acts 18.4) refers unequivocally to a meeting place rather than to the congregation, wherever assembled (Kee 1990: 4). Kee adds, 'It would be more accurate to say, "Synagogues met in homes and public spaces". This judgment is confirmed, not only on the basis of evidence from Palestinian sites, but from the wider Mediterranean area as well' (pp. 8-9). He states that Acts 16.13 is the one time in Acts when a specific *place* is mentioned where Jews gathered, and that there the term is *proseuchē* rather than *sunagōgē* (Kee 1990: 18-19).

However, as Oster has pointed out, there are two indisputable uses of *sunagōgē* in Luke–Acts in which it refers to a place: Luke 7.5 and Acts 18.7 (1993: 185). Luke 7.5 reads, 'For he (the centurion) loves our people, and it is he who built our *sunagōgē* for us', and Acts 18.7, 'Then he (Paul) left the synagogue and went to the house of a man

4. The Historicity of the Nazareth Synagogue Scene

named Titius Justus, a worshipper of God; his house was next door to the synagogue'.

Kee insists that in the first century a synagogue building was not distinguishable architecturally from a private house (Kee 1990: 8-9). This might appear to be borne out by the fact that the excavations of the Capernaum synagogue detected five strata, the first a late-hellenistic building (second cent. BC to first cent. AD), on top of which was the foundation for a public building, dated only to the first century AD.

Griffiths adds that it was not until the first century AD, or perhaps a little before, that the first synagogue is attested in Palestine (1987: 4). Having argued that the later rabbinic tradition that there was a synagogue within the Temple precincts has no support, Hoenig (1975) claimed that the synagogue began to emerge as a distinctive institution with its own characteristic structure only after 70 AD. The earliest distinct buildings date from the third century AD (Gutmann 1975, Levine 1987, and Meyers and Strange 1981). The only other candidate for a synagogue prior to 70 AD, in the Theodotus inscription, should be dated no earlier than the second half of the second century. Kee appeals to the authority of Meyers and Strange in asserting that it is highly likely that in the period when the temple stood, a synagogue could have been nothing more than a private home or part of a larger structure set apart for worship (Kee 1990: 8).

Kee and others argue that, since no building from the first century AD has been positively identified as a synagogue, the places of worship were indistinguishable from private houses, or were areas set apart in public buildings. They stress that there is evidence of meeting places in private homes and in public buildings, but none of places with distinctive architectural features prior to 200 AD. Of the so-called synagogues at Masada and the Herodium, Gutmann remarks, 'There is no proof of piety or of a definite place of worship other than (the excavator's) wishful thinking' (Gutmann 1975: xi). But, against this, Oster produces convincing evidence which suggests that Gamala was a Jewish synagogue in the Second Temple era: the large ritual bath adjacent to it, the Jewishness of the city, the presence of Second Temple Jewish iconography on a lintel within the synagogue, and the size and design of the building.

In his survey of the architectural evidence for the synagogue in the diaspora, Kraabel (1979) showed that with the exception of that at Sardis, all other synagogues (Dura-Europos, Miletus, Priene, Delos, Stobi and Ostia) were private houses. The Jews in Sardis met in a large gymnasium which they remodelled for their own purposes. It served three purposes: a place of worship, an educational centre and a place for community meetings. Only in the third century AD did it become primarily a place of worship and instruction. The features of synagogues of the third century are altogether absent from those meeting places which were originally residences. The same is true of the synagogue in Delos, which is the only Second Temple one hitherto discovered. However, the fact that this one Second Temple synagogue, from the second century BC, was originally a home, and was later converted into a synagogue, should not result in a conclusion which ignores substantial contrary evidence.

Kee, therefore, is not correct in insisting that Luke's picture of Jews assembling in specifically synagogue buildings is anachronistic, since, in his view, they did so only in private houses, or in (parts of) public buildings sporadically used by them (Oster 1993: 195-96). There is sufficient evidence from the Diaspora in particular, and also from Gamala, that in the period of the Second Temple Jews congregated also in purpose-built synagogal buildings.

The conclusion is that Kee's argument, from the near silence of the archaeological evidence to the idea that synagogues were never distinctive buildings prior to 200 AD, lacks persuasiveness. There is no single piece of evidence from any papyrus or inscription of the Second Temple period supporting the view that Jewish communities met in private houses. Indeed, the evidence to the contrary is abundant. Even if there were no other inscriptional evidence, the text of four inscriptions from Egypt which refer to the *construction* of a meeting-place (in each case *proseuchē*: Horsley 1983: 121) invalidates the revisionist conclusion: the Jews *built* the *proseuchē* (in Schedia: *IGA* 2.11, 246–221 BC; in Arsinoe-Crocodilopolis: *CPJ* 3, App.1, no. 1532a; in Alexandria: *IGA* 2.116, from the second century BC; in Alexandria: *IGA* 2.41, 37 BC). These confirm that, at least in the Egyptian diaspora, meeting-places *were* built, and, presumably, purpose-built long before the turn of the Christian era.

It is desirable to develop a picture of the scene in the Nazareth synagogue on the fateful day of Jesus' visit, recorded in Lk. 4.16-30. Kee claims that the details of the activity recorded there are anachronistic also—in other words, that they reflect the period of the writer, and not that of the period being described. But before enquiring into

4. *The Historicity of the Nazareth Synagogue Scene* 109

what happened in the synagogue in Nazareth we review here Jesus' relationship with the synagogue in general.

Jesus and the Synagogue

According to Lk. 4.16 it was the custom of Jesus to go to the synagogue on the Sabbath day. In several other places in the Gospels it is mentioned that he visited synagogues (e.g. Lk. 4.33, 44; Mt. 12.9; Mk 3.1). He taught (*didaskō*) in them (e.g. Mt. 4.23; 9.35; 13.54; Mk 1.21, 39; 6.2; Lk. 4.15, 16-30, 31-32, 44; 6.6; 13.10; Jn 6.59; 18.20), and proclaimed (*kērussō*) in them (Mt. 4.23; 9.35; Mk 1.39; Lk. 4.44). Like his teaching elsewhere (Mt. 7.28; 22.23; Mk 11.18; Lk. 4.32), it made a great impression (Mt. 13.54; Mk 6.2). It was a new teaching (Mk 1.22, 27).

The Gospels also record acts of exorcism and healings in the synagogue (e.g. Lk. 4.33; 6.6-11; Mk 1.39; Mt. 4.23). The first record of his conflict with, and victory over the demonic powers occurs in one (Mk 1.23-28; Lk. 4.33-37). He also healed in them (e.g. Mt. 12.9-14; Mk 3.1-6; Lk. 6.6-11; 13.10-17).

Jesus appears to be quite at home in the synagogue. Where his words might be interpreted as unfavourable to the institution it is the abuse of the synagogue, rather than the synagogue itself, which is the object of his criticism (e.g. Mt. 6.5; Mk 12.39, par.). Nevertheless he is aware of the opposition that his followers will experience in the synagogue (Mk 13.9 par.), and of the function of the synagogue as a place of scourging (Mt. 23.34). Many scholars believe that the references to persecution in the synagogues come from the experience of the Christian Church rather than from the time of Jesus himself.

From the New Testament we learn that synagogue activities included giving alms (Mt. 6.2), saying prayers (Mt. 6.5, standing up), conducting 'trials' (Lk. 12.11; 21.12), scourgings (Mt. 10.17; 23.34; Mk 13.9, beaten), imprisonings and floggings (Acts 22.19). We read of the front seats being taken by Pharisees (Mt. 23.6; Lk. 11.43), and scribes (Mk 12.39; Lk. 20.46). The Fourth Gospel refers to expulsion from the synagogue (Jn 9.22; 12.42; 16.2).

In addition to the Gospels' description of Jesus' visits to the synagogue, we learn from the Acts of the Apostles that it was Paul's custom also to visit synagogues (Acts 17.2; cf. Lk. 4.16), and that he used them as the bases for his missionary work. Saul asked for letters addressed to the synagogues in Damascus (9.2), and after his encounter on the way there he began preaching in its synagogues (9.20). Paul visited the synagogue in Salamis (Acts 13.5, proclaiming...), Antioch in Pisidia (Acts 13.14, reading, preaching), Iconium (Acts 14.1), Thessalonica (Acts 17.1); Beroea (Acts 17.10), Athens (Acts 17.17), Corinth (Acts 18.4), Ephesus (Acts 18.19; 19.8); and in general (Acts 24.12; 26.11). Paul's practice conforms to his view that the good news of salvation was to be brought to the Jews first, then the Gentiles (Rom. 1.16; 10.14-16; 1 Cor. 9.20-21, etc.). In addition to meeting Jews there he also encountered those on the fringe (e.g. Acts 13.16, 43; 14.1; 17.4; 18.4).

The Functions of the Synagogue

It appears that the early synagogue fulfilled many roles, ranging from a place of prayer and study, a social and political assembly room, a judicial tribunal, a lodging-place, an advisory legal office or information centre, and a place of asylum. However, the two main activities were prayer and study (Griffiths 1987: 5-6).

The most important possessions in the synagogue were the scrolls of the Scriptures, especially the Torah and the Prophets, and the transportable wooden ark for the Torah. Teaching and propagation of the Law was an activity of primary significance within Judaism. The synagogue was also a place of prayer, of instruction, and a place of assembly for various purposes.

Readings, Preaching, Debating
The tractate *Megillah* in the Mishnah (c. 200 AD), which represents Palestinian practice, prescribes details of the readings and manner of reading for a variety of occasions (Passover 3.5, Hanukkah 3.6, Sabbath, 4.2, etc.). Concerning the Sabbath we learn,

> On the Sabbath, seven [read]. [On that day] they do not assign fewer, but they do assign more, to their number. And they do conclude with a reading of a prophetic lection. And he who begins the reading of the Torah and he who completes the reading of the Torah says a blessing before and afterward. They do not recite the *Shema* [with the blessings before and after], they do not pass before the ark...(*m. Meg.* 4.2-3).

It goes on,

> He who reads in the Torah should read no fewer than three verses. He may not read to the translator more than a single verse [at a time, so the translator will not err], and in the case of the prophetic lection, three. If the three

4. The Historicity of the Nazareth Synagogue Scene

constitute three distinct pericopae, they read them one by one. They skip [from place to place] in the prophetic lections but not in the Torah lections. And how far may one skip? [Only] so much that the translator will not have stopped [during the rolling of the scroll]. He who concludes with the prophetic lection is the one who recites the *Shema* [with its blessings fore and aft], and passes before the ark, and raises his hands [in the priestly benediction] (*m. Meg.* 4.4-5).

It appears that the order of service in the synagogue on the Sabbath, then, included the recitation of the *Shema* (Deut. 6.4-9; 11.13-21; Num. 15.37-41), the Prayer (*Tephilah*), a reading from the Torah, and then one from the Prophets (*m. Meg.* 4.3). The Scripture readings could be done by any member of the congregation (*m. Meg.* 4.5-6). Several members of the congregation were invited by the officer to take part in the reading. There were at least seven readers on the Sabbath (*m. Meg.* 4.2), and each had to read a minimum of three verses of the Torah (*m. Meg.* 4.4). The service was completed by a priestly blessing (Num. 6.24-26).

However, the Talmud (the massive collection of Jewish lore, compiled in the fifth century AD, but containing much earlier traditions) assures us that outside of Palestine, the reading was done by one person (*y. Meg* 75a). The Prophets were read by one person alone (*m. Meg.* 4.5). An Aramaic translation of the readings was provided, with the Torah being translated verse by verse, and the Prophets every three verses (*m. Meg.* 4.4, 6, 10). Since the first attestation of the Aramaic translation in written form comes from the fourth century AD (*y. Meg.* 74d), we presume that it was oral in the first instance. The readings were followed by an address or sermon, which gave an exposition, and application of the reading.

We would like to know how much of the details of the later Mishnaic practice was in operation at the time of Jesus. Our primary interest in this context is the activity of Scripture reading and interpretation which went on in the synagogue. In the case of Lk. 4.16-30, in Kee's words, are we dealing with 'later forms of synagogal worship read back into the time of Jesus' (Kee 1990: 18)? In his terms, the formalities of the occasion are,

The standing up to read the scripture; the scroll of scripture handed by the attendant; Jesus finding the apparently appointed place at which to begin the reading; his returning the scroll to the attendant; his sitting down (in Moses' seat?) to begin the exposition of the text in terms of its relevance for his hearers. The term for the attendant, *hupēretēs*, is found with this meaning only here in the New Testament (Kee 1990: 18).

He summarizes his case as follows: 'Of these details there is no hint in either Mark's or Matthew's reports of this event (Mt. 13.54-58), nor is there any evidence in the gospels or elsewhere of such a set pattern for a service of preaching in synagogues from the period prior to 70' (Kee 1990: 18). As we shall see, Kee's insistence on this point is no more secure than that on the informal nature of synagogue gatherings.

In addition to the abundant references in the Gospels to Jesus teaching in the synagogues, and the account of the reading, and comment in Nazareth (Lk. 4.16-30), there is abundant evidence to show that there were readings from the Scriptures, comments on them, and theological debates in several synagogues. The Nazareth scene (Lk. 4.16-30) gives a reading from the Prophets, followed by an interpretation. The preacher, who could be any competent member of the congregation, sat on a raised place (cf. Lk. 4.20).

We can deduce from the Acts of the Apostles that it was normal for the Jewish community to gather in the synagogues, especially on the Sabbath, and that 'in every city' 'Moses' is read and discussed (Acts 15.21). The Antioch in Pisidia account (Acts 13.15) makes explicit that there was a reading from both the Law and the Prophets, followed by a *word of exhortation* for the people:

> And on the sabbath day they went into the synagogue and sat down. After the reading of the law and the prophets, the rulers of the synagogue sent to them, saying, 'Brethren, if you have any word of exhortation for the people, say it'...As they went out the people begged that these things might be told them the next sabbath...The next sabbath almost the whole city gathered together to hear the word of God (Acts 13.13-44).

Moreover, it is clear from the 'sermons' delivered that theological debate and argumentation was normal. Much of this involved interpretations of the history of salvation, and justification of one's position by the support of texts of the Scriptures (e.g. Acts 13.33-35 using Ps. 2.7, Isa. 55.3 and Ps. 16.10). At Thessalonica, for example, 'for three weeks he (Paul) argued with them from the scriptures, explaining and proving that it was necessary for the Christ to suffer and to rise from the dead' (Acts 17.2). Without pretending that we have the very words of the speaker in the accounts in Acts, it is clear that arguing from Scripture, or scriptural hermeneutics, was a normal part of theological debate (e.g. Acts 15.15-18 using Amos 9.11-12; Jer. 12.15; Isa. 45.21). The critical question, of course, is whether the Lukan accounts conform to what happened at the period they purport to describe. There are indications

4. The Historicity of the Nazareth Synagogue Scene

elsewhere which suggest that the pattern described in Luke–Acts is not anachronistic.

The Jewish synagogue did not come into existence in a cultural vacuum. It would be very strange indeed if there were no pattern in synagogal meetings, even though the institution had been in operation for a few centuries. We should not be surprised to find that the patterns reflected the different styles in different places. It is clear that patterns of organization developed as needs demanded, and these reflected the manner of doing things in the wider society, and in its various organizations (see Schürer 1986: 87-149). Since we are aware from many sources of various activities in the synagogue, it is not conceivable that the activities took place without order, and some degree of formalization. And since we know full well that such patterns were in operation later, why must it be the case that the pattern developed only after 70 AD?

Oster points to additional evidence which shows that elements of formal processes took place in synagogues. First, there is evidence of the formal liberation of slaves in a synagogue service, attested in first-century Jewish inscriptions (41 and 81 AD) from Gorgippia and Panticapaeum, on the northern bank of the Black Sea. These vouch for the stipulated ceremony of manumission in the synagogue, the supervisory role of the congregation, and the stipulation that the former slave demonstrate sincere and constant zeal for the synagogue (Oster 1993: 198-99). Secondly, the organization and overseeing of the Temple Tax could not have been effected without supervision, and synagogal officers, as is clear from Philo (*Spec. Leg.* 1.78). Thirdly, in all probability, some of the Jewish common meals would have taken place in synagogues, and would have required the appropriate level of formalization (cf. the use of Greek banquet terms in Mk 6.39; 12.39; Jn 2.8-9). While the evidence is not as compelling as one might wish, one's common sense is supported by clear witness to patterns of organization in the synagogue, prior to the destruction of the Jerusalem Temple. Let us now return to the specifics of the formalization of the synagogal service as indicated in Lk. 4.16-30.

Reading the Scriptures in the Synagogue

There is substantial evidence suggesting that reading from the Torah was normal in the first century AD. Josephus records, '(Moses) ordered...that every week men should desert their other occupations and assemble to listen to the Law and to obtain a thorough and accurate knowledge of it' (*Apion* 2.175). He refers to Jews having copies of the Scripture with them on Sabbaths in the synagogue ('the laws', *War* 2.291, and 'the holy books', *Ant.* 16.164).

From Alexandria, Philo mentions the reading of the sacred books, which was followed by an explanation of passages which were obscure (*Somn.* 2.127). He also records that 'on the sabbath days in all the cities thousands of houses of learning were opened, in which discernment and moderation and proficiency and righteous living and indeed all virtues were taught' (*Spec. Leg.* 2.62). Perhaps Paul is referring to synagogal services where he attests to the public reading of the covenant/Moses (2 Cor. 3.14-15). The inscription of Theodotus, found in the Jerusalem Ophel in 1914, although dated no earlier than the second half of the second century, perhaps, contains the following: 'Theodotus... constructed the synagogue for the reading of the Law and the teaching of the commandments' (*CIJ*, II, 1404.3-5).

Luke's portrayal of Jesus standing to read is consistent with the practice as indicated by Philo (*Spec. Leg.* 2.62). Neither is it strange that there should be an 'attendant'/'assistant' (*hupēretēs*) in the synagogue (Lk. 4.20). On simple principles of organization, it is to be expected that there would be an attendant/assistant overseeing the good order of a synagogal meeting. The term *hupēretēs* is a very common one, and is used frequently in the papyri, both before and after the turn of the Christian era (e.g. *Hibeh* papyri 29.21 [c. 265 BC] and 92.22 [c. 263 BC]; *Tebtunis* papyri 45.5 [113 BC]; 186 [105 BC]); it is often used as an official title (e.g. *P. Oxy* 475.2, 28 [182 AD], 476.12, 485.49 [178 AD], 1409 [278 AD], 1556 [247 AD], 1573 [late third century AD]). In a papyrus, possibly from the Fayum, it refers to a cult official of Zeus *Hupsistos* (dated mid first century BC: *SB* 5.2(1938).7835), line 11—see Horsley 1981: 28). The term occurs on a Roman Jewish epitaph (*CIJ* I.2—Schürer 1986: 101). A fragmentary Jewish papyrus from pre-Roman Egypt contains the titles of several officers, and each in the plural, who had duties in the synagogal services. These included chief-assistants (*archupēretai*) (*CPJ*, n. 138). There is evidence of other synagogue officials also, for example, *neokoros* in a 218 BC papyrus, and even *hiereus* in a Jewish inscription of 56 AD, as well as the much more commonly attested *archisunagōgos*, head of the synagogue, and *archōn*, synagogue leader (see Oster 1993: 202-203).

Seen against the background of the witness of Josephus (c. 37–100

AD), Philo (c. 30 BC–45 AD), the inscriptions and papyri, and of the other items detailed above, all from the Jewish diaspora, Luke's details of the scene in the synagogue in Nazareth do not appear out of place in the pre-70 AD period. But we need to investigate the matter further.

A Jewish Lectionary?

One would like to know how the reading was organized. Did first-century AD Jews have a fixed lectionary, or if not, how did they organize their Liturgy of the Word?

In his earlier work of immense scholarship, Goulder claimed that the synagogue readings were precisely fixed in an *annual cycle* which began in the month Nisan, our mid-March to mid-April (1978: 52-53). According to him, right down to the second century AD, the Liturgy of the Word in the synagogue consisted of a reading from the Torah followed by its Aramaic paraphrase, then a reading from the Prophets (and the Writings also, perhaps), and a corresponding Targum. This involved 'perhaps an hour and a quarter in all, spent listening', which, he says, is wearisome and unedifying. The problem of liturgical fatigue was solved subsequently, that is, later than 200 AD, by spreading the readings over a *three year cycle*.

Goulder claimed that each of the Gospels was a collection of reflections of a Christian preacher recording events and teachings from the life of Jesus in a sequence determined by the material of the synagogue–church readings on the Sundays or feasts. With reference to the Nazareth scene, he argued that Lk. 4.16-30 promoted Mark's account of the rejection at Nazareth (Mk 6.1-6). The reason was that the thirteenth Torah reading (*Sidra*) was Exod. 1–6.1, which describes Moses' forty years in Midian, his being sent to his people, and their disobeying him (cf. Acts 7). The sequence of readings from the Law, then, evoked the record of another Moses who was rejected by his own.

In general, Goulder was driven more by the momentum of his enthusiasm than by the strength of the evidence he adduced. At times he seemed to be afflicted with Midas' gift that everything biblical he touched became liturgical gold. Goulder was not the first to argue a case for a relationship between the synagogue readings and the writings of the New Testament. Finch argued that the readings in the synagogue services lie behind most of the New Testament (1939). Levertoff argued the case for Matthew (1928). Guilding presented the case for John, and saw in her work 'the clearest possible proof of the influence of the *three year* lectionary system on the pattern of the Gospel' (1960: 50). Carrington related Mark to the Jewish lectionary tradition, and assured his readers that the facts fitted his theory 'like a glove' (1952: 26).

Drury also related the gospel of Luke to the Jewish Scriptures. In his reconstruction, Luke presided at the weekly Christian assembly, at which there were three readings: one from the Old Testament, one from Mark or Matthew, and one, perhaps, from Paul's Letter to the Corinthians. Luke was the preacher, and when he preached he expounded the texts, linked them, and related them to the needs of his community (like any good homilist) (Drury 1976: 174-75).

This way of exegeting the scriptures is sometimes termed 'midrash', a word which is used in biblical studies with a great variety of meanings (cf. Bloch 1957, which lists about ten different types of biblical interpretation which she classifies as 'midrash'), with the result that 'the word as used currently in biblical studies is approaching the point where it is no longer really meaningful' (Wright 1967: 21-22).

The readings and homily were followed by prayer and the Eucharist. But Luke was no monk: and he was as much at home in the market place and at the dinner parties of the privileged as he was in the eucharistic assembly. When he went to his desk to compose his Gospel he had before him his Old Testament scrolls, his Christian writings and, perhaps, his own sermon notes, and from these he wrote the first thoroughgoing exposition of the relation between Christianity and unecclesiastical experience—a kind of *Gaudium et Spes* (the title of Vatican Council II's 'Pastoral Constitution on the Church in the Modern World'), presenting Christianity in dialogue with the Modern World of the first half of the second century.

Drury argues that like Matthew, Luke presents Jesus as fulfilling Old Testament prophecy, but in a more subtle and smooth way, so much so that the modern reader might miss some of the resonances. He places Luke firmly within the tradition of Jewish historiography with its great love of midrash and story. He estimates Luke to be 'one of the greatest narrative midrashists' (1976: 12). He sees the LXX as a major source for his Gospel, especially in his Infancy Narrative, where Drury finds that 'septuagintal words and phrases are as thick on the ground as autumn leaves (p. 49, and Appendix A, pp. 185-86). After Luke 2, however, the LXX has to compete with Mark as Luke's main source for narrative and with Matthew as the main source for his teaching. The source for

4. *The Historicity of the Nazareth Synagogue Scene*   117

Luke's special material is right under the nose of source critics: the Old Testament itself. Indeed!

That there was a fixed cycle, annual or triennial, of readings in the New Testament period is denied by McNamara: 'To postulate any cycle, be it annual, triennial or of some other sort, for Palestine goes beyond the evidence at our disposal. Theories based on any such cycle are founded on very insecure premises' (1972: 47). Perrot argues that there was no fixed standard, triennial or annual cycle until about 200 AD (1973). Le Déaut concludes that the cycle became fixed only in the second and third centuries AD (1977: 36). Morris, too, rejects all theories based on a fixed cycle in New Testament times:

> the fundamental reason for postulating a number of different cycles is that the evidence is not clear enough to establish any one cycle as generally accepted...The evidence as we have it seems to indicate that the early Christians were more like Free Churchmen (who read from the Old and New Testament regularly, but did not use a lectionary) than those who follow a lectionary...At the beginning of the Christian era there were no fixed lessons...It is scarcely an exaggeration to say that everyone who has written on this subject seems to have a different idea from everyone else...Their handling of the evidence in some of its aspects will seem to most to be more ingenious than convincing (Morris 1964: 19, 24-26, 47).

A vivid illustration of the confusion on the matter is provided by the fact that Schürer seems to contradict itself: The text reads, 'The Torah reading was so ordered that the whole of the Pentateuch was read consecutively in a three-yearly cycle' (rev. Vermes, vol. II: 450), whereas n. 118 reads, 'As the existence of the triennial cycle is nowhere attested in Tannaitic literature, its currency in the age of Jesus is merely conjectural'.

In his later work on Luke, Goulder looks back at his earlier attempt to reconstruct the week-by-week Sabbath readings in the first-century synagogue, and acknowledges that, on the basis of the present state of knowledge, any attempt to determine the synagogal readings is speculative. He concedes that the correspondences with the Gospel texts are patchy, and confesses that the Sabbath hypothesis needs to be shelved, though it does not need to be abandoned. However, he emphasizes the correspondences between the Gospels and the main feasts and fasts of a (Jewish-) Christian Year (1989: 147). Thus, in his hypothesis, the opening chapters of Mark gave Christian readings for the autumn festal season, and the subsequent chapters of Mark led on to the April festival of Passover, for which the Passion Narrative was provided.

Mark's Gospel, then, provided Christian readings from October to April. But what of April to September? With such rich lessons provided for half the year peoples' appetites were roused, and the evangelists after Mark felt pressurized to begin their lessons after Easter, and thus provide a full year of Gospel readings.

Matthew does so by providing in chs. 1–11 substantially new material prefixed to the main Markan outline (1989: 156-59). For his part, Luke, who in Goulder's view knew Matthew, also produced a year-long set of readings, arranged too in terms of the Jewish feasts. In the case of both Matthew and Luke the Christian Jewish New Year reading is provided by material concerning John the Baptist (Mt. 11 and Lk. 7.18-35).

Goulder considers it inconceivable that Christians would not celebrate a Christian Atonement service, and argues that Mark 2 provided ideal readings for the occasion. For his Christian Atonement service Matthew preferred the Beelzebul healing and its attendant discourse (Mt. 12.22-45). Luke settled for the narrative of the woman pardoned (Lk. 7.36-50).

Mark provided the harvest parables of 4.1-34 for the Christian Feast of Tabernacles. Matthew gives an expanded collection of parables in Mt. 13.1-52, while Luke, who has his people in church only on Sundays, settles for the Parable of the Sower, its interpretation, and so forth (Lk. 8.1-21). 'Thus all three evangelists saw the primary message of a Christian Tabernacles as the harvesting of souls' (1989: 166).

Unlike Mark, who had catered for things only from October (*Tishri*) to April (*Nisan*), Matthew and Luke felt constrained to supply a full annual cycle, beginning after Easter, and finishing with Easter, and provided suitable readings for a Christian Pentecost. Matthew does it by way of the Sermon on the Mount (Mt. 5), and Luke in the form of John's preaching (Lk. 3.1-20).

Goulder, then, has effectively abandoned his earlier hypothesis that the sequence of readings from the Gospels reflects the putative weekly synagogal readings, as well as readings of the Jewish festivals. He now restricts the connections between the readings from the three Gospels to the readings of the Jewish *festivals* only.

As far as Luke 4.16-30 is concerned Goulder puts it on the tenth week of the year, which begins after Easter, situated between the Jewish/Christian festivals for Pentecost and New Year. He claims that Luke, in composing his Gospel at this point, had Mark and Matthew before him. Luke took Matthew's account of Jesus leaving Nazareth (Mt. 4.13a), and developed it in a major way, aligning Mt. 4.13a with

Mark's account of Jesus' preaching, stating that the time is fulfilled, and God's kingdom is at hand (Mk 1.14c-15). The combination of these two provides Luke with the theme of Jesus preaching in Nazareth, and a more than adequate explanation of why he left Nazareth.

Jewish Interpretations of the Scriptures

Jesus in Lk. 4.16-30 is presented as an interpreter of the Scriptures, a Teacher of God's Mercy. A major, and perhaps the most significant factor separating Jewish factions in the New Testament period is their interpretation of the Scriptures. That which was written in the past required an interpreter.

Philo of Alexandria (c. 30 BC—45 AD)

It is likely that Philo was a zealous participant in the affairs of the synagogue in Alexandria. He interpreted the biblical texts with the purpose of strengthening the Alexandrian Jews in their faith. The application of earlier texts from a different life setting (e.g. from desert/exile, etc. to the contemporary setting of city life) is a sophisticated process, which sometimes required some intellectual somersaulting. For example, having introduced the biblical text, 'And God brought a trance upon Adam, and he fell asleep; and he took one of his sides' and what follows (Gen. 2.21), he gives his allegorical interpretation of the text:

> These words in their literal sense are of the nature of a myth. For how could anyone admit that a woman, or a human being at all, came into existence out of a man's side?...And why, when there were so many parts to choose from, did He form the woman not from some other part but from the side? And which side did he take?...What then are we to say? 'Sides' is a term of ordinary life for 'strength'. To say that a man has 'sides' is equivalent to saying that he is strong...(*Leg. All.* 2.19-21).

Philo speaks with great approval of the practices of the Therapeutae, a contemplative sect which resided by the Mareotic Lake: On the Sabbath they meet in the synagogue, with men and women separate, and they listen to a sermon: 'And this does not lodge just outside the ears of the audience, but passes through the hearing into the soul and there stays securely. All the others sit still and listen, showing their approval merely by their looks or nods' (*Vit. Cont.* 30–31). We learn also that after the meal there is a discourse by the president (*proedros*) on a scriptural point, bringing out lessons which the literal text provides. It is listened to attentively, and there is applause at the end (*Vit. Cont.* 75–79). The discourse is followed by hymns, first of all by the president, then the congregation in turn, and thirdly all join in the refrain at the end (80–81).

Qumran

For the community at Qumran the Scriptures were a treasured possession. There is an abundance of copies of 'biblical' scrolls, which represent the oldest manuscripts of the Hebrew Bible. The community saw itself as a 'House of Torah' (*CD* 7.10), engaged in the correct interpretation of Scripture which was *the* way to salvation (*CD* 14.1-2). For the Qumran community the Scriptures were an expression of the divine Truth, but it was only they who were able to interpret them properly (e.g. *1 QpHab* 2.1-10). Just as ancient Israel had Moses, so the sectarians had their own Teacher and Seeker. The Scriptures required legitimate and proper interpretation. The Qumran community defined itself in its attitude to biblical interpretation, and the consequences of its unique understanding of revelation.

In every settlement there was to be an interpreter of the Torah (*dôreš b^{e}tôrâ*) in every group of ten (*1QS* 6.6-8). In the Torah, properly exegeted, everything could be found (*CD* 16.1-2). Virtually the whole of the Scriptures was used and reused to support the community's beliefs and practices. The Scriptures consisted of the revelation of God, 'which he commanded through Moses and through all his servants the prophets' (*1QS* 1.3; cf. 8.15-16). What separated the community at Qumran from other factions within Judaism was its unique interpretation of the Scriptures, carried out under the direction of the authoritative teachers of the community. In this matter the role of the Unique Teacher (*CD* 20.1) was determinative. Outside the community's authoritative interpretation of Scripture there was no salvation (see Fishbane 1988: 375-77). The interpretation of prophecy was a major feature of Qumran exegesis. Fitzmyer has drawn attention to the similarity between Luke's manner of quoting the Hebrew Scriptures (in Greek), and that which obtained in the Qumran Scrolls (Fitzmyer 1992: 527-30).

Targumim

The Hebrew Bible was so difficult in its language, and its imagery, that it required translation for the congregation. For that reason, after the Hebrew reading the interpreter (*meturgeman*) rose to translate. A passage in the Babylonian Talmud (*Meg.* 21b) indicates that the interpretations were so popular that some congregations desired to hear more than one targumic rendering of the same Hebrew passage (Chilton 1986: 113).

That the Hebrew Scriptures were paraphrased into Aramaic in the late Second Temple Period is attested by the existence of the Qumran Targumim of Job and Leviticus, and the *Genesis Apocryphon*. Aramaic paraphrases were used in the synagogue and in private places, and served as a link between the original Hebrew text and the Aramaic vernacular, although it is clear that the Aramaic of the Targumim is literary, and not merely colloquial. Close study of the Targumim shows that they were the works of scholars. It would be unwarranted to imagine them to have come spontaneously from hearing the Hebrew text being read in the synagogue.

In the vast corpus of Targumim we have Aramaic renderings that are almost literal translations of the Hebrew text, and others that are more elaborate paraphrases (See the examples and discussion in Alexander 1988: 228-37). There was a tendency to 'update' Scripture, by identifying biblical people and places with contemporary people and places. There is a tendency to elaborate on one word by two associated ones. Frequently a translation of one text is influenced by association with another, similar text. In some instances the targum appears to reflect a meaning opposite to that of the original Hebrew (Alexander 1988: 226-28).

Rabbinic literature points to three distinct settings for the Targumim: synagogue, private devotion and school. The synagogue was the primary setting, and is the one of most interest here. As the reading of the Hebrew *Torah* and *Haftara* (from the Prophets) was being done, there was a 'simultaneous' rendering into Aramaic. The Hebrew text was read by one person and the Aramaic rendering had to be done by somebody else. The Scripture reader was to be seen reading from the text, while the *meturgeman* had to recite the Targum from memory. According to *b. Meg.* 32a the *meturgeman* was not allowed to read from a text, nor to glance at the Torah scroll, lest the people think that the translation was written in the Torah. In the case of the Pentateuch, each verse was followed by the corresponding verse of targum, while for the Prophets up to three verses could be given (Alexander 1988: 238). It is clear from the Rabbis that the purpose of the targum was to exegete, interpret and make clear the Scripture, so that the people understood the reading (*j. Meg.* 74d).

122   *Jesus the Liberator*

Although the liturgical use of the targum began to die out in the middle ages, it continues in Yemenite synagogues to this day. But after its liturgical demise it never lost its place in the *Beit ha-Midrash* (Alexander 1988: 250). Unfortunately, there is as yet no indication of a lectionary setting for the Torah, and hence no liturgical setting for the Qumran targumim (Fishbane 1988: 344).

There is no mention of the reading of the Targum in the synagogue of Nazareth. Safrai wrongly concludes from Luke 4.16 that there is reference to the reading from the Torah (1990: 191). Moreover, there is no mention of the reading of the Targum in the synagogue at Antioch in Pisidia (Acts 13.15). On the basis of these two references Safrai concludes that the Targum was not read either in the land of Israel (Nazareth), or in the diaspora (Antioch of Pisidia). Safrai suggests, 'with some caution' that the synagogal reading from the Targum began only in the Usha period, that is, after the defeat of the Bar Kochba revolt (p. 191). Before that time it was used only for private study. We do not know whether the practice of giving an Aramaic Targum of the Hebrew Scripture goes back to the New Testament period.

Conclusion

As one reflects on the fact that Jesus is pictured as entering the synagogue in Nazareth and engaging in Torah exegesis, it should not be forgotten that he presented himself in general as much more than an authoritative interpreter of the Hebrew Scriptures. The Gospels present him as introducing the Kingdom of God. 'According to Jesus, the coming of the Kingdom of God is the determinative factor in his ministry of word and deed; it culminates in his death and resurrection and leads to his parousia at an undefined time' (Beasley-Murray 1986: 338-39). While the proclamation of the Kingdom of God constitutes the opening of the ministry of Jesus in Matthew and Mark, in Luke it is his teaching in the synagogues of Galilee (Lk. 4.15) which does so.

Like so much of the two-volume work of Luke the account of the Nazareth synagogue scene is presented with an abundance of dramatic and literary skill. The dramatic character of the context should not be glossed over. The scene was the Nazareth synagogue on a Sabbath.

There is no mention of a reading from the Law in Luke 4, nor of the other elements of the service. Jesus' Old Testament text is from Isaiah, at the section we number ch. 61 (and 58.6). We simply do not know

4. The Historicity of the Nazareth Synagogue Scene

whether there was a fixed reading from the Prophets for each Sabbath service in the first century. If there was, Jesus had no choice but 'to stand under the Word' of the day. The other possibility is that he searched out his choice of reading for the day. Jesus gave the scroll back to the president, and sat down for the sermon the 'word of encouragement' (Acts 13.15) was given *ex cathedra*. The Lukan setting is firmly in the tradition of first-century Jewish synagogal practice. 'The eyes of all in the synagogue were fixed on him' (v. 20). Luke's readers share in the anticipation.

Another feature of Luke's literary skill is his incorporation in the reading and sermon of several of the main themes of Luke–Acts:

1. the action of the Holy Spirit (e.g. John the Baptist will be filled with the Holy Spirit)—the phrase 'filled with the Holy Spirit' occurs in the New Testament only in Luke–Acts, and is used of Elizabeth (Lk. 1.41), Zechariah (1.67), Jesus (4.1), and in Acts of the group (2.4), Peter (4.8), 'all' (4.31), Saul (9.17), Paul (13.52)—see also of Stephen (6.5), Barnabas (11.24), and of disciples (13.52)
2. the fulfilment of Old Testament prophecy in the person of Jesus (cf. Lk. 24.26-27; Acts 2.23, 31; 3.18, 24; 4.11; 10.43; 13.33). Luke also shows how people responded to Jesus as a prophet (Lk. 7.16, 39; 9.8, 19; 24.19; Acts 2.30; 3.22; 7.37), and how he spoke of himself as accepting the destiny of a prophet (Lk. 11.49-50; 13.33)
3. the use of Isaiah 61, with its emphasis on the poor (cf. Lk. 7.22), to which we shall return
4. the present as the acceptable year of the Lord (Lk. 19.9; cf. 23.43)
5. the universal character of salvation which runs through the double work, climaxing in the movement of the gospel from the sacred city of Jerusalem ('...and that repentance and forgiveness of sins should be preached in his name to all nations, beginning from Jerusalem...stay in the city, until you are clothed with power from on high', Lk. 24.27-29) to the secular city, Rome, the capital of the Empire (Acts 28.28-30). The double work might well be entitled, 'On How they brought the Good News from Jerusalem to Rome'. It appears from the text of Luke that it was precisely Jesus' universalization of God's Good News which prevented the Jews present in the synagogue

from accepting that the day of salvation was being ushered in by Jesus. The examples from their own sacred writings of Elijah and Elisha served only to rub salt into their wounds.

The author concludes the passage by returning to the dramatic dimension of the event. Some scholars see in the mysterious escape of Jesus a reference to his future destination ('but passing through the midst of them he went away'—the verb *poreuō* is used of Jesus setting his face to go to Jerusalem, Lk. 9.51, and again in Lk. 13.33: 'I must go on my way today...for it cannot be that a prophet should perish away from Jerusalem'). LaVerdiere suggests that for Luke the hill of Nazareth is symbolic of the hill of Calvary, that the Jews of Nazareth prefigure the Jewish authorities who had him put to death, and that the escape evokes the resurrection and ascension (1980: 68). This seems to me too fanciful. The mixed reaction to the message of Jesus prefigures the polarity of reactions to him in the course of his ministry: acceptance (Lk. 4.42; 5.15) and rejection. The readers of Luke's Gospel had already been introduced to the rejection of Jesus in the Canticle of Simeon (Lk. 2.34), and in due course will see how the Jewish establishment brought on his crucifixion.

The rejection of Jesus by those Jews in the synagogue of his own town, coupled with the movement towards the Gentiles, which is clear in the two examples of the Zarephath widow and Naaman, suggests to some readers the ultimate rejection of Jesus by 'the Jewish people'. We shall argue that this is not the case. The reader will also relate it to the movement of the Christian preaching from Jerusalem, the centre of Jewish religion, to Rome, the centre of the non-Christian empire, which is such a feature of the second volume, the Acts.

These are some of the reasons why the section is regarded as a preview, or foretaste of the remainder of the Gospel, or as a 'microcosm of the whole of Luke–Acts' (Tiede 1980: 54). They represent some of the conclusions which derive from examining Luke as an accomplished artist, that is, from the perspective of redaction criticism, the most popular method of gospel study from the fifties to the eighties.

***

The questions about Lk. 4.16-30 considered so far have reflected the changing moods and emphases of modern scholarship. The question of the historicity of the account was forced upon us by the quite different openings of the Galilean ministry as recorded in Mark and Matthew, and

4. The Historicity of the Nazareth Synagogue Scene

by consideration of some of the details in Luke's account. I do not subscribe to the view that the account reflects no historical tradition, being 'only' a literary construct due to Luke's artistic expansion of the scene hinted at in Mk 6.1-6. I have argued that Luke's account preserves a scene which took place in the synagogue at Nazareth. At what stage of the Galilean ministry of Jesus it happened must be left open.

So much for the question of historicity, which has dominated the discussion from the end of the nineteenth century to the late forties of this one. We shall now examine further Luke's account of Jesus' part in the Sabbath synagogue service in Nazareth.

Chapter 5

LUKE'S JESUS AS EXEGETE

Although it does not mention several of the elements which later texts record, Luke's scene of the synagogue of Nazareth gives us the oldest known account of a synagogue service. At face value, it appears that Jesus goes up to the place of reading, reads from the prophet Isaiah, delivers an explanation which astounds the audience, and develops his programme of novel liberation, in which the poor and outcasts are the beneficiaries. He develops his argument by reference to two major Hebrew prophetic figures.

Until recently scholarly accounts of the history of synagogue preaching have had little to say about the period prior to 200 AD. The so-called Amoraic period (ca. 200–500 AD) was the golden age of synagogue preaching, and there is an abundance of examples of the genre extant. In the most general terms, the purpose of the sermon, then as today, was to strengthen the faith of the congregation, to correct error, to instruct people on the demands of the Law, and to relate the text of Scripture to the changing demands of the day.

Analysis of the extant examples has shown that the most common sermon type in the period 200–500 AD was the *proem*. This consisted of a short homily that introduced the Torah reading for the week. It was not an explanation of the reading from the Torah. Instead, the preacher began with a verse from outside the Torah, but was required to end his sermon by quoting the first verse of the Torah lesson of the day. Although usually the opening of the *proem* was from the Writings, occasionally it was from the Prophets. It is suggested that in the period, 200–500 AD, the *proem*, which begins outside of the text of the Pentateuchal reading, and climaxes with a verse from the Torah, *preceded* the reading of the Law and the Prophets. Its brevity is accounted for by the suggestion that the extant written form is an abbreviation of what was actually said originally (Stegner 1988: 58).

5. *Luke's Jesus as Exegete* 127

A second extant sermon-form, preserved in the collection of sermons called the *Tanchuma*, and edited some time after the sixth century AD, consists of a statement of the first verse of the passage from the Scripture reading. A key word is chosen and commented on throughout. Other biblical verses are cited in support. Illustrations are drawn from Scripture or contemporary life. The ending usually reiterates a word from the beginning, and generally the main thrust is summarized in the conclusion (see the discussion of the Homily on Noah in Stegner 1988).

Some recent studies, however, have examined examples of the early Christian preaching, the so-called *word of exhortation/encouragement* (*logos paraklēseōs*) we encounter in Acts 13.15 and Heb. 13.22 (cf. Acts 2.40; 1 Macc. 10.24; 2 Macc. 7.24; 15.11; *Apostolic Constitutions* 8.5). Wills has examined Paul's missionary sermon in Pisidian Antioch, and discovered a pattern of argument that comprises three elements: *examples* from authoritative sources, such as Scripture (Acts 13.16b-37); a *conclusion* from those examples pointing out their significance (Acts 13.38-39); and an exhortation based on that conclusion (Acts 13.40-41) (Wills 1984). Wills sees this basic pattern recurring in Hebrews, *1 Clement*, 1 and 2 Corinthians, 1 and 2 Peter, the Ignatian Epistles, *Barnabas*, the old LXX version of Susanna, the *Epistle of Jeremiah*, the *Testament of the Twelve Patriarchs*, Eusebius' *Preparatio evangelica*, and Josephus' *The Jewish War*. Accepting the analysis of Wills, Clifton Black goes further, and locates first-century Jewish and Christian preaching within the mainstream of classical rhetoric. He demonstrates that the form of *the word of exhortation* manifests a remarkable consanguinity with the standards of classical oratory (Black 1988: 16).

Clearly there are features which distinguish Luke's account of Jesus' preaching from that of later Jewish examples. Apart from the differences in form, the most significant one is that of content, reflected in Jesus' claim that the prophetic fulfilment occurs *today, in your hearing*. With regard to the pattern of the sermon form in Hellenistic Judaism and Early Christianity, one notes in Lk. 4.16-30 the use of the *examples* of Elijah and Elisha, as well as the fundamental appeal to the authority of Scripture. The major teaching point (*conclusion*?) is that the word is being fulfilled *today in your hearing* (v. 21). Whatever *exhortation* is present is left implicit, since the narrative describes what happened, rather than presses the sermon to an exhortatory conclusion.

We shall discuss the possible liturgical setting of the Isaiah text, as well as Jesus' exegesis of it. But before enquiring into the significance of his application of the composite text from Isaiah, we shall review the Old Testament background against which one ought to view the Lukan Jesus.

Jesus and the Hebrew Scriptures

Jesus, a Palestinian Jew was nourished, and his mission was stimulated by the record of the Israelites' dealings with God preserved in the Hebrew Scriptures. There can be no doubt that behind the great number of references to his use of the Scriptures is the fact that they were constantly in his mind and heart, and on his lips. It is no less clear that the writers of the New Testament used the Hebrew Scriptures (in Greek translation—the LXX) abundantly.

Luke–Acts, constituting approximately one quarter of the entire New Testament, and written by one person, is an invaluable source for examining the intimate part the Old Testament plays in Early Christianity. Indeed, it is increasingly realized that Luke composed his account of Jesus and of the nascent Church after the fashion of the historical narratives of the Old Testament.

In addition to a great number of phrases from, or allusions to, the Old Testament, Luke explicitly quotes the Old Testament no less than 23 times in his Gospel, and 22 times in Acts. Since Lk. 4.18-19 and 19.46, and Acts 3.22-23 combine two Old Testament quotations each, we see that Luke has 25 Old Testament quotes in the Gospel, and 23 in Acts. Luke thereby shows that in his perspective the mission of Jesus and of the nascent Church is in continuity with that of the Old Testament (Fitzmyer 1992: 526). Sixteen of Luke's Old Testament quotations come from the Pentateuch (10 in the Gospel, and 6 in Acts), 16 from the Prophets (7 in the Gospel, and 9 in Acts), and 14 from the Psalms (with 7 in each) (Fitzmyer 1992: 532).

Moreover, the theme of the fulfilment of Old Testament prophecy runs through the double work (Lk. 3.4-6; 4.18-19; 18.31; 21.22; 22.37; 24.26, 44, 46, 47; Acts 3.18; 10.43; 13.22-23, 29-31; 15.15-18; 26.23). A distinctive feature of Luke's use of the prophecy–fulfilment theme is his introduction of a predictive element within his narrative: what has been predicted will be fulfilled within the text. For example, Lk. 4.18-19 is fulfilled in 4.21; 18.31 is fulfilled in 22–24; 22.37 is fulfilled in 22.47-53 and 23.33; and 24.47 is fulfilled in Acts 2. It has been pointed out that whereas Matthew and John frequently identify details, and sometimes even trivial ones, of the life of Jesus as being fulfilments of particular Old Testament texts, Luke virtually restricts the fulfilment to the high points of Jesus' life: his mission, death, resurrection and ascension, the gift of the Holy Spirit, the Gentile mission and the destruction of Jerusalem (Maddox 1982: 142). As Squires has pointed out, the beginning and ending of each volume, Lk. 1.1; Acts 1.16-20 and Lk. 24.44; Acts 28.25-28, respectively, point to the importance of fulfilled prophecies in Luke's literary and theological purposes (1993: 137). Prophecy–fulfilment is a major theme of Luke–Acts, even though it is not the only one (Talbert 1984a: 101).

The above figures and references add statistical support to the reported speech of the Risen Jesus, 'Everything written about me in the law of Moses and the prophets and the psalms must be fulfilled' (Lk. 24.44). For Luke, then, 'the things that have come to fulfilment among us' (Lk. 1.1) are in conformity with what was promised in the Hebrew Scriptures. Indeed, according to Lk. 24.46-47, Jesus gave an exegesis of the Hebrew Scriptures, globally, in terms of his own identity and mission: 'Thus it stands written, that the Christ must suffer, and rise from the dead on the third day. Then he began with Moses and all the prophets and interpreted for them what pertained to himself in every part of Scripture'. Here great prominence is given to an interpretation of the Law and the Prophets as a hermeneutical key to understanding the suffering, death and vindication of Jesus. 'Luke is the most explicit of the evangelists in insisting that to understand what God was doing in Christ one had to know Scripture' (J.A. Sanders 1987: 78).

In the Lukan Jesus' perspective, then, the hermeneutical key to understanding the Hebrew Scriptures is Christ, Christology. The Law and the Prophets cease with John, unless they are interpreted christologically. 'Interpretation of scripture that does not point to Jesus is, in Luke's scheme of things, misinterpretation' (Tyson 1992: 543).

The Use of Isaiah in Luke

The quotation in Luke 4 of Isa. 61.1-2 and 58.6 is only one of several instances in which Luke relates the ministry of Jesus to the pronouncements of the Israelite prophet. Isaiah was the richest quarry of suitable texts for the writers of the New Testament, and no other book of the Hebrew Bible is used as extensively in the New Testament. The statistics are as follows (cited in J.A. Sanders 1987: 75):

There are no fewer than 590 references in the New Testament to Isaiah, from 63 of its 66 chapters, with 239 from Isaiah 1–39, 240 from Isaiah 40–55, and 111 from Isaiah 56–66. The distribution in the New Testament books is 155 in Revelation; 87 in Matthew; 78 in Luke; 46 in Romans; 39 in Acts; 37 in John; 28 in Mark; and 23 in Hebrews.

In addition to contributing significantly to an understanding and appreciation of the sufferings of Jesus, Isaiah was useful for comprehending many other aspects of the life of Jesus. In addition, Isaiah enabled the early Christian communities to understand their saviour in the light of Hebrew thought, and their own place in God's plans.

The most remarkable religious experience of the writers of the New Testament derived from the experience of Jesus, who died and was raised up. The God who raised him was the God of Abraham, Isaac, and Jacob, and the God of David. A particular problem for the early Christians was to explain how God's favoured one met an ignominious death on the cross as a common criminal. Searching the Scriptures for some light on the matter brought them to the oracles of Isaiah, and his dealing with the theme of triumph through adversity.

Isa. 6.9-10 offered certain explanations of why some of Jesus' own people did not accept him. The Songs of the Suffering Servant of Isaiah 42, 49 and 53, together with some of the Psalms (e.g. 22 and 118), served as vehicles to come to terms with the sufferings and rejection of Jesus, and his vindication by God.

Luke has three quotations of Isaiah with the citation formula: Lk. 3.4-6 quoting Isa. 40.3-5, Lk. 4.18-19 quoting Isa. 61.1-2 and 58.6, and Lk. 22.37 quoting Isa. 53.12. In addition, explicitly clear Isaianic phrases appear at Lk. 2.30-32 (Isa. 52.10; 42.6; 49.6); Lk. 7.22 (Isa. 26.19; 29.18; 35.5-6; 61.1); Lk. 8.10 (Isa. 6.9-10); Lk. 19.46 (Isa. 56.7); and Lk. 20.9 (Isa. 5.1-2). One sees immediately that Luke confines his quotation to one or two verses.

According to J.A. Sanders, Isa. 49.6, which is explicitly cited in Acts 13.47, and is reflected in Lk. 1.79 and 24.47, as well as in Acts 1.8 and 26.20, influenced the shape of the whole of Luke's work (Sanders 1987: 80). Probably even more significant than the quotation of, and allusions to individual passages in Isaiah is the manner in which fundamental patterns in Isaiah serve as a framework for the central thrust of Luke–Acts.

The Song of the Servant of Isaiah 49 encapsulates many of the striking features of Luke–Acts:

Listen to me, coastlands, and hearken you peoples from afar, The Lord called me from the womb, from the body of my mother he named my name. ²He made my mouth like a sharp sword, in the shadow of his hand he hid me; he made me like a polished arrow, in his quiver he hid me away. ³And he said to me, 'You are my servant, Israel, in whom I will be glorified'. ⁴But I said, 'I have laboured in vain, I have spent my strength for nothing and vanity; yet surely my right is with the Lord, and my recompense with my God'.⁵ But now the Lord says, who formed me from the womb to be his servant, to bring Jacob back to him, and that Israel might be gathered to him, for I am honoured in the eyes of the Lord, and my God has become my strength—

> ⁶he says: 'It is too light a thing that you should be my servant to raise up the tribes of Jacob and to restore the preserved of Israel; I will give you as a light to the nations, that my salvation may reach to the end of the earth'.

⁷Thus says the Lord, the Redeemer of Israel and his Holy One, to one deeply despised, abhorred by the nations, the servant of rulers: 'Kings shall see and arise; princes, and they shall prostrate themselves; because of the Lord, who is faithful, the Holy One of Israel, who has chosen you'. ⁸Thus says the Lord: 'In a time of favour I have answered you, in a day of salvation I have helped you; I have kept you and given you as a covenant to the people,
to establish the land,
to apportion the desolate heritages
⁹saying to the prisoners, 'Come forth',
to those who are in darkness, 'Appear'.
They shall feed along the ways, on all bare heights shall be their pasture;
¹⁰they shall not hunger or thirst, neither scorching wind nor sun shall smite them,
for he who has pity on them will lead them, and by springs of water will guide them.
¹¹And I will make all my mountains a way, and my highways shall be raised up.
¹²Lo, these shall come from afar, and lo, these from the north and from the west, and these from the land of Syene...

The Song of Simeon (*Nunc Dimittus*, Lk. 2.29-32) resonates with the sentiments of the key verse 6: the servant's mission to his own people, and to all nations was being ushered in:

²⁹'Lord, now let your servant depart in peace, according to your word; ³⁰for my eyes have seen your salvation ³¹which you have prepared in the presence of all peoples, ³²a light for revelation to the Gentiles, and for the glory of my people Israel'.

The theme of light for the Gentiles appears again in Paul's word of exhortation in the synagogue of Antioch in Pisidia (Acts 13.47):

> For so the Lord has commanded us, saying,
> 'I have set you to be a light for the Gentiles,
> that you may bring salvation to the uttermost parts of the earth'.

Thirdly, Paul proclaimed before King Agrippa,

> [22]...To this day I have had the help that comes from God, and so I stand here testifying both to small and great, saying nothing but what the prophets and Moses said would come to pass: [23]that the Christ must suffer, and that, by being the first to rise from the dead, he would proclaim light both to the people and to the Gentiles (Acts 26.22-23).

The Liturgical Setting of the Isaiah Texts

Later synagogal liturgical practice (c. second and third centuries) attests to a triennial cycle of readings from the Torah. A section of the Torah (*sidra*) was read every Sabbath, with all five books covered in three years. Alas, as we have already seen, we do not know if there was a fixed lectionary in the first century AD. It is clear from Lk. 4.16-30 and Acts 13.14 that already in the New Testament period there was also a reading from the Prophets. While the reading from one of the prophets (*haftarah*) was fixed in the post-Mishnaic period, we have no way of knowing whether this was so in the New Testament period. It is commonly held that Jesus read from Isaiah 61, as indicated in Luke, and for those who presume there was a fixed reading from the Prophets also, that it was in fact the *haftarah* appropriate to the occasion.

However, as Monshouwer has shown, there are good reasons to believe that this was not the case. First, the fifth- and sixth-century collections of the prophetic *haftaroth* do not include Isa. 61.1 as one (1991: 91). This fact alone renders unlikely the various suggestions about the placing of the Isaian *haftarah* at a definite place within the liturgical cycle (e.g. on *Yom Kippur*). It is virtually certain, however, that there was a reading from the Torah before Jesus ascended to the *bimah*. It is not likely that the composite Isaiah text in Luke was a reading as such, especially since it introduces an earlier verse (58.6) into Isaiah 61. Moreover, since the examples of *haftaroth* from a later period were normally some ten verses long, the text in Isaiah is too short.

In Monshouwer's view, the best way to understand the composite Isaiah text in Luke is to see it, not as the text of the reading, but as the text for the opening of a sermon (1991: 93). He cites a number of texts which suggest that it was suitable for preaching (e.g. from Qumran, *1QH* 18.14-15; *11QMelch*). Against that view, however, is the clear statement of Lk. 4.17, that 'he found the place where it is written...' Of course, strictly speaking, the text does not actually say that he read that

5. Luke's Jesus as Exegete 133

particular text as the *haftarah* after he had found it. Nevertheless, the Isaiah text occurs between Jesus 'finding the place...' and closing the book. Monshouwer's suggested interpretation is strained: 'He stood up to read [the lesson]. And [after that] He was handed the scroll of Isaiah and opening the scroll, found the passage...' (pp. 91-92). Does Monshouwer mean that Jesus read from the Torah, as one of perhaps seven readers? I consider it more likely that Jesus is presented as having read from the prophet Isaiah, and that the composite text in Luke crystallizes the substance of what he said by way of interpretation of the text read.

Isaiah 61 in Luke

The celebrated phrase, *evangelizare pauperibus misit me* ('He sent me to preach the good news to the poor') is only one of several which occur in the reading from Isaiah 61, which in its turn is only part of the drama which unfolded in the synagogue in Nazareth on that fateful day. Before examining the Lukan account of Jesus' use of this text, it is important to respect the richness of the full text, and the whole context of the event. We give here the Isaiah text in the Septuagint (LXX), Luke's Greek text, a translation of Luke's Greek text, and a translation of the corresponding Hebrew text (Heb).

LXX	*pneuma kuriou ep' eme hou heineken echrisen me*
Luke	*pneuma kuriou ep' eme hou heineken echrisen me*
	The spirit of the Lord is upon me, because he has anointed me
Heb	The spirit of the Lord YHWH is upon me, because the Lord has anointed me
LXX	*euangelisasthai ptōchois apestalken me*
Luke	*euangelisasthai ptōchois apestalken me*
	He sent me to evangelize poor (people)
Heb	to bring good tidings to the poor he sent me
LXX	*iasasthai tous suntetrimmenous tē kardia*
Luke	
Heb	he has sent me to bind up the brokenhearted
LXX	*kēruxai aichmalōtois aphesin*
Luke	*kēruxai aichmalōtois aphesin*
	to proclaim release to captives
Heb	to proclaim release to the captives

LXX	*kai tuphlois anablepsin*
Luke	*kai tuphlois anablepsin*
	and recovery of sight to the blind
Heb	

	(not in LXX Isa 61)
LXX 58.6	*apostelle tethrausmenous en aphesei*
Luke	*aposteilai tethrausmenous en aphesei*
	to set at liberty those who are oppressed
Heb	and the opening of the prison to those who are bound

LXX	*kalesai eniauton kuriou dekton*
Luke	*kēruxai eniauton kuriou dekton*
	to proclaim the acceptable year of the Lord
Heb	to proclaim the year of the Lord's favour

LXX	*kai hēmeran antapodoseōs*
Luke	
Heb	and the day of vengeance of our God

The LXX and Hebrew text continue, in translation: 'to comfort all who mourn; to grant to those who mourn in Zion—to give them a garland instead of ashes, the oil of gladness instead of mourning, the mantle of praise instead of a faint spirit...' The city will be rebuilt (v. 4), and the misfortunes of the exiles will be reversed (vv. 5-11).

The Historical Context of Isaiah 61
The historical context of the Isaiah text is of some significance for the meaning the text receives in the ministry of Jesus. The position taken here is that the material in Isa. 60.1–62.12 reflects the period of the return of the Jewish exiles to devastated Jerusalem in 538, after the half-century of captivity in Babylon. It is a series of songs of praise of the new Jerusalem (60.1-22), in which glad tidings are brought to the lowly (61.1-11), and Jerusalem is feted as God's delight (62.1-12).

Isaiah 61 is rich in the abundance of metaphors used to convey the sense of the total salvation of God's people, in their bodies and spirits, both individually and socially. The prophet is announcing salvation for the returned exiles of that period. If some of the signs of salvation are in the future, it is not a distant future. Needless to say, the rebuilding of the city and the recovery of wealth will take time to achieve. However, while it is a time of favour for the exiles, it is also the occasion of God's vengeance being shown to their enemies.

The introduction of Isa. 58.6 into the discussion should establish resonances of a different kind in the hearers. Isaiah 58 is a prophetic critique of the type of religious practice which is contradicted by unjust behaviour to the neighbour:

> v. 3b Behold in the days of your fast you seek your own pleasure, and oppress all your workers...
> v. 6 Is not this the fast that I choose:
> to loose the bonds of wickedness,
> to undo the thongs of the yoke,
> to let the oppressed go free,
> and to break every yoke?
> v. 7 Is it not to share your bread with the hungry,
> and bring the homeless poor into your house;
> when you see the naked, to cover him,
> and not to hide yourself from your own flesh...
> v. 10 If you pour yourself out for the hungry
> and satisfy the desire of the afflicted,
> then shall your light rise in the darkness
> and your gloom be as the noonday.

The association of Isaiah 58 with Isaiah 61 intensifies the social dimension of the prophetic message, and provides a striking corrective to any religious practice which is carried on without concern for the poor, and especially so when religious activity continues in the very act of oppressing them. It suggests that in addition to Jesus' message being good news for the poor, it is bad news for the rich. The only chance for the rich is to share their bread with the hungry, to bring the homeless poor into their houses, to cover the naked, to pour themselves out for the hungry, and to satisfy the desire of the afflicted (Isa. 58.7-10). This is in keeping with a major thrust of Luke–Acts, that the disciples should alienate their possessions (cf. Lk. 3.10-14; 5.11, 28; 14.33), and that the rich should give to the poor (Lk. 16.19-31; 18.22; 19.8; Acts 2.44-45; 4.32-37; 5.1-11).

Jesus' Interpretation of Isaiah 61
One must take notice of some of the differences between the LXX text of Isaiah 61, and that section of it quoted in Lk. 4.18-19. The most obvious difference is that Luke records only two of the eleven verses of Isaiah 61. The tone of the whole of Isaiah 61 is triumphalistic and nationalistic. The restoration of Israel will be all the more enriching when one compares it with the reverse which the 'foreigners' will experience: 'Aliens shall stand and feed your flocks, foreigners shall be your ploughmen and

vinedressers...You shall eat the wealth of the nations, and in their riches you shall glory' (vv. 5-6). Jesus, by omitting any reference to that part of the context of Isaiah 61, appears to abandon that kind of nationalistic religious fervour. This impression is strengthened by Jesus' sad conclusion, 'Truly, I say to you, no prophet is acceptable in his own country' (v. 24), and even more so by the reference to the two prophetic actions in favour of the foreigners as displayed by Elijah and Elisha (vv. 25-27).

Less spectacular than that omission, but in line with it, Luke omits the LXX phrase, 'to soothe the broken hearted', and adds in, 'to set at liberty those who are oppressed'. While it is not impossible that these changes were introduced by Luke, it is more likely that they reflect the style of Jesus' preaching. Jesus omits any reference to the destruction of Israel's enemies. The omission of the reference to the soothing of the brokenhearted is understandable on the basis that in the Isaiah text the mourners in Zion are promised not only restoration, but wealth at the expense of other nations (vv. 3-6). Jesus' alteration of the Isaiah passage is significant, then, and reflects both his characteristic theology and his method of preaching (Chilton 1984: 182-83).

J.A. Sanders states that recent work indicates that Isa. 58 and 61, or portions of them, constituted the *haftarah* lesson, attached to the Torah account of the death of Israel (J.A. Sanders 1987; see J.A. Sanders 1975 and Sloan 1977). Sanders claims that it was Jesus' hermeneutics of one of the people's favourite passages which offended the audience. His *today* electrified the people living under Roman occupation.

Isaiah 61 was one of the favourite passages in Judaism at the time of Jesus (see J.A. Sanders 1975: 89ff. n. 10). The audience would have identified Jesus' proclamation as really good news for them, who were poor, and captive to Roman authority, blind with prison blindness, and oppressed. They were very pleased with him, because he had read one of their favourite passages of God's mercy, and declared its fulfilment immediately.

Jesus omitted *the day of vengeance* (of enemies) and (Israel's) comfort, and stopped at the *dektos*, the year acceptable to God, and not just to them. God's mercy extended beyond the boundaries of Judaism, which was exemplified by the behaviour of Elijah and Elisha. The offence in what Jesus said was that God was not a chauvinistic nationalist—he could not be boxed in and domesticated. God could be gracious to whomever. 'Grace is a form of divine injustice' (J.A. Sanders 1987: 85).

J.A. Sanders argues that there were two basic hermeneutical axioms in operation among the Qumran community, but not restricted to it: 1. each generation considered itself to be the 'True Israel of the End Time'; 2. At the End Time, God's wrath would be directed against Israel's enemies, and his blessing would be generously bestowed on Israel (J.A. Sanders 1975: 94-97). Jesus' *today* concurs with the first, but clearly he did not subscribe to the second.

Jesus: Prophet or Messiah?
Scholars are divided as to whether Lk. 4.16-30 portrays Jesus as a prophet or as a messiah. The tendency has been to force the issue into one of these categories which are taken to be opposed. For some, Luke presents Jesus as the Moses-like prophet. Bo Reicke suggests that the scene depicts Jesus as the true prophet, whom the locals attempt to stone after the manner of the treatment to be meted out to false prophets (Deut. 13.1-11; 17.2-7) (1973: 51)—against this view is the obvious fact that the locals intended to throw him from the hill, not stone him. For others the portrayal of Jesus as Messiah precludes any reference to his being a prophet.

A straightforward reading of the text as indicating that Jesus is presented as either prophet or messiah is complicated by the fact that the citation from Isaiah is from two texts, with our Isa. 58.6 (a messianic liberation figure) imported into Isaiah 61 (a non-messianic prophetic figure). Clearly Jesus is presented as incorporating both the prophetic and messianic.

In his comment on the Isaiah text, Jesus makes it clear that he identifies himself with the prophet who announced the vindication of Israel in the name of God. This identification would be even clearer if the hearers were familiar with the targum of Isa. 61.1 (the novel elements are in italics):

> *The prophet said,* A spirit *of prophecy before* the LORD God is upon me, because the LORD has *exalted* me to announce good tidings to *the* poor; he has sent me to *strengthen* the brokenhearted, to proclaim liberty to the captives, to those who are bound. *Be revealed to light;* 61.2 to proclaim *the* year of *pleasure before* the LORD and *the* day of vengeance *before* our God; to comfort all those who mourn; 61.3 to *confuse* those who mourn in Zion...

The targum of Isa. 56.8 reads,

> Is not *this it*, the fast that I *take pleasure in:* disperse a wicked *congregation*, undo *bands, writings of perverted judgement*, let *those who were robbed depart* free, and *remove every perverted judgement*?

When the *meturgeman* (one who translates) says, 'The prophet said', it is an emphatic reminder of the prophetic nature of the work. Chilton points out that the relevance of the Targumim to the New Testament requires two conditions: 1. that the Targumic traditions be shown to be early enough to warrant the suspicion that they influenced the New Testament; 2. that the New Testament texts concerned be better explicable in this way than by other methods (Chilton 1986: 3). Chilton argues that *traditions* contained within the Targum, not the document itself, may have been current at the time of Jesus (1986: 5). 'The Targumic portrait of the Messiah as a prayerful teacher, not merely a victorious leader (cf. 52.13–53.12), may help to explain why some, at least, came to see the forceful rabbi from Nazareth in messianic terms' (Chilton 1987: xxvii).

Before his account of the scene in Nazareth Luke had presented Jesus' baptism in a manner evocative of the outpouring of the Spirit on a prophet (Lk. 3.22). He was full of the Holy Spirit when he returned from the Jordan, and during his wandering in the desert he was led by the Spirit (Lk. 4.1-2). Armed with the power of the Spirit he returned to Galilee (4.14). In the Nazareth scene he claims to be anointed with the Spirit (of prophecy), and in his own defence he cites the proverb that no prophet is acceptable in his own country (Lk. 4.24).

The status of Jesus as prophet is more prominent in Luke than in any other Gospel. The raising of the widow's son at Nain, a scene unique to Luke, evokes the crowd's reaction that 'A great prophet has arisen among us!' (7.16). In the scene of the anointing of Jesus by the woman only Luke reports the saying, 'If this man were a prophet, he would have known who and what sort of woman this is who is touching him' (7.39). The prophetic aspect of Jesus occurs again at Lk. 9.8 // Mk 6.15, and Lk. 9.19 // Mk 8.28 // Mt. 16.14, and in the Emmaus scene, unique to Luke, 'Concerning Jesus of Nazareth, who was a prophet mighty in deed and word before God and all the people' (24.19). Acts also reflects the Moses-like prophetic character of Jesus (3.22-23; 7.37), and describes his fate as conforming to the inevitability of that of the genuine prophet (7.52; cf. Neh. 9.26). This familiar Jewish theme of the persecution of the prophet is shared with Matthew: Lk. 6.22-23 // Mt. 5.11-12;

Lk. 11.47-48 // Mt. 23.29-31; Lk. 11.49-51 // Mt. 23.34-36; and Lk. 13.34-35 // Mt. 23.37-39.

The Acceptable Year—Year of Jubilee?
Much recent writing situates the Lukan text in the context of the Jewish *Year of Jubilee*. Despite the popularity of the notion, it remains to be proven that the 'acceptable year' of Isaiah 61 must be understood to mean the *Jubilee Year*, and that the Nazareth text must be understood against the background of the features of that year. What is the justification for concluding that the acceptable year of Isaiah 61 is the Jubilee Year of Lev. 25.13, 28?

The Holy Years prescribed in the book of Leviticus (ch. 25) are aimed at extending to the land itself a rest corresponding to that provided for humans and beasts by the weekly Sabbath (Exod. 20.8-11; Deut. 5.12-15). Orientals left the land uncultivated at stated intervals to assure its future fertility. The Israelites added to that practice a theological motivation: as Yahweh's property, the land should enjoy a Sabbath of solemn rest, a Sabbath to the Lord, a full Sabbatical Year (Lev. 25.2-7). During the Sabbatical Year, planting, pruning and harvesting were forbidden. The year after the seventh sabbatical, that is, every fiftieth year, was a Jubilee Year (Lev. 25.8-55). The year began on the Day of Atonement, and was a celebration of liberty (LXX *aphesis*, v. 10) for all the inhabitants of the land.

Of course, the link word, *aphesis* (liberation) occurs in several contexts in the Old Testament, for example, Jer. 41.8 (LXX) in which the king proclaims freedom, and Deut. 15.12 in which slaves are freed. But Luke does not use the terminology peculiar to Jubilee (no sowing, no pruning, no rest for the land, no day of atonement, and so on, although the *eis tēn patrida autou*, 'each returning to his family', of Lev. 25.10 LXX finds a resonance). Neither does he develop peculiarly Jubilee concepts in the course of his writing.

Luke's own understanding of *aphesis* must be an important element in the discussion. He uses the word five times in the Gospel (1.77; 3.3; 4.18 twice; and 24.47), and five in Acts (2.38; 5.31; 10.43; 13.38; 26.18). In every case, with the one exception of the quotation from Isaiah 61, the freedom under discussion is that of liberation from sin. The forgiveness of sins is an important element in the ministry of John the Baptist (Lk. 1.77 and 3.3), and of Jesus (Lk. 5.17-26; 7.36-50; 24.46-47). It is reasonable to conclude that in his use of the word from Isaiah 61 Luke understood the forgiveness of sins to be a major element of the liberation he had in mind. Forgiveness of sins, for Luke, requires repentance. The good news of liberation from sin is no cheap grace—it involves stripping oneself of possessions, and giving to the poor.

The eschatological element of Jesus' ministry should also be kept in mind. Note that Luke has the reference to *the day of vengeance* (Isa. 61.2b) at a later point in his Gospel (21.22), referring to the end time.

Monshouwer suggests that Isaiah 61 may have been used in the proclamation of the year of Jubilee every fiftieth year. But now Jesus' proclamation assumes an eschatological aspect, namely that *today* is the End Time. The Gospel, as we know, is focused on the events of the Christian Passover, which is celebrated in the springtime. The Year of Jubilee begins at *Yom Kippur* in the Autumn. Isa. 61.1, in Monshouwer's view, unites the celebration of the Christian Passover and the Year of Jubilee, suggesting that the New Era in Jesus can be described in the language of the Year of Jubilee (1991: 94). He gives in support an argument based on the later triennial cycle of readings, for which, he suggests, Isa. 61.1 would have been a suitable text. It brings together the themes of the three hypothetical *haftaroth* for the three years. These were, respectively, Isa. 42.7-15, 21, after Gen. 8.15–9.17; Isa. 33.13-22, after Exod. 18.1–19.5; and Isa. 52.5-7, after Num. 14.11-45. He points out that the keyword, *aphesis*, occurs in each of the *sedarim* for the second Sabbath of the month *Iyyar* (April–May). It would not have been possible to find a more suitable prophetic text for the 'Jubilee Year' for each year of the three year cycle!

Luke, then, in Monshouwer's view, used Isa. 61.1 at the beginning of Jesus' ministry as suited to presenting Jesus' programme after the fashion of a Jubilee Year. But now the Jubilee would not occur only every fifty years, but, liturgically, each year, when Isa. 61.1 would serve as a model for the End Time of the Messiah, which is *Today* (Lk. 4.21). The reading of Lk. 4.16-30, then, when it recurs each year introduces a year of favour. 'The prophet and his proclamation coincide. The prophet who is read, and the prophet who reads, converge' (Monshouwer 1991: 98). Luke's Gospel is a *diēgēsis* (Lk. 1.1), a continuous retelling of the deeds of the Lord, and very much so by way of fulfilment of the Law and the Prophets.

Those scholars, like Monshouwer, who regard the *Year of Jubilee* as the controlling element in Lk. 4.16-30, and go so far as to suggest a specific date for its celebration, either in the ministry of Jesus, or in the liturgical calendar of Luke's community, are indulging in interesting speculation. It is difficult to refute such imaginative hypotheses, except by pointing out that they require the coincidence of a great number of variables.

Conclusion

In what is virtually the first scene of the Galilean ministry, Lk. 4.16-30 situates Jesus in the context of his own town, in lively discussion with his own people, in their synagogue. In line with Luke's general determination to situate Jesus' ministry within his own religious tradition, the focus of the encounter is on their Scriptures, in particular that section from the scroll of the prophet Isaiah which Jesus interpreted. Insofar as the brief Lukan account reflects what actually happened, it could do no more than summarize the lively debate which ensued. The core of Jesus' message is that the good news of Isaiah 61, originally directed at the consolation of the returned exiles from Babylon, is transposed into good news for all who are oppressed. We have seen that the Isaiah text as recorded by Luke is free of any reference to that exclusiveness which is a feature of many religious traditions. Ethnicity and 'nationalism' are being challenged. The introduction of Isa. 58.6 into the Isaiah 61 text intensifies the social implications of Jesus' message of freedom. Moreover, Jesus declares the moment of liberation to be *Today*. The Lukan Jesus' radical reinterpretation of the concept of election, challenging the notion of God's choice of one specific people, is intensified by his appeal to the example of two of the great Hebrew prophets, Elijah and Elisha. As we shall see, the Lukan prophecy–fulfilment motif is elaborated.

Chapter 6

ELIJAH AND ELISHA

The introduction of these two prophetic characters into the narrative is an important element in understanding the import of the Nazareth scene. It provides a justification from within the Hebrew tradition of Jesus' revolutionary reinterpretation of divine election. A major thrust of Luke–Acts, the inclusion of Gentiles among God's chosen ones, is outlined at the opening of Jesus' public ministry. The acceptable year of the Lord is to benefit outsiders as well as those within the Jewish tradition. Luke–Acts concerns itself with the reversal of fortunes for Gentiles, without implying a rejection of the Jews. This startling revelation is made in a thoroughly Jewish context, in Jesus' own synagogue, and in a discourse on the sacred writings of the Jews. The authenticity of the divine plan for the inclusion of Gentiles is guaranteed by recourse to these same Scriptures, in the openness of Elijah and Elisha to outsiders.

However, the prevailing view is that the references to Elijah and Elisha in Lk. 4.25-27 allude to an exclusively Gentile mission. Elijah and Elisha are taken to represent a turning to the Gentiles, in view of the failure of Israel to respond positively. Lk. 4.25-27, then, is taken as a prototype of the end of God's covenant with Israel. In my view, this is a caricature of the reality of Luke's view of salvation for all.

Elijah and Elisha: Prophets for Gentiles as Well as Israel

The text of 1 Kings 17 makes clear that Elijah's sojourn in Zarephath was temporary, and by way of flight from King Ahab, 'who did evil in the sight of the LORD more than all that were before him' (1 Kgs 16.30). The good fortune which Elijah's visit brought the widow was enough to convince her that he was a man of God, and that the word of the LORD in his mouth was the truth (1 Kgs 17.24).

In response to the word of the LORD, Elijah returned to his own people, and arranged a dramatic showdown between himself and the four hundred and fifty prophets each of Baal and Asherah (1 Kgs 18.1-19). On Mount Carmel Elijah addressed all the people, 'How long will you go limping with two different opinions? If the LORD is God, follow him; but if Baal, then follow him' (18.21). The ministry to his own people continues, for Elijah is very jealous for the LORD, and for the people who have forsaken the covenant (cf. 1 Kgs 19.14).

With regard to the ministry of Elijah's successor, Elisha, his favour to the people of Israel is registered in his purifying of the water of Jericho (2 Kgs 2.19-22). On his way to Bethel he cursed his mockers, and was obliged by two she-bears, who savaged forty-two of the boys (vv. 23-24). He came to the rescue of the combined forces of the King of Israel, Judah and Edom against Mesha, the King of Moab (2 Kgs 3). His next acts of mercy were in favour of the wife of one of the sons of the prophets (2 Kgs 4.1-7), the Shunnamite woman (2 Kgs 4.8-37), and the people of Gilgal (2 Kgs 4.38-44).

Hence, any suggestion that the references in Lk. 4.25-27 herald a turning away from the Jews in favour of an *exclusive* mission to Gentiles is unwarranted. The Lukan reference highlights the universal call to conversion and repentance, addressed alike to *both* Jews and Gentiles. The Gentile interests of Elijah and Elisha are best understood as stimuli to *Jews* to conversion (Koet 1986: 389-91).

This view is consistent with what I regard as the overall thrust of Luke–Acts, namely, that it is concerned with bringing the good news from Jerusalem, the 'Jewish' capital, to Rome, the 'Gentile' capital of the empire. The missionary dynamic of the work is the bringing of the good news to the Gentiles after it has first been presented to the Jews. Acts 28.17-28 presents the penultimate picture of Paul in Rome, arguing his case with Roman Jews within the Jewish theological framework, and after only partial success, quoting Isaiah against them, and concluding, 'Let it be known to you then that this salvation of God has been sent to the Gentiles; they will listen' (Acts 28.28).

I agree with the conclusion of B.-J. Koet's examination of 1 and 2 Kings, that the major concern of Elijah and Elisha was to restore the covenant between *Israel* and its God. Indeed, they are 'zealots for restoring the covenant and for offering the people...the choice: either YHWH or Baal' (Koet 1986: 385).

Elijah and Elisha Elsewhere in Luke

That Elijah in particular was a figure of importance in early Judaism is well attested (see Wiener 1978). That the Baptist was considered to be Elijah (cf. Mt. 11.14; 17.10-12) is evidence that the Elijah traditions held special significance for the early Christians. However, Luke has nothing corresponding to the disciples' question, 'Then why do the scribes say that first Elijah must come...?' Jesus answered, 'Elijah has already come...' (Mt. 17.10-13; Mk 9.11-13). It has been argued that the idea that Elijah would immediately precede the Messiah is not to be found in first-century Judaism (or earlier), but is more likely a distinctively Christian interpretation (Faierstein 1981). Evans proposes the following nuanced position:

> However, Mal. 4.5-6 ('Behold, I will send you Elijah the prophet before the great and terrible day of the Lord...'), especially if combined with 3.1-2 ('Behold, I send my messenger to prepare the way before me, and the Lord (Jesus?) whom you seek will suddenly come to his temple...'), may have provided early Christians or Jewish apocalypticists with the understanding that Elijah was immediately to precede the Messiah (C.A. Evans 1987: 77-78 n. 16).

Recent studies have suggested that the fourth evangelist also internalized large portions of Kings (see Bostock 1980; Brodie 1981).

In addition to examining the reference to Elijah and Elisha in the Nazareth scene we shall see that these two figures form part of the backdrop to the Lukan presentation of Jesus.

It is possible to link other elements of the Gospel to the Gentile mission alluded to in 4.25-27. The following passages in Luke make clear reference to the Elijah–Elisha traditions. Lk. 7.1-16, for example, can be considered to fulfil the allusion to Elijah and Elisha made in Lk. 4.25-27, by having Jesus perform wonders which mirror theirs. The Gentile centurion of 7.1-10 reminds one of Naaman, the Syrian commander (4.27; cf. 2 Kgs 5.1-14), who may be taken as signifying the Gentiles. The raising of the son of the widow of Nain (Lk. 7.11-17) brings to mind the miraculous work done for the widow of Zarephath (2 Kgs 4.32-37; cf. 1 Kgs 17.8-24). The incident highlights Jesus' favour to a poor woman. When seen as sandwiched between the healing of the centurion's servant (7.1-10) and the Baptist's question (7.18-23), it is clearly a statement in action of the place of the salvation of the the outsider and the disadvantaged in Jesus' ministry, and clearly relates to the

6. *Elijah and Elisha*

quotation of Isaiah in the Nazareth pericope (see the discussion in Siker 1992: 86-89).

The account of the Samaritans who refused to receive Jesus, whose face was set on Jerusalem, and on whom the disciples wanted fire to be brought down (Lk. 9.52-55), brings to mind 2 Kgs 1.9-16. Here Elijah brought down fire from heaven, which consumed first one captain and his fifty men, and then another captain and his fifty, while the third was spared, although the king died, as Elijah predicted. Jesus rebukes his disciples, refusing to destroy the Samaritans. The hostility between Jews and Samaritans in that period is well known. Of all non-Jews, perhaps, they were the ones, in Jewish eyes, most deserving of God's judgment. But contrary to what one would expect of a Jew, Jesus rebuked his disciples, and refused to permit such a judgment. The Lukan Jesus' attitude of clemency and mercy, coming at the critical moment of Jesus setting his face for Jerusalem, is a clear challenge to the prevailing Jewish assumptions regarding God's election of a chosen people (see C.A. Evans 1987: 80-81).

Another allusion to the Elijah–Elisha cycle is encountered at Lk. 9.61-62: 'Another said, "I will follow you, Lord; but let me first say farewell to those at my home". Jesus said to him, "No one who puts his hand to the plough and looks back is fit for the kingdom of God"'. The text has several verbal contacts with 1 Kgs 19.19-21. One notes that Jesus' demands on a disciple are more stringent than those demanded by Elijah on Elisha—for example, Elisha was allowed return to parents and burn the plough.

Jesus' healing of the Samaritan leper of 17.11-19 also may remind one of Elisha's healing of the Gentile leper. However, it is probably going too far to suggest that the mention of Elijah's visit to the widow of Zarephath is intended to anticipate the reality that Jews and Gentiles live and eat together (Acts 10–11), and the suggestion that Luke's allusion to Naaman's washing in the Jordan in some way adumbrates the baptism of Gentiles strains the imagination somewhat.

Luke's use of the Elijah–Elisha cycle reaches its zenith at what I regard as the hinge of Luke–Acts, the accounts of the ascension and the promise of the empowering Spirit. Just as Elijah left Elisha a 'double share' of the prophetic Spirit when he departed in a fiery chariot (2 Kgs 2.1-14), so too did the prophet Jesus endow his prophetic followers with a 'double share' of the Spirit, so that they could perform deeds as great as, or even greater than his (Lk. 24.51-53; Acts 1.9-11; 2.1-13).

The Elijah–Elisha stories indicate that the Gentiles, too, would receive the benefits and blessings of the messianic era. It is clear from the passages discussed that the Lukan Jesus is presented as extending significantly the boundaries of the elect. The requirements for membership in the kingdom of God are fundamentally expanded. Gentiles and Samaritans, as representatives of the nonelect, together with the poor, come within the reign of God. Indeed, there is even an element of reversal. Pious and wealthy Jews who say 'I will follow you' may in fact be excluded. The Lukan Jesus, then, has radically expanded the boundaries of election, and, as I have argued earlier, his universalism is one of his most distinctive contributions to New Testament thought. However, there is no question of the abandonment of the appeal to the Jews.

Jew First, then Gentile

It must be kept in mind that the missionary thrust of Luke–Acts is very much an invitation to conversion of heart of Jews first, and then Gentiles (*pace* Siker 1992). This is illustrated abundantly in Jesus' own mission to the Jews in the Gospel of Luke, and in the insistence on the Jewish provenance of the Gospel in the mission of the Jerusalem Church in the Acts. According to the Acts it was always Paul's missionary practice to go to the Jewish synagogue first, and then to the Gentiles. Siker is quite right, however, in stressing the centrality of the inclusion of outsiders, right from the very beginning of Luke's work.

Indeed the double work of Luke–Acts could be understood to be an exegesis in practice of the seminal theme of Paul's Letter to the Romans, which is a crystallization of his reflection on the gospel: 'For I am not ashamed of the gospel: it is the power of God for salvation to every one who believes, to the Jew first, and also to the Greek' (Rom. 1.16). In my view Paul's missionary zeal as expressed most systematically in the Letter to the Romans embraces *both* Jew and Gentile without distinction. This view can be supported abundantly in several places in Romans, and is reflected in Rom. 3.9: 'What then? Are we Jews any better off? No, not at all; for I have already charged that all men, both Jews and Greeks, are under the power of sin'; and Rom. 10.12: 'For there is no distinction between Jew and Greek; the same Lord is Lord of all and bestows his riches upon all who call upon him' (see Prior 1989: 130-38).

It is important to keep this insight in mind for many reasons. Firstly, it respects the reality that the Christian Way was a reform movement within Judaism, inviting Jews to accept Jesus of Nazareth as the Christ who brought salvation to *both* Jew and Greek. Secondly, it serves as a fundamental corrective to the common view of the virtual incompatibility between the picture of Paul as reflected in his own letters and that revealed in Acts.

The issue is central for understanding properly the theological perspective of the author of Luke–Acts. Did he envision a gospel for Gentiles only, or did he retain an interest in a Jewish conversion of heart also? It seems to me that no reading of Luke–Acts can justify the author's exclusive interest in only one category. If the Jews in the synagogue of Nazareth did reject the message of Jesus, and thence his person, there is no reason to conclude that Luke's Jesus in his turn rejected either Nazareth itself, or the Jews in general. Right up to the end, the author of Luke–Acts never abandoned a mission to the Jews. In Paul's final encounter with Jews in Rome he records that 'some were convinced by what he said, while others disbelieved' (Acts 28.24), and that during the two years of house custody he welcomed *all* who came to him (Acts 28.30).

It goes well beyond the evidence to conclude, as J.T. Sanders has, that the Nazareth synagogue scene, 'sums up and presents in a dramatic way Luke's theology of the rejection of the gospel by the Jews and of the divine intent to send it to the Gentiles' (1987: 165). A sensitivity to the missiological thrust of the whole of Luke–Acts, and of the missionary strategy of Jesus, the Jerusalem community and Paul, makes such a conclusion untenable. The most that can be said is that Lk. 4.16-30 illustrates how the people of the synagogue in his own town rejected his message and then his person. There is nothing whatsoever in the text to suggest that Luke is presenting Jesus as going to the Gentiles only after that point. Indeed, immediately after the scene he goes to the synagogue in Capernaum!

Conclusion

Our examination of the Elijah–Elisha tradition helps us to appreciate even more that the Nazareth text (Lk. 4.16-30) redefines in a very radical way the traditional Jewish concept of election, and participation within the domain of God's reign. Jesus' focus on the Isaiah texts, with their absence of any reference to a preference for ethnicity or nationalism, is reinforced by the references to Elijah and Elisha. From this point on, as the Lukan Gospel unfolds, God's chosen ones will include the poor, the blind, the lame, the Samaritan, the Gentile, the tax-collector, the sinner, and the outcast. This revolutionary message is good news for the outsider, and a great disappointment to those who have trusted in ethnicity and tradition to give them their status. It did not go down well with the audience in his hometown.

Chapter 7

A LITERARY APPRECIATION OF LUKE 4.16-30

Biblical Literary Criticism

The subject of biblical literary criticism is an elusive one. As soon as one settles for some definition of it, one is forced into excluding some methods and practitioners. It has developed by way of reaction to, and in some cases rebellion against, the prevailing historical-critical method, which venerates the search into the original context in which a document arose. One of the distinctive features of the practitioners of the different methods of literary criticism is a willing suspension of historical questions. The hope is that the text as we have it is likely to provide more significant results than any amount of enquiry into the history of its composition, or its interpretation down the ages. Insofar as it has prioritized the relation of the contemporary reader to the ancient text, it is to be welcomed. Insofar as any one of the approaches presents itself as the only, or most productive and viable method, the welcome is to be cautious.

Over the last ten years there has grown up a range of approaches to biblical criticism, which is conveniently surveyed by Parsons (1992). Each method justifies the title 'literary criticism', but as the following summary (following Parsons 1992) shows, they differ considerably from one another. *Formalism* regards the meaning of a text as being contained within its linguistic structure. Tannehill's work on Luke–Acts (1986–90) is broadly representative of the technique. *Feminist Biblical Criticism* criticizes the patriarchal nature of much of the biblical deposit. *Poststructuralist Criticism* applies the philosophies of contemporary theorists such as Derrida, Lacan and Foucault to the biblical text. *Media Criticism* criticizes conventional biblical criticism for being too textual, and for ignoring the fact that the texts were not originally read in silence by a solitary reader, but often were celebrated in liturgy. Moreover, since we live in an increasingly electronic, rather than literary, culture, biblical criticism must move away from concentration on the text. It is time to move on to its performance, in the way that 'the musician ceases to study the score and instead plays the music' (Fowler 1989: 24, in Parsons 1992: 18). *(Socio-) Rhetorical Criticism* enquires into the most likely social and rhetorical context of a work. *Reader-Response Criticism* attends to the implied reader, and the real reader of a text. *Cultural-Literary Analysis* stresses the fundamentally political nature of biblical interpretation, whose goal is liberation from any kind of oppression. The social context of the reader assumes a position of fundamental importance.

All of these different literary-critical approaches to the Bible move away from the historico-critical approach, which has dominated the discipline since the advent of what we arrogantly call *the critical period* since the Enlightenment. Such diversity of new approaches makes it difficult to identify which trends will define the approaches of the next generation. It is highly unlikely that any one method will win universal support quickly, and we will probably have several emphases in interpretation held together in creative tension.

I shall discuss here the application of one type of text-centred literary criticism to the Nazareth text, and then suggest a way forward which pays more attention to what I consider to be at the heart of the text, namely, liberation from oppression.

The Literary Setting in Luke–Acts

Literary criticism, as exemplified above, tends not to concern itself particularly with the different stages of the composition of a document, but stresses rather the literary characteristics of the finished work. Its emphasis, then, is not on the past history of the text (*diachronic*, through time), but on the ability of the text to create the possibility of meaning in any and every reading encounter with it (*synchronic*, contemporaneous). It considers how the meaning of a text is conveyed through all of the elements of the literary language. It concerns itself with the flow and texture of the narrative, with its pace, its portrayal of the characters (see Siker 1992). In examining Luke's report of the Nazareth scene at this point we shall pay particular attention to some of the literary qualities of the completed account.

The Structure of Luke 4.16-30

That Lk. 4.16-30 constitutes a literary unit is clear. It begins in Nazareth (v. 16) and ends there (v. 30). It is fixed in place, the synagogue (v. 16,

20, 28) and time, a Sabbath (v. 16). After the Nazareth incident the scene shifts to Capernaum, on a different Sabbath (4.31) and in another synagogue (4.33). Lk. 4.31-32 marks the transition from the Nazareth scene to what happened in Capernaum (4.33-43) (Chiappini 1990).

Verses 14-15 mark a transition from 4.1-13 to 4.16-30, and 4.31-44. The overture of vv. 14-15 which introduces Jesus' teaching and reputation is developed in the two scenes in Nazareth and Capernaum which follow. The teaching is recorded in 4.16-28, 31-32, 43-44, and attention is drawn to his reputation in 4.22, 32, 37, 42.

An Analysis of Luke 4.16-30

The story develops in three phases. The actors are Jesus, the synagogue attendant, and the synagogue crowd.

Phase 1: *Jesus' Action and the Crowd's Reaction (vv. 16-20)*
Three actors appear: Jesus, the attendant and the crowd. The phase begins with Jesus, and ends with the expectation of the crowd. Setting out vv. 16-20a in the following ways is enlightening:

Simple Chiastic Structure of vv. 16-20:
The style of composition of a literary unit often reflects a rhythm which indicates wherein the stress of the piece resides. A careful literary structure is taken to indicate that the material is fully under the control of the author. The literary critic at this point begins to draw conclusions about the author's intentions, which are effected through the literary structure. One can arrange vv. 16-20 in a way which shows the first part to be mirrored in the second, with the mirror, so to speak, being at the critical point of contact between the two parts (see Tiede 1980: 35).

A common way of arranging the material is as follows:

A He *stood up* to read;
    B there *was given to him* the book of the prophet Isaiah
        C *He opened the book* and found the place...
            D *'The Spirit of the Lord is upon me...*
        C' *He closed the book*,
    B' and *gave it back* to the attendant,
A' and *sat down*.

In this way of arranging the material there are two actors, Jesus and the attendant. The latter's role is purely passive, while that of Jesus is very active. The arrangement also focuses attention on the passage(s) from the prophet Isaiah. I have never been altogether convinced of the efficacy of this method of investigation, mainly because of the temptation to force a significance on a section by a somewhat arbitrary arrangement of the parts. For example, in arranging the material in this way one omits the conclusion of the section, 'And the eyes of all in the synagogue were fixed on him' (v. 20b). In my reading and hearing of the text this last element is a critical element of the section, and should not in any circumstances be omitted from consideration. I propose an extension of the common division, which recognizes the context more completely, by respecting the synagogue setting of the scene, and above all the role of the congregation, who are the first witnesses and hearers of Jesus' deeds and words.

A Second Approach

A And he came to Nazareth...and went to *the synagogue*...
    B He *stood up* to read;
        C there *was given to him* the book of the prophet Isaiah
            D *He opened the book* and found the place...
                E *'The Spirit of the Lord is upon me*...
            D´ *He closed the book*,
        C´ and *gave it back* to the attendant,
    B´ and *sat down*;
A´ And the eyes of all *in the synagogue* were fixed on him

While this arrangement also reflects a literary focusing on the Isaiah texts, the note of expectation at the end of the section stimulates the interest of the hearer/reader. The role of the first audience is no merely passive one. Their excitement is infectious.

A Third Approach

Neither of the above arrangements, however, does justice to the content of the Isaiah passages. Giving them their full place yields the following.

A And he came to Nazareth...and went to *the synagogue*...
  B He *stood up* to read;
    C there *was given to him* the book of the prophet Isaiah
      D *He opened the book* and found the place...
        E The *Spirit of the Lord* is upon me, because he has anointed me,
          F to *proclaim* good news to the poor.
            G He has sent me to proclaim *release to the captives*
              H and recovering of sight to the blind,
            G' to *set at liberty* those who are oppressed,
          F' to *proclaim*
        E' the acceptable year *of the Lord*
      D' *He closed the book*,
    C' and *gave it back* to the attendant,
  B' and *sat down*;
A' And the eyes of all *in the synagogue* were fixed on him

The reader may object that the separation of E' from F' is forced, and I can only agree. However forced one or two elements of the analysis may be, there is a striking overall concentricity between the elements A–G, and G'–A', hinged around H. This arrangement suggests that the phrase, 'recovering of sight to the blind' occupies a place of centrality in the section, a subject to which I return below.

The concentric arrangement of the narrative of Phase 1 focuses the emphasis on the combined quotation from Isaiah. Several elements may be behind the association of the two texts Isa. 61.1-2b and 58.6. The link-word, *aphesis* (liberation), occurs in each, and there is a common context of poverty. This suggests that one of the seven rules of interpretation associated with Rabbi Hillel in the later midrashic interpretation of the Torah, the so-called *gezerah-shawah*, may be anticipated here. This rule allowed one text to illuminate and enrich another, provided, of course, that they had elements in common.

Phase 2: *Jesus' Action and Crowd's Reaction (vv. 21-22)*

There are two actors this time, Jesus and the audience.

A   And he began to say to them,
   B 'Today this scripture has been fulfilled in your hearing'.
A' And all spoke well of him, and wondered at the gracious words which proceeded
      out of his mouth; and they said, 'Is not this Joseph's son?'

Phase 3: *Crowd's Action and Jesus' Reaction (vv. 23-29)*

The actors here are the crowd and Jesus.

A And they said, 'Is not this Joseph's son?'
   B And he said to them, 'Doubtless you will quote to me this proverb,
       "Physician, heal yourself; what we have heard you did at
       Capernaum, do here also in your own country."'
      C And he said, 'Truly I say to you, no prophet is acceptable in his own
         country...
         D there were many widows in Israel in the days of Elijah...many
           lepers in Israel in the time of the prophet Elisha...
      C' When they heard this, all in the synagogue were filled with wrath.
   B' And they rose up and put him out of the city, and led him to the brow of the
     hill on which their city was built, that they might throw him down
     headlong.
A' But passing through the midst of them he went away.

Results

At the core of each of the three phases there is a link between the mission of Jesus and the Old Testament: a combined quotation from Isa. 61.1-2b; 58.6, a radical interpretation of the prophecy at 4.21, and a justification of it by reference to Elijah and Elisha. The incorporation of these Old Testament texts shows the centrality of the presentation of Jesus as one on whom the prophetic spirit has descended. The reader of Luke will already have met this revelation in the scene of Jesus' baptism (Lk. 3.22). The expectancy of the audience is introduced, and the interest of the reader also is stimulated: 'and the eyes of all in the synagogue were fixed on him' (v. 20b).

We shall now offer some comments on the fruits of our chiastic arrangement of the text in each of the three phases:

Phase 1: *Recovering of Sight to the Blind*

It is tempting to see in this arrangement a focus on a more complete recognition of who Jesus is, expressed in the metaphor of the recovery of sight. I summarize here the impressive evidence accumulated by Hamm (1986), and his very illuminating insights.

Seeing *in Luke–Acts*

Seeing is a common metaphor for understanding in general, and in religious contexts for spiritual insight. All four evangelists portray Jesus as giving sight (back) to the blind. Luke begins his two volume work

7. A Literary Appreciation of Luke 4.16-30   155

with references to the metaphor of seeing as coming to an appreciation of the time of salvation (cf. the *Nunc Dimittis* of Lk. 2.29-32; and, 'All flesh shall see the salvation of God', as the final element of the quotation of Isa. 40.3-5 at Lk. 3.6). Seeing is also prominent at the conclusion, with Acts 28.26-28 quoting Isa. 6.9-10. It is noteworthy that while Luke's text is identical with that of the LXX at this point, there is no reference to the recovery of sight to the blind in the Hebrew text of Isa. 61.1.

Although the question of John the Baptist's emissaries, and Jesus' answer are in Mt. 11.2-6 as well as in Lk. 7.18-23, Luke's v. 21 is unique to his Gospel. It gives a summary of Jesus' activity, sandwiched between the question and the answer: 'In that hour he cured many of diseases and plagues and evil spirits, and on many that were blind he bestowed sight'. Jesus' answer to John's emissaries is to report, 'The blind receive their sight, the lame walk, lepers are cleansed, and the deaf hear, the dead are raised up, poor people are evangelized. And blessed is he who takes no offence at me' (Lk. 7.22-23). In the Lukan account, then, the receiving of sight is the hinge around which the list of Jesus' healing activity revolves. In Hamm's reading, it is given pride of place (1986: 460-61). When one recalls the elements of renewal associated with the *One who is to Come*, as predicted in Isa. 61.1 LXX (blind, poor), 35.6 (blind, deaf, lame), and 29.18 (blind, deaf, poor), those who have eyes to see, and ears to hear will recognize him to have arrived in Jesus.

Actors in the gospel narrative, and readers/hearers who are open to it are led through a series of eye-openings concerning the identity of Jesus. The reader is introduced to it in the prophetic images of Isaiah. Luke's arrangement of his narrative in 18.18–19.10 is particularly revealing. It consists of the dialogue with the rich ruler (18.18-30), a passion prediction (18.31-34), the healing of the blind beggar near Jericho (18.35-43), and the conversion of Zacchaeus (19.1-10). The blind beggar coming to see is placed between the story of the rich ruler who remained in the darkness of his riches, and the conversion of Zacchaeus who gave away half his goods. The cure of the anonymous blind beggar near Jericho may stimulate in the reader a recognition of the true identity of Jesus of Nazareth, as not only Son of David (Lk. 18.38), but as Lord (*kurios*, v. 41). With the cure coming between the dialogues with the rich ruler (18.18-30), and Zacchaeus (19.1-10), the reader is also challenged to abandon the blindness of riches.

Luke also deals with false modes of seeing. In a passage unique to Luke, Herod Agrippa I is depicted as 'trying to see Jesus' (9.9). When he finally got his chance, however, he wants only the performance of a sign (23.8). Luke places his saying about the eye being the lamp of the body (11.34-36) in between two scenes: after the account of the evil generation which sought a sign, but did not recognize someone greater than Jonah (11.29-32), and before his denunciation of the Pharisees (11.37-44) and lawyers (11.45-52). Hamm sees the whole of Lk. 11.14-53 as unified by critique of an Israel, especially as personified in its leadership, which fails to hear and see Jesus properly (1986: 466). Hamm suggests that the blindness with which the multitudes are charged in Luke 12.56 is that of failing to perceive Jesus correctly (p. 467). Finally, the verb Luke uses to describe the Jewish leadership's interest in seeing Jesus (*paratēreō*) has the pejorative sense of 'spying out' (Lk. 6.7; 14.1; 20.20 and Acts 9.24). The only New Testament use of the noun is in the phrase, 'The reign of God does not come *meta paratērēseōs*' (Lk. 17.20), which should be paraphrased, 'The kingdom of God is not perceivable to those who would try to "check it out" in an uncommitted way' (Hamm 1986: 468).

True seeing is evident in a number of Lukan scenes: in the reaction of the crowd to the healing of the paralytic (Lk. 5.26); in the apostolic seeing (Lk. 10.23-24); in the action of the Samaritan leper, who when he *saw* that he was cured went back to Jesus and thanked him as God (Lk. 17.11-19); and in the scenes of the lament over, and entry into Jerusalem (Lk. 13.34-35; 19.37-38).

Luke's use of the vocabulary of seeing in the Calvary scene highlights the role of the crowd, previously hostile and calling out for Jesus' crucifixion (Lk. 23.13, 18), but which returned beating their breasts (Lk. 23.48). They function as a paradigm of conversion for the reader. In the Emmaus story the eyes of the two were kept from recognizing the risen Jesus (Lk. 26.16), a reference not to a failure to see in the physical sense, but in the sense of recognition. After the breaking and sharing of the bread their eyes are opened and they recognize him (v. 35). Their hearts burned when, in speaking to them on the road, he opened the Scriptures to them (v. 32), showing that it was necessary for the Christ to suffer and enter into his glory (v. 26). The link between the true recognition of Jesus and understanding the Scriptures is confirmed when Jesus opens the minds of the Eleven to understand them (v. 45). Seeing at one level allows one to recognize that the Risen Jesus is the one who died. But a deeper vision reveals that he is the Christ of Scripture who must suffer and enter into his glory. In his name forgiveness of sins should be preached to all nations, beginning from Jerusalem. The Eleven are witnesses to these things. They are to stay in the city until they are empowered from on high.

The second volume of Luke's work marks significant stages in the bringing of the Good News from Jerusalem to Rome. Paul bore his witness before King Agrippa, and described his missionary vocation as an opening of the eyes of the Gentiles (Acts 26.17-18). Later, in Rome itself, the hearing/seeing imagery of Isa. 6.9-10 is his justification for bringing the witness to the Gentiles (Acts 28.26-28). Other significant references in Luke–Acts to sight as a coming to see salvation include Simeon's song (the *Nunc Dimittis*, Lk. 2.29-32), Lk. 3.6, and Acts 13.47; 26.17-18, 23.

The high point of the significance of Jesus in the *Nunc Dimittis* (Lk. 2.29-32) is that he will be, 'A light for revelation to the Gentiles, and for glory to thy people Israel'. That Jesus was a light to the Gentiles (Isa. 42.6; 49.6) was not realized during his earthly ministry, and had to await the ministry of the church in the second volume of the work, as indicated by Paul in Acts 13.47, quoting Isa. 49.6, and in Acts 26.17-18, 23. Interest in the combined mission to both Jew and Gentile, then, is sustained in Luke–Acts.

Phase 2: *'Today this scripture has been fulfilled in your hearing'*
In Phase 2 the Lukan Jesus presents himself as the fulfilment of the Scripture, *in your ears*. Jesus is not only an interpreter of Isaiah 61, but is the one in whom the prophecy is fulfilled. The significance of the prophetic word is stressed further by the concentration on the vocabulary of saying and pronouncing: 'he began to say' (v. 21); 'the gracious words' (v. 22).

Today
Luke emphasizes the imminence of salvation in his use of *today*. The graceful day of the Lord, that utopian period when Israel's misfortunes would be righted, was on that very day being ushered in in the ministry of Jesus of Nazareth. The liberation inaugurated by him was not only a matter of words, but would be supported by actions of grace, which are recorded throughout the Gospel of Luke.

Luke presents the acceptable year as being inaugurated on the historic occasion on which Jesus spoke the gracious words. The fact of recording this event in writing and its consequent proclamation brings up another *today*, the *today* of subsequent hearers and readers. The hearing and reading of the account invite later disciples of Jesus to respond to what has been revealed. The message may have had a particularly striking significance for the disciples of Luke's congregation (whatever that may have looked like). The message, however, should not be reduced to one of merely ecclesial significance.

The immediacy of salvation is highlighted in other places in the Gospel of Luke. The angel says to the shepherds, 'For to you is born *this day* in the city of David a Saviour, who is Christ the Lord' (2.11). On seeing the healing of the paralytic the reaction of the crowd is, 'We have seen strange things *today*' (5.26). Luke records Jesus' message to Herod, 'Behold, I cast out demons and perform cures *today* and tomorrow, and the third day I finish my course. Nevertheless I must go on my way *today* and tomorrow and the day following; for it cannot be that a prophet should perish away from Jerusalem. O Jerusalem, Jerusalem, killing the prophets and stoning those who are sent to you' (13.32-34). In Jericho, Jesus says to Zacchaeus, '"Zacchaeus, make haste and come down; for I must stay at your house *today*"...And Jesus said to him, "*Today* salvation has come to this house, since he also is a son of Abraham. For the Son of man came to seek out and to save the lost"' (19.5-9). Finally, Jesus on the Cross says to the repentant thief, 'Truly, I say to you, *today* you will be with me in Paradise' (23.43).

The reader learns that Jesus' interpretation of the Isaiah text is no mere rhetoric, but is manifested throughout the Gospel in his ministry to people. This point is made dramatically in the exorcism and several healings which continue in the narrative of ch. 4, and are summarized in vv. 40-41: 'Now when the sun was setting, all those who had any that were sick with various diseases brought them to him; and he laid his hands on every one of them and healed them. And demons also came out of many...'

Each of the elements of the Isaiah text can be seen to be fulfilled throughout the Gospel of Luke. That Jesus was *empowered by the Spirit* is a recurring theme (e.g. Lk. 1.35; 3.22; 4.1,14; 10.21; cf. Acts 1.2; 10.38). This puts him in line with Moses (Num. 11.17), Gideon (Judg. 6.34), David and Saul (1 Sam. 16.13-14), Elizabeth (Lk. 1.41), Zechariah (Lk. 1.67), John the Baptist (Lk. 1.16-17), and Simeon (Lk. 2.25). The activity of the Spirit in the lives of Jesus' disciples is a feature of Acts also (e.g. Acts 4.8, 31; 5.32; 6.3, 5, 10). *His concern for evangelizing* is made explicit again in Lk. 4.43; 7.22; 8.1 and 20.1. *His concern for the poor* surfaces again at Lk. 6.20; 14.13, 21; 16.20; 18.22; 19.9 and 21.3.

7. *A Literary Appreciation of Luke 4.16-30* 159

In your Hearing
The statement that the Scriptures have been fulfilled *in your ears* implies more than a passive communication. The audacious claim of Jesus that the Scriptures are being fulfilled for the audience opens up the way for it to react in whatever way it wishes. The account continues, 'And all spoke well of him, and wondered at the gracious words which proceeded out of his mouth; and they said, "Is not this Joseph's son?"' (v. 22). I have discussed already the different meanings one can give to v. 22, as to whether it indicates that Jesus was received favourably, or not. While the common view considers the people up to this point to be in admiration of Jesus, there is much to be said for the view that already resentment is breeding.

Phase 3: *'There were many widows in Israel in the days of Elijah...and many lepers in Israel in the time of the prophet Elisha...'*
The bringing into the narrative of two great prophetic figures of Jewish history, Elijah and Elisha, sustains the revelation of Jesus as prophet. The universalist ministry of these two prophets, who went out to non-Jews, is mentioned in the same breath as Jesus' interpretation of Isaiah. Jesus is not only the biblical interpreter, *par excellence*, but is the person in whom the prophetic ministry comes to its fulfilment.

In my reading of the literary drama, resentment to the message of Jesus has already surfaced, and finds expression in a rhetorical question which I take to be aimed at bringing Jesus down to earth: 'Is not this Joseph's son?' (v. 22). From this point on, Jesus goes into the attack.

Physician, heal yourself (Luke 4.23)
As if by way of reading the minds of the audience (a quality Luke frequently attributes to him: cf. 5.22; 6.8; 7.39-40; 9.47 and 11.17), Jesus confronts them with, 'Doubtless you will quote to me this proverb, "Physician, heal yourself; what we have heard you did at Capernaum, do here also in your own country"' (v. 23).

This is likely to have been an aphorism in common usage. Noorda (1982) has drawn attention to classical parallels to it. A similar sentiment is found in a funerary inscription from Stratonikeia in Caria (later second century), marking the death of a doctor, Epaphroditos: 'Having become a doctor you were most companionable to all, both good at your craft and diligent in character, for you learned to be wiser than your knowledge. But you could not save yourself from sickness, for Fate is stronger than doctors'. The Greek text is reproduced in Horsley (1987:

20). The Synoptic Gospels record a similar sentiment in the mocking of Jesus, 'He saved others; he cannot save himself' (Mt. 27.42 = Mk 15.31; cf. Lk. 23.35).

The theme of a doctor who could not save herself is reflected also in a husband's epitaph for his wife, a midwife: 'To the divine spirits. I, Julia Primigenia the midwife, saved many women, yet I did not escape the Fates. After a good life I departed (for) home (*anelusa eis oikon*), where a place of piety has been reserved for me. Tiberius Julius Hierax her husband inscribed this for his wife for the sake of a good remembrance, since he loved (her)' (*IGUR* 1240, Rome, early Imperial?; plate on p. 96—the Greek text is reproduced, and a translation is given in Horsley 1987: 23).

Capernaum
The activity of Jesus in Capernaum is a novelty for the reader of Luke, since he records Jesus' ministry there only after the Nazareth scene (Lk. 4.31-41), although there is the general summary of his activity in Galilee in Lk. 4.14-15.

'No prophet is acceptable in his own country'
The prophetic role of Jesus is clear in his quotation of the aphorism, 'No prophet is acceptable in his own country' (v. 24), a point illustrated dramatically at the end of the section. Again Scripture in adduced in the prophetic figures, Elijah and Elisha. The rejection of Jesus by the people of Nazareth intensifies the reader's realization that Jesus is indeed a prophet.

There are some striking similarities between the Nazareth synagogue scene, and that of Stephen before the Council in Jerusalem. Already it has been noted that Philip spoke with wisdom and with the Spirit (Acts 6.10). Very abruptly at the end of his summary of the stages of Israelite salvation, Stephen harangued his audience, 'You stiff-necked people, uncircumcised in heart and ears, you always resist the Holy Spirit. As your fathers did, so do you. Which of the prophets did not your fathers persecute?' (Acts 7.51). The audience cried out with a loud voice, and stopped their ears, and rushed together upon him. Then they cast him out of the city and stoned him (Acts 7.57-58).

Conclusion

The application of modern literary criticism to New Testament texts offers much, but when one measures the reward it is modest. It is true that our investigation of some techniques of the discipline has drawn attention to some elements of the text which might have escaped the reader. Nevertheless, one is left with a certain unease. Several factors contribute to an explanation of this discomfort. Much literary criticism assumes a *privatization* of the encounter between a reader and the text. The experience is often a function of a private, isolated, and hermetically sealed confrontation between a sole reader and a text. Moreover, the text is presumed to be read for the first time, and has been chosen for all kinds of different reasons that evade narrow classification.

In the case of readings from the Bible, by way of contrast, the context is normally communal. There are links joining the values of the transmitting community and those of the receiving one. In traditional theological terms, the spirit in the text and the spirit in the reader/hearer recognize each other. The context of the group reading/hearing is often a very powerful one in promoting the impact of the text.

When the text is read in the Christian assembly, for example, it is often a part of the drama of re-enactment of the saving acts of Jesus. When the texts re-present his teaching, the drama of the liturgy moves on to the offering of gifts, the great Prayer of Thanksgiving, with its focus on the Passion, Death, Resurrection and Future Coming of Christ. Then comes the Communion Meal, in which the Body and Blood are consumed as enlivening food and drink.

Furthermore, the Christian Church is very conscious of its traditions. The generations which have preceded ours have heard the message, and offered their interpretations, both practical and academic. There is, then, a tradition of interpretation into which each new generation enters.

But there is a factor which is more fundamental. The self-revelation of Jesus recorded by Luke involves good news for the poor, release for captives and recovering of sight for the blind. It is a *programme* which sets at liberty those who are oppressed, and proclaims the acceptable year of the Lord. As with the case of Jesus' statement in the synagogue, the re-announcement of the programme in a liturgical context ought to be followed by actions, anticipatory signs of the liberation which will find its final expression in God's good time. Since the Christian Church sees itself as manifesting the mission of Jesus, it must do so, and do so particularly in concrete actions of liberation of the poor, those who suffer, and those who are oppressed. The proclamation of the good news of liberation from all forms of bondage, and the blessings of the day of the Lord, require *programmes of action* in favour of the oppressed. Otherwise the Church will merit the correction offered by a preacher of an earlier generation, 'Be doers of the word, and not hearers only, deceiving yourselves' (Jas 1.22).

Literary criticism which leads only to an enrichment of the intellect, and a greater sensitivity to the drama of the text, leaves much undealt with. I shall now discuss a reading of the text which in my view goes closer to the heart of its message.

Chapter 8

THE INVITATION OF LUKE–ACTS—YESTERDAY:
THE SOCIOLOGICAL SETTING OF THE TEXT

The Lukan Nazareth text is an obvious one for developing a liberation theology. At the heart of contemporary liberation theologies is the urge to improve the lot of the poor and the oppressed. Two questions spring to mind immediately: who are the poor, and how does one go about improving their lot?

Luke–Acts: The Gospel of the Poor?

The Gospel of Luke is commonly regarded as 'the Gospel of the poor'. The claim of Richard Cassidy reflects a common view: 'An unmistakable feature of the Jesus described in Luke's account is that he displays a specific and consistent concern for the sick and the poor' (1987: 2). He cites the Nazareth synagogue scene (4.18-19), the banquet of the poor and disabled (14.12-14), the reference to diseases and infirmities (14.21), the parable of Lazarus (16.19-26), all of which are peculiar to Luke. In addition he highlights Luke's references to Jesus' concern for less regarded groups, such as Samaritans, Gentiles, women and tax-collectors.

Are the poor in Luke's Gospel to be identified with the hungry, those who weep, the sick, those who labour, those who bear burdens, the last, the simple, the lost, the sinners? It is prudent in the first instance to distinguish between Jesus' attitude to the poor, and that to tax-collectors and sinners (Karris 1978). In this chapter we shall examine whether Luke–Acts stresses the poor, and, if so, consider why. But before examining the relevant texts it is important to be sensitive to one's own dispositions.

The Standpoint of the Reader

We must be aware of the influence our own social circumstances impose on our understanding of any text, and this applies no less to the Gospels than to any other literature, old or new. Any reader of any text, but particularly of one which is likely to provoke a moral response, will do well to enquire into her or his dispositions *prior* to engaging the text. Contact with any literature has the possibility of correcting, reshaping and enlarging the individual reader's standpoint.

Does one embark on the examination of a text in the hope of having one's own predispositions confirmed, or is one prepared to place oneself under the power of the word of the text even if it should invite a radical change of values and lifestyle? To be sensitive to one's own pre-understanding may turn out to be more fundamental to understanding a text than any enquiry into its putative meaning.

Suppose our enquiry into the meaning of 'the poor' in Luke concludes that 'the poor' are to be identified with the destitute and the beggars of society. Is a subscriber to the Lukan programme of liberation required, or at least invited, to align her or his energies to the evangelization of the destitute and the beggars of our society?

Suppose, on the other hand, that our enquiry concludes that 'the poor' are those who because they are so deficient in material possessions put all their trust in God. Are contemporary disciples of the Lukan Jesus true to their vocation invited, or even required, to divest themselves of all material possessions in order to share the blessedness of the poor?

These questions ought to be borne in mind as we now enquire into the meaning of the term *the poor*, and examine whether the Gospel of Luke is 'the Gospel of the poor'. In considering the context of that Gospel I bring into the discussion some of the conclusions of the most recent scholarship which uses methods which derive from the science of sociology. All of this is done in an attempt to help us arrive at an understanding of the key phrase, 'he sent me to evangelize the poor'.

The Poor and Oppressed in Luke's Gospel

Over the last twenty years I have participated in lively discussion centring on the question, 'Who are the poor and the oppressed?' That scholars need to pose this question constantly reflects the distance from which most scholastic practitioners view the real world.

A major development in recent biblical exegesis enquires into the social setting of Luke's Gospel. For biblical interpretation to have anything of substance to offer theology, it is necessary for it to uncover as much as possible of the real life-context in which the biblical documents developed. Armed with these perspectives authentic theology must also enquire into the social, economic and political circumstances of contemporary society. We shall attempt here to go beyond a merely textual investigation, and consider some question of socio economic import.

Who are the Poor in New Testament Times?

Good scholarship avoids the pitfall of regarding the New Testament period as monochromatic in terms of its social, political and religious structure. Although some patterns were general, it is more accurate to presume that each writing in the New Testament reflects circumstances which are particular to the communities in which, or for which, the writings were composed.

We ought to concede readily that the thrust of the message of Jesus may be understood distinctively in contemporary London, Rwanda, Gaza, Latin America or Australia, as it was in rural Palestine, and the sophisticated cities of Paul's missionary activity. It is reasonable to suspect that in addition to indicating Jesus' and Paul's views on *the poor*, the New Testament writings may also contain clues to the social, political, and religious circumstances of the communities reflected in each of the writings.

The Meaning of ptōchos

If one were guided only by Greek usage, the word, *ptōchos*, which we translate 'poor' (*pauperes*), should be translated by 'destitute', or 'beggar'. It marked a more severe form of poverty than the other common Greek term *penēs* (which occurs in the New Testament only at 2 Cor. 9.9). *penēs* refers to a person who could make a living, albeit with some difficulty at times. Another common Greek word for poverty, *endeēs* occurs in the New Testament only at Acts 4.34. The *ptōchoi* were on the fringe of Greek society, since they had no place in the economy, and for their survival depended entirely on the hospitality of others.

One has sympathy for the person who asks, 'If *ptōchos* means "destitute", why not translate it as such?' There is a problem in adopting such a swift solution, and as the following discussion shows, the difficulty is not easily solved. We are not dealing with purely Hellenistic culture, and hence account must also be taken of the Jewish terminology. Every effort should be made to uncover the true meaning of *ptōchos* in Lk. 4.18, since so much depends on getting it right. But patience is required when one is attempting to clarify nuances of meanings of words which have been used over hundreds of years in quite different social, political and religious contexts.

The most common words for *poor* in the Hebrew Scriptures are *'anî* (80 times), and *'ebyôn* (61 times). *'anî* involves some dependence on others, but *'ebyôn* suggests a much more fundamental need—if *'anî* needed help, *'ebyôn* needed it immediately as a condition of survival. It would seem appropriate to translate *'anî* by *penēs*, and *'ebyôn* by *ptōchos*. However, the situation in the Septuagint is not so straightforward. *ptōchos* translates *'anî* 38 (out of 80) times, and *penēs* translates *'ebyôn* 29 (out of 61) times. Moreover, *'ebyôn* is rendered by *ptōchos* (or equivalent) 10 times, and *'anî* is translated by *penēs* (or equivalent) 13 times. Furthermore, where the context makes it clear that the poor person is in need of immediate relief, *'ebyôn* is rendered by *ptōchos* or *endeēs*. Perhaps the fact that the term *'anî* came to have the religious meaning of being totally dependent on God contributed to its being translated by *ptōchos*, albeit that term had negative secular connotations (see Hamel 1990: 167-73; and Gillingham's discussion of the terminology in the Psalms: 1988).

Another interesting insight into the meaning of the term 'poor' is provided by the specifically religious use of the terminology in the documents of the Dead Sea community. The author of the *Hymns of Thanksgiving* refers to himself as *'anî* (*1QH* 5.1; 5.21, etc.) and *'ebyôn* (*1QH* 2.32; 3.25, etc.), and in the *War Rule* the 'sons of light' are called the 'poor in spirit' (*'ānāwey rûaḥ, 1QM* 14.7). In the *Commentary on Psalm* 37.11 the author refers to the Qumran community as 'the Congregation of the Poor Ones' (*4QpPs* 2.11-12). Although living conditions by the shore of the Dead Sea were not luxurious, to put it mildly, subsistence was possible. Moreover, the architectural remains suggest a standard of sufficiency that would rival many religious foundations today.

Yet another piece of evidence should be brought in. In two passages Paul speaks of the *ptōchoi* (Gal. 2.10), or 'the *ptōchoi* of the saints in Jerusalem' (Rom. 15.26). Were these destitute in the economic sense, or was their poverty to be measured by their total dependence on God?

ptōchos in the New Testament

In the New Testament alone the word *ptōchos* occurs 34 times: ten times in the Gospel of Luke, five in Matthew, five in Mark, and four in John. Surprisingly, it does not occur in Acts, the second volume of Luke–Acts. In Paul it occurs only in Rom. 15.26; 2 Cor. 6.10; Gal. 2.10; 4.9. It occurs four times in James (2.2, 3, 5, 6), and elsewhere in the New Testament only in Rev. 3.17 and 13.16.

ptōchos in Luke

A certain perspective on the significance of the theme of the poor in Luke can be gauged by examining his ten occurrences of the term *ptōchos*, and seeing these against the background of the term in the rest of the New Testament. The reader may readily see from the layout which follows which references are unique to Luke, and which are shared by the other Gospels. If one accepts the common view of the literary relationships between the Gospels one will use phrases like, 'Luke modified Mark...', or 'Luke's version of the material shared with Matthew reflects his emphasis...' For my part, I use the more neutral, 'In Luke's version we find stress on...'

1. Nazareth Synagogue Homily:
Luke 4.18   he sent me to evangelize *poor people* (no parallel)

2. Beatitude:
Luke 6.20   Blessed are you *poor*,
Matt 5.3   Blessed are *the poor in spirit*,

Luke 6.20   for yours is the kingdom of God
Matt 5.3   for theirs is the kingdom of heaven

3. John the Baptist's Witness to Jesus:
Luke 7.22   Go and tell John what you have seen and heard:
Matt 11.4   Go and tell John what you   hear and see:

Luke 7.22   the blind receive their sight,   the lame walk,
Matt 11.5   the blind receive their sight and the lame walk,

Luke 7.22   lepers are cleansed, and the deaf hear,
Matt 11.5   lepers are cleansed, and the deaf hear,

Luke 7.22   the dead are raised up,   *poor people are evangelized*
Matt 11.5   and the dead are raised up, and *poor people are evangelized*

Luke 7.23	And blessed is he who takes no offence at me
Matt 11.6	And blessed is he who takes no offence at me

4. Parable of Places at Marriage Feast (Luke 14.12-14):
¹²When you give a dinner or a banquet, do not invite your friends or your brothers or your kinsmen or rich neighbours, lest they also invite you in return, and you be repaid. ¹³But when you give a feast, invite *poor people*, maimed, lame, blind, ¹⁴and you will be blessed, because they cannot repay you. You will be repaid at the resurrection of the just (no parallel).

5. Parable of the Great Supper:
Luke 14.21	Go out quickly to the streets and lanes of the city, and bring in *the poor* and maimed and blind and lame
Matt 22.9	Go therefore to the thoroughfares and invite to the marriage feast as many as you find

6, 7. Lazarus:
Luke 16.20	And at his gate lay *a poor man* named Lazarus... ²²*The poor man* died...(no parallel)

8. The Rich Ruler:
Luke 18.22	One thing you still lack,
Matt 19.21	If you would be perfect,
Mark 10.21	One thing you lack,

Luke 18.22	Sell all (*panta*) that you have
Matt 19.21	go, sell what you possess
Mark 10.21	go, sell what you have

Luke 18.22	and distribute it to *poor people*,
Matt 19.21	and give it to *poor people*,
Mark 10.21	and give it to *poor people*,

Luke 18.22	and you will have treasure in the heavens
Matt 19.21	and you will have treasure in heavens
Mark 10.21	and you will have treasure in heaven

Luke 18.22	and come, follow me
Matt 19.21	and come, follow me
Mark 10.21	and come, follow me

9. Zacchaeus:
Luke 19.8	Half of my goods I give to *the poor*... (no parallel)

10. The Widow's Mite:
Luke 21.3	...this *poor* widow has put in more than all of them
Mark 12.43	...this *poor* widow has put in more than all those...

ptōchos in the other Gospels
Matthew uses the word *ptōchos* five times: 5.3 (par. Lk. 6.20); 11.5 (par. Lk. 7.22); 19.21 (par. Mk 10.21; Lk. 18.22); 26.9 (par. Mk 14.5; cf. Jn 12.5), 11 (par. Mk 14.7; Jn 12.8). Mark similarly uses the word five times 10.21 (par. Mt. 19.21; Lk. 18.22); 12.42, 43 (par. Lk. 21.3); 14.5 (par. Mt. 26.9), 7 (par. Mt. 26.11; Jn 12.8). John has the word four times, three in the context of the Bethany anointing (12.5, 6, 8), and the fourth concerning what the eleven at the Last Supper supposed Jesus to have said to Judas ('that he should give something to the *poor*', 13.29).

Luke, then, shares with both Matthew and Mark the incident of the Rich Man only. He shares with Matthew alone the Beatitude, and John's Witness to Jesus, and shares with Mark alone the incident of the Widow's Mite. Luke alone has the Nazareth homily, the places at a feast parable, (the use of *ptōchos* in the parable of the Great Supper), the Lazarus parable, and the Zacchaeus incident.

On the other hand, Luke's scene of the anointing of Jesus (7.36-50) deals with the question of sin, while that of Mt. 26.6-13, Mk 14.3-9 and Jn 12.1-8 bring in the theme of the poor. Luke, therefore, does not have the phrases, 'For this ointment might have been sold...and given to *the poor*' (Mt. 26.9; Mk 14.5; and cf. Jn 12.5), and, 'For you always have *the poor* with you' (Mt. 26.11; Mk 14.7; Jn 12.8).

ptōchos in Paul
Rom. 15.26 uses the word in connection with the collection in favour of *the poor* of Jerusalem. In 2 Cor. 6.10 Paul and Timothy describe themselves as '*poor*, yet making many rich'. Gal. 2.10 describes the help of *the poor* as a condition in the agreement of Paul and Barnabas with James, Cephas and John. Gal. 4.9 uses the adjective of 'the elements', in the pejorative sense of *beggarly*.

ptōchos in James
In his celebrated passage criticizing the attitude of a preferential option for the rich, James contrasts a man with gold rings and in fine clothing, with a *poor* man (2.2, 3). He gives the core of his theological reflection: 'Has not God chosen those who are *poor* in the world to be rich in faith and heirs of the kingdom which he has promised to those who love him?' (v. 5), and he chastises his readers for their having dishonoured the *poor* (v. 6).

ptōchos in Revelation
In the Letter to the Church of Laodicea, the author writes, 'For you say, I am rich, I have prospered, and I need nothing; not knowing that you are wretched, pitiable, *poor*, blind and naked' (Rev. 3.17). The author of the Apocalypse completes the New Testament usage of the term with his description of all people, under the headings, 'the small and the great, the rich and the *poor*, the free and the slave...' (Rev. 13.16).

Cognate Noun and Verb
The cognate noun *ptōcheia* also reflects the root meaning. Paul and Timothy remind the Corinthians that in the churches in Macedonia, while in a severe test of affliction, 'their abundance of joy and their extreme *poverty* have overflowed in a wealth of liberality on their part' (2 Cor. 8.2). The *poverty* of Christ is invoked in 2 Cor. 8.9. The association of tribulation with *poverty* occurs also in Rev. 2.9: 'I know your tribulation and your poverty, but you are rich'.

The cognate verb *ptōcheuō* occurs just once in the New Testament, with reference to the grace of our Lord Jesus Christ, 'that though he was rich, yet for your sake *he became poor (eptōcheusen)*, so that by his poverty you might become rich' (2 Cor. 8.9).

Conclusions
Clearly one must respect the possibility that the same term *ptōchos* may refer to a person in somewhat different social circumstances from one place to another. As we know, the social circumstances of a London *ptōchos*, living in 'cardboard city', will not be quite the same as those living in a shanty town on the fringe of Lima. Nevertheless, from the survey of the occurrence of *ptōchos* in the New Testament it appears that

1. *the poor* are the opposite of the rich (Lk. 6.24; Lk. 16.20, 22; 2 Cor. 8.9; Jas 2.2, 3). However, the author of Revelation turns the term on its head when he assures the rich, prosperous and self-sufficient that they are in fact wretched, pitiable, *poor*, blind and naked (Rev. 3.17);
2. the path to discipleship for the rich ruler of Lk. 18.22 (cf. Mt. 19.21; Mk 10.21) is to sell all that he has, and give to the poor—compare Zacchaeus who gave half of his goods to *the poor* (Lk. 19.8). The importance of caring for the poor is reflected also in its being a condition of the agreement struck

8. The Invitation of Luke–Acts—Yesterday

by Paul and Barnabas with James, Cephas and John (Gal. 2.10). The care of *the poor* of Jerusalem spurred on the collection referred to in Rom. 15.26. James chastises his readers for their having dishonoured the *poor* (2.6);

3. the evangelization of the poor is of the same order as the liberation of prisoners, the restoring of sight to the blind, the freeing of the oppressed (Lk. 4.18), the healing of the lame, lepers, and the deaf, and the raising of the dead (Lk. 7.22; Mt. 11.5);

4. the poor are classed with the non-rich, the maimed, the lame, and the blind (Lk. 14.13; cf. Lk. 14.21), perhaps because, while they are all quite distinct disabilities, they reflect different modes of disadvantage in society.

The Rich

In addition to enquiring into the use of *ptōchos* in the New Testament, and especially in Luke–Acts, it is significant to examine the use of the term which expresses the other end of the spectrum, *plousios*, a rich person. While it occurs in Matthew three times (Mt. 19.23, 24; 25.27), twice in Mark (Mk 10.25; 12.41), and not at all in John, it occurs eleven times in Luke. Elsewhere in the New Testament it occurs in 2 Cor. 8.9; Eph. 2.4; 1 Tim. 6.17; Jas 1.10, 11; 2.5, 6; 5.1; and Rev. 2.9; 3.17; 6.15; 13.16. Statistics alone, then, suggest that Luke has a particular interest in the rich. Luke's Jesus is critical of the *rich man* who brought forth plentifully, and who was tempted to eat, drink, and be merry (12.16). He also criticizes the host who invited only *rich* neighbours (14.12).

But it is in those passages in which he contrasts the rich with the poor that his teaching is at its starkest (Beatitude/Woe of 6.20, 24, and *a rich man* and Lazarus at 16.19, and the poor widow who gave her all, Lk. 21.1-4; Mk 12.41-44). Luke records incidents which reflect a total selfishness (the rich ruler of 18.22-25; parallels in Mt. 19, Mk 10), and a total selflessness (the poor widow of 21.1-4; Mk 12.41-44), separated by the example of Zacchaeus who gave half his possessions away (Lk. 19).

Luke's arrangement of his narrative in 18.18–19.10 is particularly revealing. It consists of the dialogue with the rich ruler (18.18-30), a passion prediction (18.31-34), the healing of the blind beggar near Jericho (18.35-43), and the conversion of Zacchaeus (19.1-10). Having acknowledged Jesus to be a 'good teacher', the rich ruler grows sad when he learns that inheriting eternal life demands that he sell all that he has and give to the poor. Zacchaeus, on the other hand, who already gives half his goods to the poor, receives Jesus with joy, and with him salvation. Between the two accounts of rich men and their dealings with Jesus we have the passion prediction and the healing of the blind beggar near Jericho. Hamm sees in the literary arrangement,

> a kind of narrative triptych, with the center panel being the story of a literal cure of a blind man, and the two wing panels being the stories of two men blinded by their riches, one of whom, the rich ruler, is not freed by his encounter with Jesus, and the other, Zacchaeus, who is open to the gift of salvation (19.9) (Hamm 1986: 464).

The placement of the passion prediction as a kind of hinge between the first and central panel, however, makes the triptych image rather forced. Nevertheless, it is clear from the narrative that the rich ruler of 18.18-30 needs to be cured of a kind of blindness associated with his wealth, while Zacchaeus has already given half his goods to the poor. Let the reader understand!

Putting these reflections on the theme of rich in Luke side by side with his remarks on the poor leaves one in little doubt that when Luke speaks of *poor people* he means people who are lacking in the essentials for subsistence. It is obvious, of course, that one is never poor only in a material sense. Material poverty involves loss of dignity, status and security, and, in a society sensitive to questions of ritual purity, uncleanness.

What Makes a Person Poor?

There are, broadly speaking, two kinds of poverty: absolute poverty, which describes the state of a person who is without the basic food, clothes and shelter required to subsist, and all other forms of relative poverty which vary according to the changing standards of every society and period. For the purposes of what follows, I will regard as poor those people who, according to the standards of their own society, are ill-fed, ill-clothed and ill-housed. The reasons for this state of poverty may be traceable to natural causes, or to human causes, or to some combination of the two. Clearly, substantial improvement of the lot of the poor will require dealing with the underlying causes.

How far does the information about the living conditions of first century Galilee bring us? As we shall see, in that context, poverty is

Diet

In first-century Palestine, food consumption differentiated the rich from the poor (see Hamel 1990). The celebration attending the return of the Prodigal Son in Luke 15, with the slaughter of the fattened calf, and the other son's complaint that not even a goat had been available to him, shows both the festive nature of the eating of meat and also its rarity. Wealth was recognized by the possession of choice meat, white wheat bread and wine, without the requirement of such inferior food as barley bread, certain legumes, wild plants, and the like.

Poor people could not eat meat or wheat, and they were recognized by their consumption of barley bread and meat (if any) or wine (vinegar) of low quality. The purity laws of Judaism made it more difficult for poor people to fulfil them. Some of the food they had to eat, because of their poverty, was unclean, being less pure or less white. Barley bread, *cibariun*, was the mark of the common person, the slave and the poor. It is only in John's Gospel that the type of bread is mentioned, in connection with the multiplication of the loaves: 'Andrew, Simon Peter's brother, said to Jesus: "There is a lad here who has five barley loaves and two fish"' (Jn 6.9). On this passage in Matthew's Gospel (14.17) Origen suggested that the Disciples' shame was that they could only offer Jesus barley loaves, and not behave to him as a true Lord. The poor people's meat came from locusts and from older domesticated animals. To be poor, from that perspective, meant having enough to eat, but with little dignity and security. Among these poor people, of course, were the needy, who for one reason or another did not have even that little security, and were reduced to begging.

There were certain categories of poor people who were entitled to regular help, and from a second-century AD text, it appears that a poor person was supposed to receive two loaves of bread per day, sufficient for two meals (*m. Pe'ah* 8.7). It has been determined that a loaf weighed between 500g and 600g (Hamel). This average loaf of whole wheat bread was deemed to be the minimum fare for one day, being just enough to survive. People who did not have this amount per day were in danger of starvation. In such cases, the duty to preserve human life took precedence over purity rules.

The wealthier people appeared to have secured a good living, although they too were subject to catastrophes, mainly of a political form. They ate good meat regularly, drank old wine, ate excellent bread and varied vegetables, fruit and nuts. Most people ate bread or porridge made of barley, various cereals and legumes, or more rarely wheat. They also supplemented them usually with salt and oil, or olives, and so forth. Sometimes, also, they had quantities of milk and cheese, and when in season they had some vegetables and fresh fruits, and out of season dried fruits which were very important sources of calcium, vitamins and riboflavin. Meat was restricted to festivities, and was normally consumed only in small quantities. To have meat every day, apparently, was the greatest food luxury, and fish also was treasured (Hamel 1990: 24). Eggs were more freely available.

The real difference between rich and poor was in terms of security. The rich people could store away food in anticipation of famines and other misadventures. The *rich man* of Lk. 12.16-21 is a good example:

> The land of a *rich man* brought forth plentifully; and he thought to himself, 'What shall I do, for I have nowhere to store my crops?' And he said, 'I will do this: I will pull down my barns, and build larger ones; and there I will store all my grain and my goods. And I will say to my soul, "Soul, you have ample goods laid up for many years; take your ease, eat, drink, be merry"...'

The poor, on the other hand, had no such stores, and they were therefore much more liable to be devastated by the various catastrophes, such as drought and famine. Reflecting such reverses, the Midrash on Lamentations says: 'While the fat one becomes lean, the lean one is dead' (*Lam. R.* 3.10).

Clothing

The account in the Acts of the Apostles of Peter's miraculous escape from jail indicates the normal pattern of dress: '"Get up quickly", and the chains fell off his hands. And the Angel said to him, "Dress yourself and put on your sandals". And he did so. And he said to him, "Wrap your mantle around you and follow me"' (Acts 12.7-8; cf. Mt. 5.40 // Lk. 6.29).

The Gospel of Luke shows the contrast between wealth and poverty in the clothing of Lazarus and the Rich Man:

> There was a rich man who was clothed in purple and fine linen and who feasted sumptuously every day. And at his gate lay a poor man named Lazarus, full of sores, who desired to be fed from what fell from the rich man's table. Moreover the dogs came and licked his sores (Lk. 16.19-21).

The two figures, Lazarus and the rich man, highlight the difference in economic terms. The rich man could dress in the greatest refinements of his time, and feast accordingly. Lazarus had no clothes worthy of mention, was afflicted with sores, perhaps due to malnutrition, and was happy to get the scraps from the table, and he did not even have the strength to drive off the dogs.

The causes of poverty were many. We know from our sources that in normal times intensive work produced an abundance of the necessary foods, but whether this was enough to go around, if the society wished it, we simply do not know. Food production was upset by such factors as famines, wars and disease. In general the existence of poverty and wealth was considered to be a question of religion and politics, rather than one related to food production (Hamel 1990: 141). The exploitation of people's labour through taxes, rents and debts also added to some people's poverty.

Biblical Overview: The Poor in the Old Testament

It is not possible to derive one agreed perspective on the poor from the vast number of references to the term in the Hebrew Bible. The biblical text includes perceptions from the wide variety of experiences over some one thousand years. It is not difficult to build up a picture of aspects of the discussion, by clustering texts from different periods around a particular emphasis. There is no shortage of texts suggesting that to be rich was a sign of God's favour (e.g. Prov. 8.18), and that to be poor was to be forsaken (e.g. Prov. 14.10; Ps. 37.25). Coggins comments, 'There is no Old Testament equivalent of Franciscanism, embracing the "Lady Poverty" as a desirable end in itself' (1987: 14). In other Old Testament strands, however, the language of destitution is applied to the domain of religion and spirituality—for example, the psalmist confesses himself to be poor, needy, godly, and one who trusts in the Lord (Ps. 86). This figurative use is reflected widely (Pss. 109.22-25, etc.), and, as Hobbs shows so tellingly, the poverty in the case of the king does not refer to absence of money, but to an absence of honour and appropriate social status (Hobbs 1989: 293).

Within the Pentateuch there are strict laws against the exploitation of widows and orphans (Exod. 22.22-24; Deut. 27.19), helpless aliens (Lev. 19.33), and of the poor in general (Exod. 23.6; Lev. 25.6; Deut. 15.17). Moreover, the condemnation of the exploitation of the poor is a significant factor in the prophetic teaching of Amos (2.7; 5.7-11; 8.4-6), as is his disdain for the exploiting upper classes (4.1-3; 6.1). The concern for the poor is prominent within some of the traditions in the Writings (e.g. Ps. 82; Job. 31.16-32). Within the Old Testament, then, there is a wide spectrum of attitudes to the poor. By selective proof-texting one could justify biblically either extreme: rampant, selfish capitalism, or the revolutionary social liberation of the poor. Weir calls for a balanced, exhaustive study of the biblical teaching on poverty (1988), while Hobbs alerts us to be sensitive to the distinctiveness of the world views of the biblical periods, and our own—the ancient world must not be manipulated to become a springboard for a larger, modern political polemic (cf. Finley, quoted in Hobbs 1989: 292). The likelihood, of course, is that the study will be done by the secure and powerful, those, like myself, who have secure positions in universities, and who are distanced from the tragedy of the reality of contemporary poverty. The poor may not have the patience to wait for the publication of such an academic study, not to speak of its employment within applied Theology.

Rich and Poor in Luke's Community

The scholarly methods applied to the study of the documents of the New Testament until recently (Source, Historical, Form and Redaction Criticism) have paid scant attention to the social, political and religious circumstances that provided the context for the composition of the documents. More recent scholarship has attempted to respect these factors. The application of the methods of sociology to the investigation of New Testament texts has proved to be both popular and enlightening. There is, however, a fundamental limitation in this methodology as far as the Gospels are concerned. Unlike the situation reflected in the letters of Paul, the authorship, time and place of composition of the Gospels is a matter of ongoing speculation. The lack of reliable evidence in these matters invites high levels of conjecture, which, however attractive, are never altogether convincing.

Moreover, all sociology-based studies of the Gospels operate on the basis of unproven solutions to the problems of the sources of, and the literary interrelationships between, the Gospels. A further limitation arises from a concentration on the final stage of gospel composition. Sparse attention is paid to the context of the material in the ministry of Jesus. Readers may like to know whether the views on the poor (and the rich) in Luke–Acts derive from Luke's free re-presentation of Jesus' attitudes, if not in part from his own composition, or whether they reflect accurately Jesus' own attitudes, if never quite *verbatim*.

Why does Luke portray Jesus as being so concerned with the poor and the rich? Scholars have proposed various answers. According to Cadbury Jesus' focus was on the rich, and their responsibility to give alms, rather than on the alleviation of the lot of the poor as such (1966: 262-63). Degenhardt argues that the admonitions to abandon wealth are given only to the travelling apostles, missionaries, wandering preachers, and resident community leaders, and the like (1965: 214-15). He argues that Luke confronted *Gentile* Christians, who because of their background, had little time for the poor (pp. 221-23). Dupont takes the view that the beatitudes of Luke are addressed to the Christian community, while the woes are addressed to those outside that community (i.e. blind Israel—cf. 1973: 149-203).

In addition to taking account of the occurrence of the terminology of the poor, it is very important to enquire into what is the overall thrust of Luke–Acts in the matter. If it is the case that the destitute/beggars are the particular concern of Luke, how does one explain that this concern is not prominent in the Acts of the Apostles? Johnston pleads that 'Any discussion of "the poor" in Luke–Acts...must take seriously the effective disappearance of that terminology after chapter 16 of the Gospel, which suggests that Luke used such language for a special literary function in his first volume' (1991: 4-5). Against that, however, it is clear that while the second volume of his work does not use the word *ptōchos*, we do find that the alienation of wealth in favour of others is a feature of the Jerusalem Church (Acts 2.45; 4.34-35; 6.1), and was practised by Cornelius (Acts 10.2, 4, 31). Moreover, the alleviation of those suffering because of famine is noted in Acts 11.28-30, and Paul's collection is mentioned in Acts 24.17.

Secondly, it is of interest to investigate whether the emphasis in Luke on the poor reflects Luke's real concern for their economic betterment, or whether it is more in the form of a polemic against the rich. Is Luke an invitation to make a preferential option for the poor, or is it more an invitation to abandon one's riches—is Luke for the poor, or is he merely against the rich?

Schmidt concludes his study on *Hostility to Wealth in the Synoptic Gospels* (1987) by claiming that there is little evidence of sympathy for the poor as such in any of the Synoptic Gospels. From the lack of any clear indication of the socio-economic circumstances of Luke's audience or of the situation described, Schmidt argues that Luke was not really interested in the poor as such, but only in communicating his judgment that the dispossession of wealth was a Christian's way of expressing trust in God (1987: 161-62).

While Schmidt does the service of showing that hostility to wealth has a history independent of socio-economic circumstances, and a place in a variety of literatures, his conclusions with respect to Luke are too doctrinaire. If some of the texts of Luke bear the interpretation that hostility to wealth rather than care for the poor is the predominant factor, others must be read differently (esp. The Rich Man and Lazarus, Lk. 16, special to Luke).

Of the recent scholars who attempt to describe the social context of Luke's community we focus on two, Robert J. Karris and Philip Esler.

Robert J. Karris
Karris challenges the view of Dupont that the beatitudes and the woes cannot be addressed to the same community (1978: 115). He concludes that Luke is more concerned with possessors than with the poor (p. 116). He holds that the summaries of Acts 2.41-47 and 4.31c-35 are of major significance, and that they show that the ideal of friendship, so rarely found in secular society, is found in the Christian community, because Christians treat each other as friends. The function of these summaries, then, is to try to bring the Gentile Christians in his community to a sense of the Christian/Jewish concern for the poor.

Luke's Christian community consists of

> propertied Christians who have been converted and cannot easily extricate themselves from their cultural mindsets. It also consists of Christians in need of alms. Luke takes great pains to show that Christians treat each other as friends and that almsgiving and care for one another is of the essence of the Way. If the converts do not learn this lesson and learn it well, there is danger that the Christian movement may splinter (p. 117).

This theme of concern for almsgiving is also to be found in Acts 1.18 (Judas); 3.2-10 (Peter and John without silver and gold to give alms); 5.1-11; 6.1d-6; 8.18d-25; 9.36; 10.2, 4, 31; 11.29; 20.28-35; 24.17.

Karris holds that the poor (*ptōchos*) of 4.18 and 7.22 are the Christian community of Luke's day, who are suffering deprivation and persecution for their faith. He adds that the woes are addressed to the rich members of the Christian community who are tempted to stick to their riches, and ignore the plight of their fellow followers of the Way.

8. *The Invitation of Luke–Acts—Yesterday*

The example of Simon, James and John (5.11), and Levi (5.28) who left everything and followed him, Karris takes to be tokens of what some people did in response to becoming disciples.

Karris asks why Luke in his Travel Narrative (Lk. 9.51–19.44) has Jesus equip his disciples with so much teaching on rich and poor. He suggests that for Luke, almsgiving is one of the signs of adherence to the law, and one of the conditions for participation in a meal (Lk. 11.41). The message of the warning against avarice (Lk. 12.13-15), and the Parable of the Rich Fool (Lk. 12.16-21), both special to Luke, is that possessions are for distribution to the poor. Karris takes these verses to be addressed to the rich in Luke's community who may be tempted to ignore the plight of the poor. Jesus' instruction to invite the poor, the maimed, and the blind to attend the festive meal (Lk. 14.12-14) was directed by Luke against those in his community with the wherewithal to host festive meals. They were encouraged to go against their Greco-Roman values of inviting only the wealthy.

Karris is on less secure ground in claiming that the Pharisees of Lk. 16.14 ('lovers of money') are the rich members of Luke's community who think that almsgiving is not important, not only because their cultural background made them blind to the needs of the poor, but for the theological reason that they imagine that riches are a sign of the divine favour. Lk. 18.18-31 (The very rich ruler in search of eternal life), and 18.28, he argues, propose the ideal of renunciation of that which is one's own for the sake of the poor in the cummunity (*koinōnia*). Read alongside Acts 2.41-47 and 4.31c-35, the possessors in Luke's community can voluntarily renounce their possessions in favour of those in need. But in Luke's community there was room also for those who gave away in favour of the poor only half of what they owned (Lk. 19.1-10—the Zacchaeus scene, unique to Luke). Karris concludes:

> Luke's community clearly had both rich and poor members. Luke is primarily taken up with the rich members, their concerns, and the problems which they pose for the community. Their concerns, as evidenced in 18.18-30 and 19.1-10, revolve around the question: do our possessions prevent us from being genuine Christians? The concerns of the rich are multiplied by the onslaught of sporadic, unofficial persecution (see 6.24-26 and 14.25-33) (1978: 124).

Karris builds up a credible picture from some hints. But he never faces the question of the setting of the words of Jesus in his lifetime *(Sitz im Leben Jesu)*, nor in that of the communities which traditioned the material

(Sitz im Leben der Kirche). Everything is related to the circumstances of Luke's community, nothing to the context in Jesus' ministry, or later.

Philip F. Esler
Esler insists that Luke has shaped the Gospel traditions at his disposal in response to social and political pressures experienced by his community. His investigations have led him to conclude that, 'it is entirely unrealistic to expect to be able to appreciate the purely religious dimension of Luke–Acts apart from an understanding of the social and political realities of the community for which it was composed' (1987: 2).

He summarizes the circumstances of the Lukan church as follows: Luke's community, living in a Hellenistic city of the Roman East in the period 85–95, experienced difficulties both from within and without. Its membership was mixed, and included people from the opposite ends of the religious and social spectra. Prior to their embracing the Christian Way some had been pagans, and others conservative Jews. Some were from the richest echelons of society, while others were beggars.

The fact that the members of Jewish origin shared table fellowship with those of Gentile origin further exacerbated the problems which the Jewish Christians were having with the synagogue. The social mix of the community also contributed to the internal tensions of the Lukan community:

> The presence within the same group of representatives from the glittering elite and from the squalid urban poor was very unusual in this society and created severe internal problems, especially since some of the traditions of Jesus' sayings known to the community counselled the rich to a generosity to the destitute quite at odds with Greco-Roman attitudes to gift-giving (Esler 1987: 221).

There was also a political problem for the members of the community who were Roman soldiers or officials, who were embarrassed by the fact that Jesus, the founder of the new movement had been put to death by the Roman Governor of Judaea, and that Paul, its leading propagator, had been before Roman courts a number of times.

This situation spurred on one of the leaders or intellectuals in the community, whom tradition named Luke, to re-interpret the traditions of Jesus in such a fashion as to reassure the different groups within the community by answering their problems. He argued that table fellowship between Gentiles and Jews had already been authorized by Peter's vision which was of divine origin (Acts 10.1-48), and was approved by the Jerusalem church on two occasions (Acts 11.1-18; 15.6-26). Moreover, Luke–Acts from beginning to end presents the Christian Way, rather than the Judaisms of the synagogue, as the genuine fulfilment of the Jewish traditions.

On the social front Luke intensified the preference for the poor which was in the traditions available to him, and which went back to Jesus himself. He also introduced a paraenetic motif, warning the rich that their way to salvation depended on their generosity to the poor. He dealt with the fear that there was conflict between Christianity and Rome, by showing that both Paul and Jesus had repeatedly been adjudged innocent of any crime against Roman law. Moreover, since it derived from the ancient religion of Judaism, it was not a new religion which might produce social unrest.

Luke's theology, then, was motivated by the religious, social and political forces active in his own community. The relevance of Luke, Esler concludes, derives from the fact that he exercised such liberty in reinterpreting the traditions in order to address the real needs of his own community, and not merely from the appeal of so much of his theology, with its interest in such contemporary themes as rich and poor. 'The freedom with which he has moulded the gospel to minister to the needs of his community constitutes a potent authority for all those struggling to realize a Christian vision and a Christian life-style attuned to the social, economic and political realities of our own time' (Esler 1987: 223).

Conclusion

This investigation into the significance of the theme of poor–rich in Luke–Acts, and into the hypothetical circumstances of the community of the author, has brought results which help us to understand the text of Lk. 4.16-30 in a new light. But there are still several questions to be posed. The past must have its say, but exegetes must strain to ensure that it is the past of reality, rather than the construct of text-proofing manipulators.

One of the major concerns of biblical interpretation—and indeed one might be forgiven for concluding that it was the only one—has been to get at the original historical context of the writings. The so-called historical-critical method has dominated biblical studies for some time. Of course, even in its own terms, the search has been only partially successful. It is important to attempt to reconstruct the world of the Lukan text, with as much detail as possible, relying on the evidence of the source material, which, of course, is never adequate. If the Lukan text has anything to say to our contemporary society, we must have security in outlining what it had to say in its own time.

The exegetical discipline in the West has been as much in captivity to its own dogmatic and academic presuppositions as any previous generation was to its ones. While much recent scholarship shows a sensitivity to the role of the reader in the art of interpretation, the pre-history of a text, and an understanding of it in its original context are still the *foci* of exegetical interest. The post-history of a text, if represented at all, is relegated to footnotes, while the search for contemporary meaning is shifted conveniently from the centre of exegetical concern to seek out a place in the domain of spirituality. A sensitivity to the power of the word of Scripture in the two thousand years of intervening history is a much needed corrective to the academic arrogance of any one age or place. Exegesis within a community and tradition of interpretation ought not to be satisfied with a mere unearthing of the past. Biblical commentary must not end with an almost idolatrous veneration of the original historical context.

But even if the historico-critical method of investigation had been completely successful in illuminating the past, the curiosity of the human mind and heart would not have been satisfied. For Christians, the Bible is the book of the Church, and church people desire more than an unearthing of the past. Even if they had the ambition to do so, they could not live in the past of the biblical period. Church people, not unreasonably, expect their religious tradition to illuminate the context of their present and future lives. The past has much wisdom to offer, and it is appropriate to let it have its say. But each new engagement of the believer with the text of the Bible unleashes a new encounter. The reality is that each generation of readers, and, more realistically, hearers of (parts of) the Bible desires to make sense of its own world. It does not find it sufficient to discover how the person and teaching of Jesus Christ was significant in first-century Nazareth, Jerusalem, or some Hellenistic city in which Luke–Acts may have been composed, but how it is consequential today in Strawberry Hill, Sarajevo, or the Appalachian Mountains. One should not attempt to evade facing major contemporary issues by expending all one's interpretative energies on questions about the past.

Part III

CONTEMPORARY READING OF LUKE 4.16-30

Chapter 9

THE INVITATION OF LUKE–ACTS—TODAY

Contemporary investigation of the biblical text reflects all the methods which are applied in modern literary criticism. But most of these are derived from an examination of literature which is very different in origin and purpose from the biblical text. Much of contemporary literature is composed by people who write in an individualistic way, although, for many reasons, no writing is purely private, if only because the act of publishing requires a sensitivity to others. The biblical texts have survived and been preserved within communities precisely because these communities recognized in them a lasting significance.

A major difference between the Bible and any example of modern literature is the fact that most of the former was written with the intention of being read aloud, while most of the latter is for private reading. In the case of the Gospels, moreover, the original context of reading was probably public, and in the company of people who were for the most part familiar with at least some of the contents, and were well disposed towards its hero. Since any contemporary comment on a biblical text must respect the realities of life, it must not be forgotten that for most people the Bible is heard in snippets, and in a context of shared values and, very likely, common worship.

I began this investigation in the hope of contributing towards discovering the meaning of Lk. 4.16-30. In the earlier parts I used the historical-critical method of investigation, considering that knowledge of the circumstances of the author and of the first audience/readership of Luke's Gospel would clear the way for us to arrive at an understanding of Lk. 4.16-30 which is not inconsistent with the message intended by the author. It must be remembered, however, that whatever the findings of such an investigation be, they are no substitute for the opportunity which every new reading of the text presents to the reader of posing the question, 'What, then, shall we do?'

In enquiring into the meaning of Lk. 4.16-30 we are not dealing with 'any old text'. Believers will see 'the hand' of the Spirit of God in the text. It derives its authority also from its position within the Canon of the Scriptures of the community of believers. The study of the post-history of a biblical text is a necessary element in arriving at its significance. The collection of essays in Burrows and Rorem (1991), ranging over some two thousand years of biblical investigation, reinforces the conclusion that texts are always read in interpretative contexts, and that the contexts of the reader play a major part in determining the meaning of the texts. The relevance of such an insight is obvious.

The historical understanding of a text can never be exhausted by enquiring only into the pre-history of the text, and the circumstances obtaining at the time of composition, with its inevitable concentration on the intention of the author. Just as texts have histories before their final form of composition, they also have histories within the experience of different generations of interpreters after the time of composition. The Scripture must be seen to be a living voice in each era of the two millenia of interpretation.

What benefit does a later interpreter derive from the different elements of the exegetical tradition which she or he inherits? At least one can say that the diversity of interpretation within the tradition cautions one against a simplistic reading of any text. Secondly, one is forced to acknowledge that the standpoint of the interpreter prior to engaging the text is a significant factor in understanding it.

It is widely conceded nowadays that the horizon of the reader of a text as well as that of the author must be brought into the discussion, and a certain interaction, and perhaps even fusion take place. The history of interpretation of a biblical text cautions against seeing the interpretative process as involving some relationship between the author and the modern reader only. The tradition of investigation also must be considered. On literary grounds alone, there is a tradition of investigation and a community of exegetes.

In addition there are theological factors. People within a religious tradition will recognize the original biblical text to have come under the influence of the Holy Spirit. The same Spirit may be considered to have been active among the generations which have engaged in the interpretation. Such activity, of course, does not protect the text from interpretations which are adjudged to be false.

The apparently simple question, 'What does the text mean?' does not allow of a correspondingly simple answer, and this for several reasons.

No literary text has 'a meaning'. A text may well have 'a meaning' for the author at the level of her or his consciousness—the influence of the author's subconscious is, by definition, excluded from the meaning of the text as consciously intended by the author. In the nature of a literary or artistic work, 'the meaning' is never locked within the confines of the work. Moreover, as soon as it leaves the hands of its author a text encounters the world-view of each of its readers. The 'meaning of the text' for the reader will reflect both the reader's world-view before encountering the text, and the impact the reading of the text has on her or him.

Before deciding on 'the authentic meaning of the text' one would be wise to respect the tradition of interpretation. An outstanding example of *practical* exegesis of the text is provided by the life-work of Vincent de Paul, who took the phrase, *Evangelizare pauperibus misit me*, as the motto of the religious community that he founded in seventeenth-century France, and of which I am a member. His indefatigable interpretation of the Gospel of Luke, in terms of ideology and practice, is such as to have him named Patron of Charity in Europe. The practical evangelization of the poor is the primary aim of the charitable societies either founded by him, or which look to him as Patron.

Religious communities look to their founder for inspiration. The more scholastic disciples of Vincent de Paul in search of their tradition work with the literature dealing with him and his period. Such study can easily develop into a form of antiquarianism, in which the end-product is the uncovering of information about the past. Ideally there should be dialogue between the past and the present. One of the lessons taught by the practitioners of liberation theology is that experience (*praxis*) is the primary element in theologizing. Gutiérrez (1983: 6-11). Reflection should follow practice. Exegesis of a text dealing with the evangelizing of the poor should begin with the personal experience of the poor (cf. Prager 1991). In a corresponding fashion, authentic exegesis of Lk. 4.16-30 should derive from a saturation in the experience of the under-class. My own sense of Christian ministry changed substantially when the gypsy families among whom I celebrated the Sunday Mass were evicted from their site by the local borough, at which point pastoral ministry was transposed into a high-profile social and political struggle for justice.

To understand better the Nazareth Synagogue text I wish to focus on that emphasis within the science of hermeneutics which concentrates on the stance/response of the reader/hearer.

9. The Invitation of Luke–Acts—Today 187

First World and the Bible

It is one of the results of recent reflection on the process of enquiring into the meaning of a text that *the reader* no less than the text is in a particular historical context and tradition. The *reader* of Lk. 4.16-30 is in a state of pre-understanding (*Vorverstehung*) before she or he embarks on the reading. In reality, the questions posed to the biblical text in learned journals are not life-or-death issues for most people today. Biblical scholars tend to set the agenda for each other and for those entering the growing community of professional biblical interpreters, and much of the world is left aside in the process. This leads to a radical dissatisfaction among many.

According to various writers from the so-called Third World the interpretation of the Bible in the Western World will always be distorted. The reason, they claim, is that the central message of the Bible is that God is on the side of the oppressed, while interpreters from North America and Europe do not know the experience of being subject to economic, personal or institutional oppression. Typically, Western interpreters of the Bible live in considerable comfort and guaranteed security, and are respected members of prestigious academic institutions. The present writer, alas, is no exception. Such circumstances become an obstacle to an authentic reading of the text.

First World difficulties with the text of the Bible, it is claimed, do not arise from the strangeness of the language, or from the time-span and the differences in culture that separate the two civilizations. Rather, they come about because the Bible witnesses to the experience of the powerless and exploited, while the modern Western interpreter reads it from her or his guaranteed and secure position of power (see, e.g., Tamez 1982, Sugirtharajah 1991). Although this assessment of the Bible is selective, and therefore somewhat inaccurate, biblical exegesis in the West has much to learn from examining how Christians in different regions, living in the midst of poverty and oppression, deal with the Bible.

The Bible and Contextualized Theology: Three Examples

Conventional Liberation Theologies, like all theologies, look to the Bible for their underpinning. It is not difficult to discern within the Hebrew Scriptures a whole range of themes which fit the concept of liberation very comfortably (e.g. liberation from oppression in Egypt, Babylon, etc.). However, does God, who is on the side of the oppressed Israelites, and who frees them from Egypt, remain on their side when they become the oppressor? And where in God's plans was the indigenous population?

I wish to draw attention to three areas of the world wherein the claim that the Bible is an agent of liberation is challenged, and indicate how the communities there deal with the matter (see further Prior 1995). They have biblical movements which enable the Christian Good News to enlighten people with regard to their social conditions, and contribute to the evangelization of the world. These communities engage the biblical text, in such a way that it becomes a basis for a programme of liberation. The text itself, of course, does not provide the strategies required.

South Africa

Takatso Mofokeng refers to a statement concerning the Bible and human liberty, which is known by young and old in South Africa: 'When the white man came to our country he had the Bible and we had the land. The white man said to us, "let us pray". After the prayer, the white man had the land and we had the Bible'. Black people of South Africa point to three dialectically related realities.

> They show the central position which the Bible occupied in the ongoing process of colonization, national oppression and exploitation. They also confess the incomprehensible paradox of being colonized by a Christian people and yet being converted to their religion and accepting the Bible, their ideological instrument of colonization, oppression and exploitation. Thirdly, they express a historic commitment that is accepted solemnly by one generation and passed onto another—a commitment to terminate exploitation of humans by other humans (Mofokeng 1988: 34).

He goes on,

> When Black Christians see all these conservative and reactionary efforts and hear the Bible being quoted in support of reactionary causes they realise that the Bible itself is a serious problem to people who want to be free (1988: 37).

Mofokeng relates two approaches of people who experience the Bible as an agent of oppression. They accuse the offending preachers of misusing the Bible, or of not practising what they preach. He himself, however, contends that there are numerous 'texts, stories, and traditions in the Bible which lend themselves to only oppressive interpretations and oppressive uses because of their inherent oppressive nature...Any

9. The Invitation of Luke–Acts—Today 189

attempt to 'save' or 'co-opt' these oppressive texts for the oppressed only serve the interests of the oppressors' (Mofokeng 1988: 38). Young blacks, he says, have identified the Bible as an oppressive document by its very nature and its very core, and call for its displacement.

G. West and J. Draper report on the activities of the recently founded South African *Institute for the Study of the Bible*, which attempts to develop an interface between biblical studies and ordinary readers of the Bible (1991: 369-70). They draw attention to the very impressive work being done by the collaboration of a great number of institutions in the land.

Brazil

Leif Vaage discusses developments at the interface between biblical reflection and social struggle in Latin America, also against a background of the use of the Bible as an instrument of oppression in that region (Vaage 1991). The Centre for the Study of the Bible in Brazil operates on the basis of three crucial commitments: to begin with reality as perceived; to read the Bible in community; and to engage in sociopolitical transformation through Bible reading. This is called Contextual Bible Study. In this process, biblical scholars become servants, who are invited to participate as the people choose. They must be committed to biblical studies from the perspective of the poor and oppressed.

Palestine

One might expect to find a thriving Liberation Theology in the land where Jesus delivered his message of freedom. Palestine has a long line of liberation theologians, from Moses to Jesus. The circumstances of the indigenous Christian communities are ripe for a theological reflection on life under military occupation within the Occupied Territories, and on life as third-, fourth-, or fifth-class citizens of the Jewish State of Israel.

The fundamental problem of the Palestinians is the price they have had to pay, and continue to pay, for the encroachment on their land by Zionists from the diaspora. The creation of the State of Israel was not brought about without the destruction of some 400 Arab villages, and the exodus and expulsion of more than 700,000 Arab inhabitants. At least a further 300,000 left Palestine as a result of the 1967 Six Day War. There can be no question of a *just* solution to the problem unless these refugees are allowed return to their former homes, or are adequately compensated in accordance with international law. There can, of course, be a pragmatic solution, based on compromise by the parties concerned.

I probed Canon Naim Ateek, author of the foundational work on Palestinian Liberation Theology (1989), on his most recent reflections on the task of Contextualized Palestinian Theology.

> There are two levels to work on, the internal and the external. We ask ourselves what we can do to help our own people by way of liberation. We are agreed that one of the things we can do is to conduct workshops. We take a theme, and develop it in a day conference, with one or two papers. We have discussion groups and allow people to *do* Theology. We have done this successfully on a number of occasions, both in Jerusalem and Galilee. We have requests now to hold workshops in several places. Our problem is to respond to the need. Another area is more long-term, where a number of people commit themselves to long-term study, in which we will work more deeply.

Other activities include working with the Christian schools, availing of the visits from theologians from abroad, producing a Newsletter, and doing more writing in Arabic. It is their hope that once a year they will bring a group of between ten and twenty theologians for a symposium, to share with, learn from, and teach. 'We want to expose them to who we are, to what is happening here.' They are particularly interested in theologians from South Africa.

> They have a situation similar to us, but they are ahead of us in theology. Serious thought is also being given to theologians from the European community, and the USA. They, too, must see the oppression of the Palestinians for themselves...We are trying to rediscover the liberation that Christ has given us—reclaim it, reuse it. *Lahut Al-Quds* (*Jerusalem Theology*) would be a beautiful name!

Palestinian theologians have to contend with a number of very sensitive issues. First, they are themselves all victims of oppression. Secondly, it is clear that some Christians see in the establishment of the State of Israel in 1948 the fulfilment of God's promises to the Children of Israel. Thirdly, the attitude of Christians throughout the world to the fate of the Palestinians, including Palestinian Christians, is ambivalent. Proponents of biblical fundamentalism, whether Christian or Jewish, read the Pentateuch as providing the guarantee of God's unconditional gift of the land to the Israelites, without any regard to those who were living in the land already. Fourthly, even when there is abundant evidence of Israeli oppression, there is a deep unease within Western Christian circles about even the most tame criticism of Israeli policies. Fifthly, in Western circles the revulsion which one expects to surface at any form of wicked behaviour is muted in the case of the State of Israel. Sixthly, some influential members of organizations committed to the noble ideal of Jewish–Christian dialogue remain silent on the oppression of the Palestinians, in spite of the presence of overwhelming, embarrassing evidence.

The Christian Palestinian voice is only one of several voices which cry out under oppression in the Holy Land. It is part of the larger Palestinian protest. By and large, it is firmly in conformity with the aspiration of most Palestinians for national independence in a democratic, secular State of Palestine. It works towards that end in the context of Israeli intransigence, and the alternative solutions proposed by *Hamas* and *Islamic Jihad*. Most important of all, the struggle for Palestinian justice and liberation depends for its success on the readiness of the United States of America to forego its virtually unqualified support for, and financing of, Israeli oppression, in the interests of its own foreign policy. Dwarfed by such political giants, Palestinian Theology may not succeed in doing much more than explicating a moral ideal, and giving its people a dignity in their suffering (see Prior 1993).

Contextualized Lukan Theology Today

Theology is constantly tempted to ignore history in favour of eternity, and to confine the salvation which the gospel offers to the private and individual dimension. The Lukan text is an obvious one for developing a theology of liberation. The underlying desire is that Christian orthodoxy be reflected also in orthopraxis. At the heart of contemporary liberation theologies is the urge to improve the lot of the oppressed. Two questions spring to mind immediately: who are the oppressed, and how does one go about improving their lot? While most of the excitement of liberation theology comes from South America, and reflects a fundamental concern with issues of economic poverty, it must be conceded that the Good News of Jesus Christ is much wider in its scope. All forms of oppression inhibit the capacity of society and individuals to realize their potential.

I suggest that the following findings are derivable from, and are consistent with the Lukan text. A reading of Luke's account of the scene in the Nazareth synagogue requires that attention be given to the following areas:

Faith in Jesus Christ as Response to Reading Luke
To profess faith in Jesus Christ is to say that his message and significance are central to one's values, give one's life its fundamental character and direction, shape one's understanding and vision, are the norms for evaluating oneself and others in our world, give grounding to one's hopes and fears and aspirations, and inform one's conscience, affections and loyalties (see MacNamara 1988: 2-3). The invitation to profess faith in Jesus Christ, then, may require that one turns one's personal and community world on its head.

Repentance as Response to Reading Luke
While the emphases of each of the evangelists diverge, they are at one in requiring of the reader repentance (*metanoia*). Whereas Matthew and Mark open the public ministry of Jesus with the call to repentance, Luke presents Jesus proclaiming the good news to the poor in the synagogue of Nazareth.

After John the Baptist had preached his message requiring repentance,

> the multitudes said to him, 'What then shall we do?' And he answered them, 'He who has two coats, let him share with him who has none; and he who has food, let him do likewise'. Tax collectors also came to be baptized, and said to him, 'Teacher, what shall we do?' And he said to them, 'Collect no more than is appointed you'. Soldiers also asked him, 'And we, what shall we do?' And he said to them, 'Rob no one by violence or by false accusation, and be content with your wages' (Lk. 3.10-14).

Responding to the invitation to repentance, then, is not merely a matter of words, and no sensitive reader can fail to be alerted to the social obligations implied in the Lukan call to repentance.

Repentance and Discipleship
In Luke's account of Jesus' movements we find him in Capernaum after the Nazareth incident, performing an exorcism (4.31-37), the healing of Peter's mother-in-law (4.38-39), and other healings and exorcisms (4.40-41). Then he left to preach in other cities (4.42-44). So far he operated alone. After the miraculous catch of fish, Simon, James and John 'left everything and followed him' (5.11). It is difficult to avoid the conclusion that discipleship of the Lukan Jesus demands frugality, and, if one has possessions, the alienation of them in favour of the poor.

9. *The Invitation of Luke–Acts—Today*

Repentance for the Rich

The objection that theology ought not to be dominated by a concern for the poor and oppressed can be answered easily by acknowledging two realities, namely, that the rich and well-off have plenty of access to channels of conscientizing society about the difficulties of their condition, while the poor as the underclass of society are relatively voiceless and politically impotent.

I find it impossible to escape the conclusion that the Lukan theme of rich and poor must leave any Christian community fundamentally disturbed in the face of serious inequalities of wealth and social security in its own community. Since Luke–Acts moves inexorably from Jerusalem, the centre of Jewish 'ethnic' religion, to Rome, the secular city and capital of the Empire, its readers should embrace the universalism of its message that all people, and in the first place poor people, fall under the grace of God, and should be beneficiaries of his Good News.

A Lukan Christian ought not to possess more than is absolutely necessary for survival, as long as others are in need. It would be a scandal if the dress and meals of disciples of the Lukan Jesus were closer in quality to those of the Rich Man than to those of Lazarus. The Lukan theme of rich–poor invites its readers to relinquish their riches in favour of the poor. The programme outlined in Lk. 4.16-30, and in the passages which speak of the poor and the rich, implies an invitation to respond. Unless one insists on so interpreting it, it is not an imperative. Readers are left free to respond in proportion to their moral generosity and perhaps in the light of their political analysis.

Social and Political Dimensions of Discipleship

A study of Lk. 4.16-30 which ended with a mere definition of the phrase, 'He sent me to evangelize the poor' would be a dereliction of one's responsibilities. If Luke's Gospel defines the message of Jesus in terms of evangelizing the poor, a disciple must ensure that the poor are not robbed of its message, by giving the impression that the gospel is a promise to the wealthy, rather than to them.

The concept of *evangelizing the poor* involves both theory and practice. In addition to getting the rhetoric right, one is presumed to effect some action, or programme of action, in favour of the poor person. What kind of betterment of the poor person is required to constitute evangelization? At this point one must acknowledge the radically different context of the Christians in Luke's church, and that of Christians today.

The inspired documents of the Early Church reflect a context in which followers of the Christian Way were in a minority, and were without any significant political power. The same cannot be said of the Christians of any period since Constantine. Even if the most that was required by Luke in his context was that the rich members of his community should come to the aid of the poor ones, and that they should live frugally, it is clear that major change is required of most Christians today if they wish to submit themselves to the power of Luke's summons.

Whether or not a Christian, or group of Christians, lives frugally is not a phenomenon of absolute significance, and is probably a matter of marginal interest to the poor. The poor do not require Christians to adopt the destitution of their life-style. In any case, because biblical scholars and all church officials are secure members of the empowered class, their 'practice of poverty' can never be more than a gesture. In our western society, at least, Christian leaders and exegetes can never share the degradation of the poor. In antiquity, as also today, professional religious people, including those vowed to a life of poverty, by designating themselves as 'living in poverty', distort the meaning of the word 'poverty', and misrepresent and probably insult those who are really poor.

What the poor can with justification require is that Christians use their power in their favour. Modern Christians true to the picture presented by Luke are invited to subvert, rather than underpin, those cultures which produce poverty and ignore the plight of the poor. The modern Lazarus is not likely to be impressed should a Rich Man imitate his life-style, even to the point of having the sores of his body licked by dogs. A Christian society which rests content with the life-style of the Rich Man of Luke 16, and allows Lazarus to languish, cannot expect to fare any better than the man who dressed in purple and feasted sumptuously every day.

Readers attracted to the ideal of the evangelization of the poor may be expected to respond to Luke's invitation with enthusiasm. To respond absolutely puts one in a position of radical discipleship—that will always be a minority response. Turning one's back on the poor leaves the rich one sad. Fortunately, as the discipleship of Zacchaeus shows, half-measures are better than none.

Lukan Liberation and Life

In much of the Western world, where there is any significant engagement with the gospel, it is generally a private, individual one. Christian preaching there tends to see its function in terms of the growth in faith of the individual member of the community, rather than in the advancement of the New Order inaugurated in the ministry of the original preacher of Good News for the Poor. Nevertheless, a certain humility is called for.

Jesus was a great prophet, but a social reformer of very modest achievement. Little or nothing in the reports we have of his itinerant ministry suggests that his programme of reform involved a socio-political upheaval that could be regarded as a serious threat to the stability of his region of the Roman empire. Neither does the transplanting of his gospel from rural Palestine to cosmopolitan Asia Minor, Greece, and beyond, appear to have offered any serious challenge to the social stability of Greco-Roman cities. By and large the early Christians appear to have taken over very smoothly the morality which prevailed in the Greco-Roman world and adapted it to their new vision.

However, one of the major achievements of the challenge which liberation theologies have offered to Western dominated theology is its insistence that authentic theological reflection cannot be divorced from the social and political realities of life. It is only when theology involves itself with the realities of the conditions of people, and particularly those in oppression, that it can be seen to offer a new order. Nevertheless, liberation rhetoric is not sufficient. Liberation requires great people who can elevate into concrete political programmes the ideals of liberation theologies.

There is no shortage of prophets, who utter attractive rhetoric in condemnation of the evils of the present and in advocacy of a better order. The world needs politicians also, who can diagnose what is astray with the present order, describe a new order, define long-term goals and strategies, prescribe short- and long-term remedies, and, finally, plan the structures of the rearrangements of society so that the goal of liberation is achieved.

It is desirable to elevate into concrete political programmes the ideals of liberation theologies. The attractive gospel of socialism in its various forms has suffered severe criticism in parts of Europe, to the extent that the ideals of socialism have been reduced almost to a vice, while the pursuit of selfish wealth has been put at the top of the social and political agenda. Great social reformers have abounded in the West. However, the political ingeniousness of such as Stalin and Hitler is matched by their moral turpitude.

The impact of liberation theologians from the Third World countries has been considerable. Until recently the theological schools, particularly those in the West, reflected the general outlook of the middle class establishment of their own societies. But the Church's experience with the poor in Third World countries has given focus to its political and social reflections. Even though circumstances differ from place to place, these theologies reflect a common interest in the lot of the poor and in their struggle against all forms of injustice and domination (see Sugirtharajah 1991).

In an ideal world, those who contribute to liberation theologies should be as skilled in the discipline of social analysis as they are in theological discourse. Specialization in human learning has the adverse effect of reducing the number of those with equal skills in diverse areas. The rare being who is academically competent in biblical exegesis, theology and even economics is not likely also to have the capacity to elevate admirable ideological insights into macroplans for national and even international economies.

The Christian gospel, clearly, is about liberation. So, too, should the Church be, if it persists in presenting itself as a sign of the Kingdom which Jesus ushered in. The question is not whether Jesus was a revolutionary like the Zealots. Even a superficial glance at the programme of Jesus and that of the Zealots highlights their different intentions. The real question, however, is whether Jesus' message already contained the seeds of revolution, significantly transforming the lives of people already in the first, second and third Christian generations, whose writings reflect the change.

Change is revolutionary when it transforms significantly and basically a segment of life. Jesus' announcement of the Good News to the Poor belongs to that class of radical change. To see the gospel as addressing only individual people, and in a private fashion, is to guarantee its social irrelevance in history. Christians were designated the salt of the earth, and the light of the world, and the leaven of the dough. They had a message of liberation for the poor.

However, Jesus did not leave a clearly worked out strategy whereby his disciples would transform the world. We have only a record of his ideals, and the example of his lifestyle and death. It is up to the ingenuity of his disciples, using their human skills, infused by Christian love, to carry the message forward, so that it becomes a light to the world, the salt of the earth, and the leaven that transforms the world in all its parts. It should be realized at the beginning that any partial transformation of the world along the lines of the gospel is a mere shadow of the fulness of the Kingdom of God. Nevertheless, it should be a sign of that Kingdom. In Jesus' new society God's favour is poured out on the underclass of society.

From being a society which looked to the transformation of the world, the Christian Church has had to accommodate itself to a long life in history. From being an agent of radical reform, it came to be the major stabilizing factor in the Roman Empire within a few hundred years, and behaved like all imperial or state religions, in propping up the present structures, and giving them the pretence of divine authorization. In most parts of the world today Christians have access to the power structures of society. The Lukan Jesus invites them to subvert all oppressive patterns in society, so that the human family can live in equality and mutual respect, where there is neither bond nor free, Jew nor Greek.

Conclusion

Our study of the first announcement of Jesus' new revolutionary order in the Nazareth synagogue, and the unfolding of that programme as detailed in the two volumes of Luke–Acts, suggests a strong challenge to contemporary society. The New Order ushered in by Jesus of Nazareth challenges those who encounter it to participate in the liberation of the oppressed. It is a blessing for those who are poor, and a woe to those who are rich while others are poor.

Those who respond generously to the invitation to incarnate the New Order of Liberation will realize quickly that the task is a very demanding one. In Lk. 4.16-30 the evangelist introduces the liberating ministry of Jesus, who preached, healed and exorcized, and expanded the perceived horizons of God's care by moving beyond ethnic and religious categories. The rejection of Jesus in the Nazareth synagogue was already hinted at in Lk. 2.34b. Under the power of the same Spirit of the Lord, the Church brought the Good News from Jerusalem to the ends of the earth (Acts 28.30). In terms of changing the society around him Jesus' success was modest, and he paid the supreme price for his efforts. The treatment he received in Nazareth foreshadows the fate of his disciples in Acts (e.g. 13.44-50; 14.19; 17.4-5; 18.12; 20.3; 22.21; 28.23-29).

Good Friday invites Christians, and victims of oppression, to grapple with the perplexity of apparent disaster. Its liturgy invites theoreticians, and liberation theologians, to face into the reality of dreams which have become nightmares, of visions which have never come off the drawing-board. Christians are invited to die with Christ, to enter the tomb with the spirit-less corpse of Jesus. As they enter the tomb with Jesus, they bring

> our body's labour, our spirit's grief, our selfish hearts, our failing faith, our daily toil, the plants in our heart's poor soil, all that we start and spoil, each hopeful dream, the chances we have missed, the graces we resist (from Kevin Nicholls, hymn, 'In Bread we Bring you, Lord').

Conclusion

At the heart of the Christian Gospel is the reality of the Cross. It is a paradox. At the level of phenomena it depicts failure. But seen in the light of faith in the Crucified God it enfleshes victory.

The gospel of Christian faith, hope and love must stand above the misery of the plight of all who suffer at the hands of powerful oppressors. The pervasiveness and ubiquity of evil in the world tempts one to abandon the struggle to continue to bring the Kingdom about, and leave things to God to sort out at the end of time. This cannot be a legitimate Christian option. Alone, or even with God on one's side, all cannot be achieved on this side of the eschatological Day of the Lord. But to do nothing is not an acceptable alternative.

The Christian Church, in collaboration with different groups, should seek always to promote the growth of the Kingdom in an energetic and humble way. Its message is fundamentally Good News which brings peace and joy. It must be striven for in the midst of the reality of human life in all its complexity: personal, interpersonal and socio-political. And even while grappling with it, Christians realize that God's Kingdom and Good News for the oppressed will never be enacted fully in history. Nevertheless, there is a certain peace and fulfilment in seeing what can be achieved, and in submitting to the constant call to conversion to goodness.

The Theology of the Cross seems to have a particular relevance for poor and oppressed people, whether in London, the Occupied Territories of the West Bank, Rwanda, or in any context in which there is an assault on human dignity. One of the features of the Gospel of Luke is the theme of reversal of fortunes. It is those who are secure, while others live in insecurity, those who already have their consolation, who are challenged by the gospel. The Gospel of Luke is full of examples of how the lowly in society (the poor, maimed, blind, deaf, marginalized, women, sinners, tax-collectors, Samaritans, Gentiles...) are rendered blessed.

All Theologies of Liberation require refinement by being subjected to the most testing examination in the light of social analysis and political options. The New Order inaugurated by Jesus in Nazareth will not be brought in by the rhetoric of the most eloquent liberation theologians alone. In contemporary society, the evangelization of the poor will come about only through the combined efforts of competent people who share the vision of Jesus. The Christian Church, which comes together and stays together precisely because of Jesus, has a critical role to play if it is to be true to its Master. But meanwhile, it must itself be subjected to the conversion involved in being evangelized.

A sensitivity to the realities of history as well as common-sense itself shows that society changes constantly, and in many places at a pace which shocks. It is the task of theologians and liberation practitioners to respect the reality of social and political change, and to refine constantly their analysis of society, and the light which the revolutionary message of Jesus throws upon the programme for the evangelization of the poor. History teaches that it is prudent to be modest in what biblical exegesis, liberation theology and even liberation praxis can achieve.

Christian 'Praxis' is another name for lived-out Christian spirituality. It will not be sufficient to blame every social evil on capitalism, or on some corrupt forms of it, and, now that Marxism has been abandoned by those who know best its political expressions, to look to some particular form of socialism as the all-embracing solution. Neither will it be acceptable to identify Jesus' notion of the Kingdom of God with the fulfilment of socialist aspirations, as outlined hitherto. However, it should be clearer still that manifestations of social and political life in which the poor are in captivity—in the world at large, and in virtually every society—stand at a great distance from the Kingdom of God.

The Christian Church, if it is faithful to its founder from Nazareth, should be at the forefront of transformation, not only by offering the world the liberation rhetoric of Lk. 4.16-30, but by contributing to the development of goals and strategies by which the poor can experience the blessedness of the gospel. Jesus' ministry acted out the programme of reform announced in Nazareth, as he testified for John the Baptist, 'Go and tell John what you have seen and heard: the blind receive their sight, the lame walk, lepers are cleansed, and the deaf hear, the dead are raised up, poor people are evangelized' (Lk. 7.22). A community which sees itself as the continuing presence of Jesus Christ in the world must strain itself in the interests of advancing God's Kingdom. The reverse suffered by Jesus and the first disciples should galvanize it in its efforts.

In God's Kingdom the poor will be enriched, captives will be set free, the blind will have their sight restored, the oppressed will be freed, and the longed-for year of God's favour will be ushered in. The disciples were shrewd, street-wise people. They included weather-beaten fishermen, a callous tax-collector, and a man always in search of a 'pound or two'. Some had left wife, family and home. They had given up their jobs, and thrown in their lot with Jesus, the prophet from

Nazareth. They were not in the business of discipleship of Jesus purely for the good of their health. There was something in it for them. Their aspirations would not have been satisfied by merely having their sins forgiven. They expected much more. Clearly things did not work out as they had hoped. Even if they had the disposition of always looking at the bright side of life, what happened on the Cross must have been a crushing let-down for Jesus' disciples.

The liberation Jesus inaugurated in Nazareth was not a national liberation. It was a liberation for all, promising a freedom not yet experienced on earth. His message of liberation, of release from bondage, his invitation to shake off oppression in a cosmic *Intifada* does not automatically eliminate the interracial barbarisms in Sarajevo or the scandalous starving in Somalia, nor does it automatically restore the dignity of a people trodden down by various forms of structural oppression. Jesus' message is an invitation to join the company of those committed to a better future, of a New Order of The Kingdom. About this Kingdom R.S. Thomas has written:

> The Kingdom
>
> It's a long way off but inside it
> There are quite different things going on:
> Festivals at which the poor man
> Is king and the consumptive is
> Healed; mirrors in which the blind look
> At themselves and love looks at them
> Back; and industry is for mending
> The bent bones and the minds fractured
> By life. It's a long way off, but to get
> There takes no time and admission
> Is free, if you will purge yourself
> Of desire, and present yourself with
> Your need only and the simple offering
> Of your faith, green as a leaf.

Alas, much more is required than the purging of one's individual malice! There is no legitimate theology that is not politically involved. The political theology which derives from the teaching and example of the crucified Lord of history exposes the institutionalized selfishness espoused by nation states and international economic communities. But the poor and exploited will not congratulate the Christian Church merely for exposing injustice. Appropriate political action must derive from theological reflection which is focused on the programme, 'He sent me to evangelize the poor', and is enlivened by the vision, 'See, I make all things new' (Rev. 21.5). The preacher in the Nazareth synagogue offers an ethic which is distinctive. His call is to bring about God's New Order within the reality of life. Only when 'the blind receive their sight, the lame walk, lepers are cleansed, and the deaf hear, the dead are raised up, poor people are evangelized' (Lk. 7.22) can the Church be at peace with its Founder, the Nazareth preacher, and its Lord.

BIBLIOGRAPHY

Aletti, J.-N.
    1985   'Jésus à Nazareth (Lc 4.16-30). Prophétie, ecriture et typologie', in *A cause de l'évangile: Etudes sur les Synoptiques et les Actes* (FS J. Dupont; LD, 123; Paris: Cerf): 431-51.
    1989   'Récit et Révélation. Lc 4,16-30', ch. 2 of *L'art de raconter Jésus Christ: L'écriture narrative de l'évangile de Luc* (Paris: Editions de Seuil): 39-61.

Alexander, L.
    1993   *The Preface to Luke's Gospel: Literary Convention and Social Context in Luke 1.1-4 and Acts 1.1* (SNTSMS, 78; Cambridge: Cambridge University Press).

Alexander, P.S.
    1988   'Jewish Aramaic Translations of Hebrew Scriptures', in Mulder 1988: 217-53.

Alter, R.
    1981   *The Art of Biblical Narrative* (New York: Basic Books).

Alter, R. and F. Kermode (eds.)
    1987   *The Literary Guide to the Bible* (London: Collins).

Anderson, H.
    1964   'Broadening Horizons. The Rejection at Nazareth Pericope of Luke 4.16-30 in Light of Recent Critical Trends', *Int* 18: 259-75.

Ateek, N.S.
    1989   *Justice and Only Justice: A Palestinian Theology of Liberation* (Maryknoll, NY: Orbis).

Aune, D.A.
    1987   *The New Testament in its Literary Environment* (Philadelphia: Westminster Press).

Aymer, B.C.P.
    1987   'A Socio-Religious Revolution. A Sociological Exegesis of "Poor" and "Rich" in Luke–Acts' (Dissertation, Boston).

Baarlink, H.
    1982   'Ein gnädiges Jahr des Herrn—und Tage der Vergeltung', *ZNW* 73: 204-20.

Barrett, C.K.
    1961   *Luke the Historian in Recent Study* (London: Epworth).

Beasley-Murray, G.R.
    1986   *Jesus and the Kingdom of God* (Exeter: Paternoster; Grand Rapids: Eerdmans).

Bellinzoni, A.J. (ed.)
    1985   *The Two-Source Hypothesis* (Macon, GA: Mercer University Press).

Black, C.C.
    1988   'The Rhetorical Form of the Hellenistic Jewish and Early Christian Sermon: A Response to Lawrence Wills', *HTR* 81: 1-18.

Bloch, R.
    1957   'Midrash', *DBSup*, 1270-75.

Bornhäuser, K.
    1921   *Das Wirken des Christus durch Taten und Worte* (Gütersloh: Bertelsmann [2nd edn 1924]).

Bostock, D.G.
    1980   'Jesus as the New Elisha', *ExpTim* 92: 39-41.

Bouwman, G.
    1989   'Le "premier livre" (Act., I.1) et la date des Actes des Apôtres', in Neirynck 1989: 553-65.

Bovon, F.
    1987   *Luke the Theologian: Thirty-Three Years of Research (1950–1983)* (Allison Park: Pickwick).

Brawley, R.L.
    1987   *Luke–Acts and the Jews: Conflict, Apology, and Conciliation* (SBLMS, 33; Atlanta: Scholars Press).

Brekelmans, C.
    1980–81   'Arm en rijk in het evangelie van Lucas', *Sacerdos* 48: 283-90.

Brodie, T.L.
    1981   'Jesus as the New Elisha: Cracking the Code', *ExpTim* 93: 39-42.

Brown, R.E.
    1977   *The Birth of the Messiah: A Commentary on the Infancy Narratives on Matthew and Luke* (London: Chapman).

Bruce, F.F.
    1977   'The History of New Testament Study', in I.H. Marshall (ed.), *New Testament Interpretation: Essays in Principles and Methods* (Exeter: Paternoster): 21-59.
    1990   *The Acts of the Apostles: Greek Text with Introduction and Commentary* (3rd edn; Grand Rapids: Eerdmans; Leicester: Apollos).

Burridge, R.A.
    1992   *What are the Gospels? A Comparison with Graeco-Roman Biography* (SNTSMS, 70; Cambridge: Cambridge University Press).

Burrows, M.S. and P. Rorem (eds.)
    1991   *Biblical Hermeneutics in Historical Perspective: Studies in Honour of Karlfried Froehlich on his Sixtieth Birthday* (Grand Rapids: Eerdmans).

Busse, U.
    1978   *Das Nazareth-Manifest Jesu: Eine Einführung in das lukanische Jesusbild nach Lk 4.16-30* (SBS, 91; Stuttgart: Katholisches Bibelwerk).

Busse, U., et al.
    1980   *Jesus zwischen Arm und Reich: Lukas-Evangelium* (Bibelauslegung für die Praxis, 18; Stuttgart: Katholisches Bibelwerk).

Cadbury, H.J.
    1927   *The Making of Luke–Acts* (London: SPCK).

Carrington, P.
1952   *The Primitive Christian Calendar* (Cambridge: Cambridge University Press).

Cassidy, R.J.
1978   *Jesus, Politics, and Society: A Study of Luke's Gospel* (Maryknoll, NY: Orbis).
1987   *Society and Politics in the Acts of the Apostles* (Maryknoll, NY: Orbis).

Chiappini, A.
1990   'Jésus de Nazareth, Prophéte et Liberateur. Luc 4,16-30', in *Peuple parmi les Peuples: Dossier pour l'animation biblique* (Essais Biblique, 18; Geneva: Labor & Fides): 229-37.

Chilton, B.D.
1981   'Announcement in Nazara: An Analysis of Luke 4.16-21', in R.T. France and D. Wenham (eds.), *Gospel Perspectives: Studies of History and Tradition in the Four Gospels*, II (Sheffield: JSOT Press): 147-72.
1984   *A Galilean Rabbi and his Bible: Jesus' own Interpretation of Isaiah* (London: SPCK).
1986   *Targumic Approaches to the Gospels: Essays in the Mutual Definition of Judaism and Christianity* (Studies in Judaism; Lanham, MD: University Press of America).
1987   *The Isaiah Targum: Introduction, Translation, Apparatus and Notes* (The Aramaic Bible, 11; Wilmington, DE: Glazier).

Coggins, R.J.
1987   'The Old Testament and the Poor', *ExpTim* 99: 11-14.

Cohen, S.J.D.
1989   *From the Maccabees to the Mishnah* (ed. W.A. Meeks; Library of Early Christianity, 7; Philadelphia: Westminster Press).

Conzelmann, H.
1960   *The Theology of St Luke* (ET; London: Faber)
1963   *Die Apostelgeschichte* (HNT, 7; Tübingen: Mohr [2nd edn 1972]).

Corbo, V.C.
1987   'La Chiesa-Sinagoga dell'Annunziata a Nazaret', *Liber Annuus* 37: 333-48.

da Spinetoli, O.
1982   *Luca: Il Vangelo dei Poveri* (Commenti e studi biblici; Assisi).

Davids, P.
1976   'The Poor Man's Gospel', *Themelios* NS 1: 37-41.

Dawsey, J.
1989   'The Literary Unity of Luke–Acts: Questions of Style—A Task for Literary Critics', *NTS* 35: 48-66.

Degenhardt, H.-J.
1965   *Lukas, Evangelist der Armen: Besitz und Besitzverzicht in den lukanischen Schriften: Eine traditions- und redaktionsgeschichtliche Untersuchung* (Stuttgart: Katholisches Bibelwerk).

Delobel, J. (ed.)
1982   *Logia: Les Paroles de Jésus—The Sayings of Jesus. Memorial Joseph Coppens* (BETL, 59; Leuven: Leuven University Press).

Dibelius, M.
   1956   *Studies in the Acts of the Apostles* (ET; London: SCM Press).
Dietrich, W.
   1985   ' "…den Armen das Evangelium zu verkünden": Vom befreienden Sinn biblischer Gesetze', *TZ* 41: 31-43.
Donelson, L.R.
   1987   'Cult Histories and the Sources of Acts', *Bib* 68: 1-21.
Drury, J.
   1976   *Tradition and Design in Luke's Gospel: A Study of Early Christian Historiography* (London: Darton Longman & Todd).
Dumais, M.
   1984   'L'évangélisation des pauvres dans l'oeuvre de Luc', *Science et Esprit* 36: 297-321.
Dupont, J.
   1958   *Les Béatitudes*, I (EBib; Paris: Gabalda).
   1960   *Les Béatitudes*, II (EBib; Paris: Gabalda).
   1973   *Les Béatitudes*, III (EBib; Paris: Gabalda).
   1978   'Jésus annonce la bonne nouvelle aux pauvres', in *Evangelizare Pauperibus* (Atti della XXIV settimana biblica; Brescia: Paideia): 127-89.
Easton, B.S.
   1936   'The Purpose of Acts', in F.C. Grant (ed.), *Early Christianity: The Purpose of Acts and other Papers* (Greenwich CT: Seabury [1954]).
Eichhorn, J.G.
   1794   'Ueber die drey ersten Evangelien', in *Allgemeine Bibliothek der biblischen Literatur*, V: 757-996.
Elias, J.W.
   1980   'The Furious Climax in Nazareth (Luke 4.28-30)', in W. Klassen (ed.), *The New Way to Jesus: Essays Presented to Howard Charles* (Newton: Faith & Life Press): 87-99.
Ellis, E.E.
   1972   *Eschatology in Luke* (Philadelphia: Fortress Press)
   1974   *The Gospel of Luke* (2nd edn; London: Marshall, Morgan & Scott).
Esler, P.F.
   1987   *Community and Gospel in Luke–Acts* (SNTSMS, 57; Cambridge: Cambridge University Press).
Evans, C.A.
   1987   'Luke's Use of the Elijah/Elisha Narratives and the Ethic of Election', *JBL* 106: 75-83.
Evans, C.F.
   1990   *Saint Luke* (Trinity Press International Commentaries; London: SCM; Philadelphia: Trinity Press International).
Farmer, W.R.
   1976   *The Synoptic Problem: A Critical Analysis* (Dillsboro: Western North Carolina Press).
Faierstein, M.M.
   1981   'Why do the Scribes Say That Elijah Must Come First?', *JBL* 100: 75-86.

Farrer, A.
1957   'On Dispensing with Q', in D.E. Nineham (ed.), *Studies in the Gospels: Essays in Memory of R.H. Lightfoot* (Oxford: Blackwell): 55-88.
Finch, R.G.
1939   *The Synagogue Lectionary and the New Testament* (London: SPCK).
Fishbane, M
1988   'Use, Authority and Interpretation of Mikra at Qumran', ch. 10 in Mulder 1988: 339-77.
Fitzmyer, J.A.
1981–85   *The Gospel according to Luke* (AB; New York: Doubleday).
1992   'The Use of the Old Testament in Luke–Acts', *SBLSP* 31: 524-38.
Foakes-Jackson, F.J. and K. Lake
1920–33   *The Beginnings of Christianity. Part I. The Acts of the Apostles.* Vol. 1: *Prolegomena I. The Jewish, Gentile and Christian Backgrounds* (London: Macmillan, 1920). Vol. 2: *Prolegomena II. Criticism* (London: Macmillan, 1922). Vol. 3: *The Text of Acts* (London: Macmillan, 1926). Vol. 4: *English Translation and Commentary* (London: Macmillan, 1933). Vol. 5: *Additional Notes* (London: Macmillan, 1933).
Fowler, R.M.
1989   'Postmodern Biblical Criticism', *Forum* 5: 3-30.
Gasque, W.W.
1975   *A History of the Criticism of the Acts of the Apostles* (Tübingen: Mohr; repr. Grand Rapids: Eerdmans).
1989   'The Historical Value of Acts', *TynBul* 40: 136-57.
Gillingham, S.E.
1988   'The Poor in the Psalms', *ExpTim* 100: 15-19.
Gottwald, N.K. (ed.)
1983   *The Bible and Liberation: Political and Social Hermeneutics* (Maryknoll, NY: Orbis).
Goulder, M.
1974   *Midrash and Lection in Matthew* (London: SPCK).
1978   *The Evangelists' Calendar: A Lectionary Explanation of the Development of Scripture* (London: SPCK).
1989   *Luke: A New Paradigm*, I (JSNTSup, 20; Sheffield: JSOT Press).
Grabbe, L.L.
1988   'Synagogues in Pre-70 Palestine: A Re-Assessment', *JTS* NS 39: 401-10.
Grelot, P.
1990   'Sur Isaie LXI: La première Consécration d'un Grand-Prêtre', *RB* 97: 414-31
Griesbach, J.J.
1774   *Libri historici Novi Testamenti Graece: Pars prior, sistens synopsin Evangeliorum Matthaei, Marci et Lucae* (Halle).
1783   'Inquisitio in fontes, unde evangelistae suas de resurrectione domini narrationes hauserint', *Griesbachii Opuscula Academica*, II (ed. Gabler, Jena): 241-56.

Griffiths, J.G.
    1987   'Egypt and the Rise of the Synagogue', *JTS* NS 38: 1-15.

Grundmann, W.
    1981   *Das Evangelium nach Lukas* (THKNT, 3; 9th edn; Berlin: Evangelische Verlagsanstalt).

Guilding, A.
    1960   *The Fourth Gospel and Jewish Worship* (Oxford: Clarendon).

Gutiérrez, G.
    1983   *A Theology of Liberation* (New York: Orbis).

Gutmann, J.
    1975   'The Origins of the Synagogue: The Current State of Research', in Gutmann (ed.), 1975: 72-76.

Gutmann, J. (ed.)
    1975   *The Synagogue: Studies in Origins, Archaeology and Architecture* (Selected with a Prolegomenon by J. Gutmann; Library of Biblical Studies; New York: KTAV).

Haenchen, E.
    1971   *The Acts of the Apostles* (trans. B. Noble and G. Shinn; 4th edn; Oxford: Blackwells [orig. Germ. edn 1965]).

Hamel, G.
    1990   *Poverty and Charity in Roman Palestine, First Three Centuries CE* (Near Eastern Studies, 23; Berkeley: University of California Press).

Hamm, D.
    1986   'Sight to the Blind: Vision as Metaphor in Luke', *Bib* 67: 457-77.

Hanson, P.D.
    1989   *The Dawn of Apocalyptic* (Philadelphia: Fortress Press).

Harnack, A. von
    1906   *Beiträge zur Einleitung in das Neue Testament. I. Lukas der Arzt: Der Verfasser des dritten Evangeliums und der Apostelgeschichte* (Leipzig: Hinrichs [ET 1907, *Luke the Physician* (London: Williams & Norgate)]).
    1908   *Beiträge zur Einleitung in das Neue Testament. II. Die Apostelgeschichte* (Leipzig: Hinrichs [ET 1909, *The Acts of the Apostles* (London: Williams & Norgate)]).
    1911   *Beiträge zur Einleitung in das Neue Testament. IV. Neue Untersuchungen zur Apostelgeschichte und zur Abfassungszeit der synoptischen Evangelien* (Leipzig: Hinrich [ET 1911, *The Date of the Acts and of the Synoptic Gospels* (London: Williams & Norgate)]).

Hemer, C.J.
    1977–78   'Luke the Historian', *BJRL* 60: 28-51.
    1989   *The Book of Acts in the Setting of Hellenistic History* (WUNT, 49; Tübingen: Mohr).

Hengel, M.
    1975   'Proseuche und Synagoge. Jüdische Gemeinde, Gotteshaus und Gottesdient in der Diaspora und in Palästina', in Gutmann 1975: 157-84.
    1979   *Acts and the History of Earliest Christianity* (trans. J. Bowden; London: SCM Press).

　　　　1983　　　*Between Jesus and Paul: Studies in the Earliest History of Christianity* (trans. J. Bowden; London: SCM Press).

Herder, J.G.
　　　　1797　　　*Christliche Schriften*, III (Riga): 303-416.

Hoenig, S.
　　　　1975　　　'The Suppositious Temple Synagogue', in Gutmann 1975: 55-71.

Hobbs, T.R.
　　　　1989　　　'Reflections on "The Poor" and the Old Testament', *ExpTim* 100: 291-94.

Holtzmann, H.J.
　　　　1863　　　*Die synoptischen Evangelien: Ihr Ursprung und ihr geschichtlicher Charakter* (Leipzig).

Horsley, G.H.R.
　　　　1981　　　*New Documents Illustrating Early Christianity*, I (North Ryde: Macquarrie University Press).
　　　　1982　　　*New Documents Illustrating Early Christianity*, II (North Ryde: Macquarrie University Press).
　　　　1983　　　*New Documents Illustrating Early Christianity*, III (North Ryde: Macquarrie University Press).

Horsley, G.H.R. *et al.*
　　　　1987　　　*New Documents Illustrating Early Christianity*, IV (North Ryde: Macquarrie University Press).
　　　　1989　　　*New Documents Illustrating Early Christianity*, V (North Ryde: Macquarrie University Press).
　　　　1992　　　*New Documents Illustrating Early Christianity*, VI (North Ryde: Macquarrie University Press).

Jeremias, J.
　　　　1956　　　*Jesu Verheissung für die Völker* (SBT, 24; Stuttgart [= *Jesus' Promise to the Nations* (trans. S.M. Hooke; London: SCM Press 1958)]).

Johnston, L.T.
　　　　1977　　　*The Literary Function of Possessions in Luke–Acts* (SBLDS, 39; Missoula, MT: Scholars Press).
　　　　1991-92　　*The Gospel of Luke: The Acts of the Apostles* (Sacra Pagina, 3, 5; Collegeville, MN: Liturgical Press).

Karris, R.J.
　　　　1978　　　'Poor and Rich: The Lukan *Sitz im Leben*', in Talbert 1978: 112-25.

Kee, H.C.
　　　　1990　　　'The Transformation of the Synagogue after 70 CE: Its Import for Early Christianity', *NTS* 36: 1-24.

Keegan, T.J.
　　　　1985　　　*Interpreting the Bible: A Popular Introduction to Biblical Hermeneutics* (New York: Paulist Press)

Koet, B.-J.
　　　　1986　　　'"Today this Scripture has been Fulfilled in your Ears". Jesus' Explanation of Scripture in Luke 4,16-30', *Bijdragen* 47: 368-94 (= *Five Studies on Interpretation of Scripture in Luke–Acts* [Studiorum Novi Testamenti Auxilia, 14; Leuven, 1989]: 24-55.

Kraabel, T.
1979 'The Diaspora Synagogue: Archaeological and Epigraphic Evidence since Sukenik', in *ANRW* II.19.1 (Berlin: de Gruyter): 477-510.

Kurz, W.S.
1987 'Narrative Approaches to Luke–Acts', *Bib* 68: 195-220.
1990 'Narrative Models for Imitation in Luke–Acts', in D.L. Balch, E. Ferguson and W.A. Meeks (eds.), *Greeks, Romans, and Christians: Essays in Honor of Abraham J. Malherbe* (Minneapolis: Fortress Press): 171-89.

Lachmann, K.
1835 'De ordine narrationum in evangeliis synopticis', *TSK*: 570-72.

LaVerdiere, E.
1980 *Luke* (New Testament Message, 5; Dublin: Veritas).

Leaney, A.R.C.
1966 *A Commentary on the Gospel according to St Luke* (BNTC; London: Black).

Le Déaut, R.
1977 *The Spirituality of Judaism* (ed. R. Le Déaut, A. Jaubert and K. Hruby; Religious Experience Series, 11; Wheathampstead: Anthony Clark).

Lessing, G.E.
1784 'Neue Hypothese ueber die Evangelisten als bloss menschliche Geschichtschreiber betrachtet', *Theologischer Nachlass* (Berlin): 45-72.

Levertoff, P.P.
1928 'Introduction to Matthew', in C. Gore, H.L. Goudge and A. Guillaume (eds.), *A New Commentary on Holy Scripture* (London).

Levine, L.I. (ed.)
1987 *The Synagogue in Late Antiquity* (Philadelphia: American Schools of Oriental Research).

Lindsey, R.L.
1963 'A Modified Two-Document Theory of the Synoptic Dependence and Interdependence', *NovT* 6: 239-63.

Liu, P.
1986 'The Poor and the Good News: A Study of the Motif of εὐαγγελίζετθαι πτωχοῖς in Isaiah 61 and Luke–Acts' (dissertation, Fuller Theological Seminary, Pasadena).

Lohfink, N.F.
1978 *Option for the Poor: The Basic Principle of Liberation Theology in the Light of the Bible* (trans. L.M. Maloney; Berkeley: Bibal Press).
1986 'Von der "Anawim-Partei" zur "Kirche der Armen": Die bibelwissenschaftliche Ahnentafel eines Hauptbegriffs der "Theologie der Befreiung"', *Bib* 67: 153-75.

Lucian of Samosata
1959 *How to Write History* 1.2-5 (cited from Lucian, VI; trans. K. Kilburn; LCL; Cambridge, MA: Harvard University Press).

Lüdemann, G.
1989 *Early Christianity according to the Traditions of Acts: A Commentary* (trans. J. Bowden; London: SCM Press [German edn 1987])

McNamara, M.
  1972   *Targum and Testament* (Shannon: Irish University Press).
MacNamara, V.
  1988   *The Truth in Love: Reflections on Christian Morality* (Dublin: Gill & Macmillan).
Maddox, R.
  1982   *The Purpose of Luke–Acts* (Edinburgh: T. & T. Clark).
Marsh, H.
  1798   'Dissertation on the Origin of our Three First Canonical Gospels', included at the end of vol. III of his translation of Michaelis' *Introduction to the New Testament* (Cambridge).
Marshall, I.H.
  1970   *Luke: Historian and Theologian* (Exeter: Paternoster Press).
  1978   *The Gospel of Luke* (NIGTC; Exeter: Paternoster Press).
Mattill, A.J., Jr
  1970   'The Purpose of Acts: Schneckenburger Reconsidered', in W. Ward Gasque and R.P. Martin (eds.), *Apostolic History and the Gospel* (Grand Rapids: Eerdmans): 108-22.
Mayer, G.
  1974   *Index Philoneus* (Berlin: de Gruyter).
Meyer, E.
  1921a   *Ursprung und Anfänge des Christentums. I. Die Evangelien* (Stuttgart/Berlin: J.G. Cotta).
  1921b   *Ursprung und Anfänge des Christentums. II. Entwicklung des Judentums und Jesus von Nazareth* (Stuttgart/Berlin: J.G. Cotta).
  1923   *Apostelgeschichte und die Anfänge des Christentums*, II (Stuttgart/Berlin: J.G. Cotta).
Meyers, E., and J. Strange
  1981   *Archaeology, the Rabbis and Early Christianity* (Nashville: Abingdon).
Mofokeng, T.
  1988   *Black Christians, the Bible and Liberation. Journal of Black Theology* 2.
Monshouwer, D.
  1991   'The Reading of the Prophet in the Synagogue at Nazareth', *Bib* 72: 90-99.
Morris, L.
  1964   *The New Testament and the Jewish Lectionaries* (London: Tyndale).
Mulder, M.J. (ed.)
  1988   *Mikra: Text, Translation, Reading and Interpretation of the Hebrew Bible in Ancient Judaism and Early Christianity* (Assen: Van Gorcum; Philadelphia: Fortress Press).
Neirynck, F.
  1989   'Synoptic Problem', in R.E. Brown, J.A. Fitzmyer and R.E. Murphy (eds.), *The New Jerome Biblical Commentary* (London: Chapman): 587-95.
Neirynck, F., (ed.)
  1989   *L'évangile de Luc: The Gospel of Luke. Revised and Enlarged Edition*

of *L'évangile de Luc: Problèmes littéraires et théologiques* (BETL, 32; Leuven: Leuven University Press).

Neyrey, J.H., (ed.)
    1991   *The Social World of Luke–Acts: Models for Interpretation* (Peabody, MA: Hendrickson).

Noorda, S.J.
    1982   ' "Cure Yourself, Doctor!" (Luke 4.23). Classical Parallels to an Alleged Saying of Jesus', in Delobel 1982: 459-67.

Noy, D.
    1992   'A Jewish Place of Prayer in Roman Egypt', *JTS* 43: 118-22.

O'Fearghail, F.
    1984   'Rejection in Nazareth: Lk 4,22', *ZNW* 75: 60-72.

O'Neill, J.C.
    1970   *The Theology of Acts in its Historical Setting* (2nd edn; London: SPCK).

Oster, R.E.
    1993   'Supposed Anachronism in Luke–Acts' Use of ΣΥΝΑΓΩΓΗ. A Rejoinder to H.C. Kee', *NTS* 39: 178-208.

Parsons, M.C.
    1987   *The Departure of Jesus in Luke–Acts: The Ascension Narratives in Context* (JSNTSup, 21; Sheffield: JSOT Press).
    1992   'What's "Literary" about Literary Aspects of the Gospels and Acts?', *SBLSP* 31: 14-39.

Perrot, C.
    1973   *La lecture de la Bible dans la Synagogue* (Hildesheim: Olms).

Pervo, R.
    1987   *Profit with Delight: The Literary Genre of the Acts of the Apostles* (Philadelphia: Fortress Press).

Plümacher, E.
    1972   *Lukas als hellenistischer Schriftsteller* (Göttingen: Vandenhoeck & Ruprecht).

Powell, M.A.
    1989   *What are they Saying about Luke?* (New York: Paulist Press).

Prager, J.P.
    1991   'The Poor as the Starting Point for Vincentian Studies: A Liberation Hermeneutic', *Vincentiana* 1991.2: 140-45.

Prior, M.
    1979   'Revisiting Luke', *ScrB* 10: 2-11.
    1986   'A "Copernican" Revolution, or, Griesbach Re-Buried?', *ScrB* 17: 14-19.
    1989   *Paul the Letter-Writer and the Second Letter to Timothy* (JSNTSup, 23; Sheffield: JSOT Press).
    1990   '*Evangelizare Pauperibus Misit Me*: Jesus in the Synagogue at Nazareth', *Colloque* 22: 250-63.
    1993   'Palestinian Christians and the Liberation of Theology', *The Month* (2nd NS) 26: 482-90.
    1994   'Isaiah and the Liberation of the Poor (Luke 4.16-30)', *ScrB* 24: 36-46.

1995	'The Bible as Instrument of Oppression', *ScrB* 25: 2-14.

Pritz, R.A.
    1988   *Nazarene Jewish Christianity: From the End of the New Testament Period until its Disappearance in the Fourth Century* (Jerusalem: Magnes; Leiden: Brill).

Ramsay, W.M.
    1890   *Historical Geography of Asia Minor* (London: Murray)
    1895–97   *The Cities and Bishoprics of Phrygia*, I (1895), II (1897) (Oxford: Clarendon).
    1915   *The Bearing of Recent Discovery on the Trustworthiness of the New Testament* (London: Hodder & Stoughton).
    1930   *St Paul the Traveller and the Roman Citizen* (17th edn; London: Hodder & Stoughton).

Reicke, B.
    1973   'Jesus in Nazareth—Lk 4,14-30', in H. Balz and S. Schulz (eds.), *Das Wort und die Wörter* (FS G. Friedrich: Stuttgart): 47-55.

Richtmyer, F.K., E.H. Kennard and J.N. Cooper
    1969   *Introduction to Modern Physics* (New York: McGraw–Hill).

Safrai, Z.
    1990   'The Origins of Reading the Aramaic Targum in Synagogue', in M. Lowe (ed.), *The New Testament and Christian–Jewish Dialogue: Studies in Honor of David Flusser (Immanuel* 24/25): 187-93.

Sampley, J.P.
    1980   *Pauline Partnership in Christ: Christian Community and Commitment in Light of Roman Law* (Philadelphia: Fortress Press).

Sanders, J.A.
    1975   'From Isaiah 61 to Luke 4', in J. Neusner (ed.), *Christianity, Judaism, and other Greco-Roman Cults: Studies for Morton Smith at Sixty*, I (Leiden: Brill): 75-106.
    1987   'Isaiah in Luke', in J.L. Mays and P.J. Achtemeier (eds.), *Interpreting the Prophets* (Philadelphia: Fortress Press): 75-85.

Sanders, J.T.
    1986   'The Jewish People', in *SBLSP* 25: 110-29.
    1987   *The Jews in Luke–Acts* (London: SCM Press).
    1991   'Who is a Jew and who is a Gentile in the Book of Acts', *NTS* 37: 434-55.

Schleiermacher, F.E.D.
    1832   'Ueber die Zeugnisse des Papias von unsern beiden ersten Evangelien', *TSK*: 736-68.

Schmidt, T.E.
    1987   *Hostility to Wealth in the Synoptic Gospels* (JSNTSup, 15; Sheffield: JSOT Press).

Schmitals, W.
    1975   'Lukas—Evangelist der Armen', *Theologia Viatorum* 12: 154-67.

Schnackenburg, R.
    1968   *The Gospel according to St John*, I (ET; New York: Herder & Herder; London: Burns & Oates).

Schottroff, L., and W. Stegemann.
  1978   *Jesus von Nazareth: Hoffnung der Armen* (Urban-Taschenbücher, 639; Stuttgart).
Schrage, W.
  1971   'συναγωγή', *TDNT*, VII, 798-852.
Schreck, C.J.
  1989   'The Nazareth Pericope: Luke 4.16-30 in Recent Study', in Neirynck 1989: 399-471.
Schürer, E.
  1979   *The History of the Jewish People in the Age of Jesus Christ (175 BC–AD 135)*, II (rev. and ed. G. Vermes, *et al.*; Edinburgh: T. & T. Clark).
  1986   *The History of the Jewish People in the Age of Jesus Christ (175 BC–AD 135)*, III.1 (rev. and ed. G. Vermes, *et al.*; Edinburgh: T. & T. Clark).
Siker, J.S.
  1992   '"First to the Gentiles": A Literary Analysis of Luke 4.16-30', *JBL* 111: 73-90.
Sloan, R.B., Jr
  1977   *The Favorable Year of the Lord: A Study of Jubilary Theology in the Gospel of Luke* (Austin, TX: Schola)
Squires, J.T.
  1993   *The Plan of God in Luke–Acts* (SNTSMS, 76; Cambridge: Cambridge University Press).
Stegner, W.R.
  1988   'The Ancient Jewish Synagogue Homily', in D.E. Aune (ed.), *Greco-Roman Literature and the New Testament* (SBLSBS, 21; Atlanta: Scholars Press): 51-69.
Storr, G.C.
  1786   *Ueber den Zweck der evangelischen Geschichte und der Briefe Johannis* (Tübingen).
Streeter, B.H.
  1924   *The Four Gospels: A Study of Origins* (London: Macmillan).
Sugirtharajah, R.S. (ed.)
  1991   *Voices from the Margin: Interpreting the Bible in the Third World* (London: SPCK).
Talbert, C.H.
  1966   *Luke and the Gnostics: An Examination of the Lucan Purpose* (Nashville: Abingdon).
  1974   *Literary Patterns, Theological Themes and the Genre of Luke–Acts* (SBLMS, 20; Missoula, MT: Scholars Press).
  1978   *What is a Gospel? The Genre of the Canonical Gospels* (London: SPCK).
  1978   *Perspectives on Luke–Acts* (Edinburgh: T. & T. Clark)
  1984   *Reading Luke: A Literary and Theological Commentary on the Third Gospel* (New York: Crossroad).
  1984a 'Promise and Fulfilment in Lucan Theology', in C.H. Talbert (ed.), *Luke–Acts: New Perspectives from the Society of Biblical Literature Seminar* (New York: Crossroad): 91-103.

1989	'Luke–Acts', in E.J. Epp and G.W. MacRae (eds.), *The New Testament and its Modern Interpreters* (Atlanta: Scholars Press): 297-320.

Tamez, E.
    1982   *Bible of the Oppressed* (New York: Orbis).

Tannehill, R.C.
    1972   'The Mission of Jesus according to Luke 4.16-30', in W. Eltester (ed.), *Jesus in Nazareth* (Berlin: de Gruyter): 51-75.
    1986   'Rejection by Jews and Turning to Gentiles: The Pattern of Paul's Mission in Acts', in *SBLSP* 25: 130-41.
    1986-89   *The Narrative Unity of Luke–Acts* (2 vols.; Philadelphia: Fortress Press).

Tiede, D.L.
    1980   *Prophecy and History in Luke–Acts* (Philadelphia: Fortress Press).
    1986   '"Glory to Thy People Israel!": Luke–Acts and the Jews', *SBLSP* 25: 142-51.

Tuckett, C.
    1982   'Luke 4.16-30, Isaiah and Q', in Delobel 1982: 343-54.
    1983   *The Revival of the Griesbach Hypothesis* (SNTSMS, 44; Cambridge: Cambridge University Press).

Tyson, J.B.
    1992   'Torah and Prophets in Luke–Acts: Temporary or Permanent?', *SBLSP* 31: 539-48.

Unnik, W.C. van
    1979   'Luke's Second Book and the Rules of Hellenistic Historiography', in J. Kremer (ed.), *Les Actes des Apôtres: Traditions, rédaction, théologie* (BETL, 48; Leuven: Leuven University Press): 37-60.

Vaage, L.E.
    1991   'Text, Context, Conquest, Quest: The Bible and Social Struggle in Latin America', in *SBLSP* 30: 357-65.

Violet, B.
    1938   'Zum rechten Verständnis der Nazarethperikope', *ZNW* 37: 251-71.

Wechsler, A.
    1991   *Geschichtsbild und Apostelstreit: Eine forschungsgeschichtliche und exegetische Studie über den antiochenischen Zwischenfall (Gal 2,11-14)* (BZNW, 62; Berlin: de Gruyter).

Weir, J.E.
    1988   'The Poor are Powerless. A Response to R.J. Coggins', *ExpTim* 100: 13-15.

Weisse, C.H.
    1838   *Die evangelische Geschichte kritisch und philosophisch bearbeitet* (Leipzig).

West, G., and J. Draper
    1991   'The Bible and Social Transformation in South Africa: A Work-in-Progress Report on the Institute for the Study of the Bible', *SBLSP* 30: 366-82.

Wiener, A.
    1978   *The Prophet Elijah in the Development of Judaism* (Boston: Routledge & Kegan Paul).

Wilkinson, J.
  1977   *Jerusalem Pilgrims before the Crusades* (Warminster: Aris & Phillips).
  1981   *Egeria's Travels to the Holy Land: Newly Translated with Supporting Documents and Notes* (rev. edn; Jerusalem: Ariel; Warminster: Aris & Phillips).

Wills, L.
  1984   'The Form of the Sermon in Hellenistic Judaism and Early Christianity', *HTR* 77: 277-99.

Wilson, S.G.
  1973   *The Gentiles and the Gentile Mission in Luke–Acts* (SNTSMS, 23; Cambridge: Cambridge University Press).

Wright, A.G.
  1967   *The Literary Genre Midrash* (New York: Alba House).

Wylie, A.B.
  1991   'The Exegesis of History in John Chrysostom's *Homilies on Acts*', in Burrows and Rorem 1991: 59-72.

Zeitlin, S.
  1930–31 'The Origin of the Synagogue', *PAAJR* 2: 69-81.

INDEXES

INDEX OF REFERENCES

OLD TESTAMENT

Genesis	
2.21	119
8.15–9.17	140

Exodus	
1.1–6.1	115
7.8–10.27	22
10–14	22
18.1–19.5	140
20.8-11	139
22.22-24	175
23.6	175

Leviticus	
19.33	175
25	139
25.2-7	139
25.6	175
25.8-55	139
25.10	139
25.13	139
25.28	139

Numbers	
6.24-26	111
11.17	158
14.11-45	140
15.37-41	111
27.16-17	104

Deuteronomy	
5.12-15	139
5.12	139
6.4-9	111
8.3	97
11.13-21	111
13.1-11	137
15.17	175
17.2-7	137
27.19	175

Judges	
6.34	158

1 Samuel	
16.13-14	158

1 Kings	
3–11	22
16.30	142
17	142
17.8-24	144
17.24	142
18.1-19	143
18.21	143
19.14	143
19.19-21	145

2 Kings	
1.9-16	145
2.1-14	145
2.19-22	143
2.23-24	143
3	143
4.1-7	143
4.8-37	143
4.32-37	144
4.38-44	143
5.1-14	144

Nehemiah	
9.26	138

Job	
31.16-32	176

Psalms	
2.7	112
16.10	112
22	130
37.25	175
51	23
82	176
86	175
109.22-25	175
118	130

Proverbs	
8.18	175
14.10	175

Isaiah	
1–39	130
5.1-2	54, 130
6.9-10	54, 130, 155, 157
26.19	54, 130
29.18-19	94
29.18	54, 130, 155
29.20	94
33.13-22	140
35.4	94
35.5-6	54, 94, 130
35.6	155
40–55	130

40.3-5	49, 54, 130, 155	58.7-10	135	*Amos*		
42	130	58.7	135	2.7	176	
42.6	54, 130, 157	58.10	135	4.1-3	176	
42.7-15	140	60.1–62.12	134	5.7-11	176	
42.21	140	60.1-22	134	6.1	176	
45.21	112	61	89, 97, 98, 122, 123, 132-37, 139-41, 157	8.4-6	176	
49	54, 130			9.11-12	112	
49.1-12	131			*Jonah*		
49.5-6	54	61.1-2b	153, 154	1	22	
49.6	54, 130, 157	61.1-11	134	1.17–2.10	22	
49.8-9	54	61.1-3	137	2	22	
52.5-7	140	61.1-2	54, 129, 130	3	22	
52.10	54, 130	61.1	54, 94, 130, 132, 137, 140, 155	4	22	
52.13–53.12	138			4.1-11	22	
53	130					
53.12	54, 130	61.2	93, 94	*Malachi*		
55.3	112	61.3-6	136	3.1-2	144	
56–66	130	61.4	134	4.5-6	144	
56	51	61.5-11	134			
56.6-7	51	61.5-6	136	*Susanna*		
56.7-8	51	61.2b	140	28	103	
56.7	51, 54, 130	62.1-12	134			
56.8	138			*1 Maccabees*		
58	135, 136	*Jeremiah*		10.24	127	
58.3	135	7.11	51			
58.6	54, 98, 122, 129, 130, 132, 134, 135, 137, 141, 153, 154	12.15	112	*2 Maccabees*		
		41.8	139	7.24	127	
				15.11	127	
		Ezekiel				
		12.18-19	22			

NEW TESTAMENT

Matthew		4.24	79	9.9-13	50
1–11	118	5–7	69	9.9	50
1–2	69	5	118	9.35–11.1	69
3.1–4.25	69	5.3	167, 169	9.35	50, 109
3.1–4.11	69	5.11-12	138	10.17	109
4.12–18.35	69	5.40	174	11	118
4.12-17	14, 79	6.2	109	11.4	167
4.12-13	77	6.5	109	11.5-6	84
4.12	78	7.28	109	11.5	167, 169, 171
4.13a	118	8	50		
4.17	77	8.1–9.34	69	11.6	168
4.18-22	14	8.5-13	50	11.14	144
4.23	50, 109	8.11	50	11.19	50

Index of References

12.1–13.35	69	1.14-15	14, 77, 79,	11.18	109		
12.9-14	109		84, 119	12.39	109, 113		
12.9	50, 109	1.14a	78	12.41-44	171		
12.22-45	118	1.16-20	14, 74	12.41	171		
13	78	1.21	50, 109	12.42	169		
13.1-52	118	1.22	109	12.43	50, 168, 169		
13.53–28.8	69	1.23-28	109	13.9	109		
13.53–14.1	66, 76, 78	1.27	109	14–15	69		
13.53-58	14, 86	1.39	50, 109	14	50		
13.53-54	79	1.40–2.22	69	14.3-9	74, 169		
13.53	78	2	118	14.5	169		
13.54-58	112	2.13-17	50	14.7	169		
13.54-57	80	2.14	50	15.31	160		
13.54	50, 78, 109	2.23–4.34	69	16	69		
13.57–14.1	81	3.1-6	109				
13.57	78, 85	3.1	50, 109	*Luke*			
13.58	78	3.31-35	74	1–2	22, 23, 48,		
16.14	138	4–5	69		56, 69		
17.10-13	144	4.1–9.41	69	1.1-5	28		
17.10-12	144	4.1-34	118	1.1-4	23, 28, 62,		
19–20	69	4.16-30	87		63		
19	171	5	50	1.1-2	90		
19.13–28.10	69	5.13	84	1.1	28, 87, 129,		
19.21	168-70	6	78		140		
19.23	171	6.1–16.8	69	1.3	21		
19.24	171	6.1-6a	14, 75	1.16-17	158		
21–25	69	6.1-6	66, 76, 77,	1.16	49		
22.9	168		82-86, 102,	1.32	49		
22.23	109		115, 125	1.34	49		
23.6	109	6.1-2	79	1.35	158		
23.29-31	139	6.1	78	1.38	49		
23.34-36	139	6.2-3	80	1.41	123, 158		
23.34	109	6.2	50, 78, 82,	1.54-55	49		
23.37-39	139		109	1.67	123, 158		
25.27	171	6.3	78	1.68-79	49		
26–27	69	6.4-7	81	1.77	139		
26	50	6.4	78, 85	1.79	54, 130		
26.6-13	169	6.5	78	2	49, 116		
26.9	169	6.15	138	2.1-2	28		
26.11	169	6.39	113	2.1	49		
27.42	160	6.45–8.26	69, 74	2.4	123		
28	69	8.28	138	2.11	158		
		9.11-13	144	2.14	49		
		10	69	2.25	158		
Mark		10.13-16.1-8	69	2.29-32	49, 131,		
1.1–3.12	69	10.21	168-70		155, 157		
1.1-39	69	10.25	171	2.30-32	54, 130		
1.1-13	69	11–13	69	2.34	124		
1.14–9.50	69						

2.34b	198		149, 184,	4.33	50, 109, 151
2.41-50	49		186, 187,	4.37	151
3–4	22		193, 198,	4.38-39	192
3.1–6.19	69		200	4.40-41	158, 192
3.1–4.13	69	4.16-21	84	4.42-44	192
3.1-20	118	4.16	50, 57, 78,	4.42	124, 151
3.1	49		84, 96, 109,	4.43-44	151
3.3	139		122	4.43	97, 158
		4.17-21	84	4.44	50, 109
3.4-6	49, 54, 128,	4.17	132	5	75
	130	4.18-19	54, 94, 98,	5.1-11	14, 75
3.6	155, 157		128, 130,	5.10b-11	74
3.8	49		135, 163	5.11	135, 179,
3.10-14	135, 192	4.18	139, 166,		192
3.22	138, 154,		167, 171,	5.12–6.11	74
	158		178	5.15	124
3.23	49	4.19	95	5.17-26	139
3.34	49	4.20	95, 112,	5.22	159
3.37	49		114, 123	5.26	156, 158
4	78, 122,	4.21	94, 95, 98,	5.27-32	50
	129, 158		127, 128,	5.27-28	50
4.1-13	151		140	5.28	135, 179
4.1-2	138	4.22	78, 80, 84,	6	75
4.1	123, 158		92, 93, 95-	6.1-6a	74
4.8	123		98	6.5	123
4.14–9.50	24, 44, 69	4.23-33	81	6.6-11	50, 109
4.14-21	79	4.23-27	98	6.6	50, 109
4.14-15	13, 14, 76,	4.23	78, 84, 88,	6.7	156
	88, 151, 160		92, 96, 97	6.8	159
4.14	24, 78, 138,	4.24	78, 84, 85,	6.20–8.3	69, 74
	158		98, 136, 138	6.20	158, 167,
4.15	50, 91, 109,	4.25-30	84		169, 171
	122	4.25-27	84, 136,	6.22-23	138
4.16–7.17	22		142-44	6.24-26	179
4.16-30	13, 15-17,	4.26-27	50	6.24	170, 171
	20, 27, 30,	4.27	144	6.29	174
	37, 38, 50,	4.28-29	15, 78, 92	7	75
	58, 66, 72,	4.29	98	7.1-16	144
	74-77, 82,	4.30	96	7.1-10	50, 144
	84, 86, 88,	4.31-44	74, 151	7.5	106
	90, 91, 102,	4.31-41	160	7.11-17	144
	108, 109,	4.31-37	88, 192	7.16	123, 138
	111-13,	4.31-33	14, 77	7.18–8.56	22
	115, 118,	4.31-32	109, 151	7.18-35	118
	119, 124,	4.31	88, 123, 151	7.18-23	144, 155
	127, 132,	4.32	109, 151	7.18-19	94
	137, 140,	4.33-43	151	7.22-23	84, 94, 155
	141, 147,	4.33-37	109		

Index of References

7.22	54, 94, 123, 130, 158, 167, 169, 171, 178, 200, 202	11.29-32	156	16.20	158, 168, 170
		11.37-52	97		
		11.37-44	156	16.22	170
		11.38	97	16.27-31	54
		11.39-44	97	17.11-19	50, 145, 156
7.23	160	11.41	179	17.11	56
7.34	50	11.43	109	17.20	156
7.36-50	74, 118, 139, 169	11.45-52	97, 156	18.15–24.12	69
		11.47-48	139	18.18–19.10	155, 171
7.39-40	159	11.49-51	139	18.18-31	179
7.39	123, 138	11.49-50	123		
7.44-50	50	11.53-54	97	18.18-30	155, 171, 172
8	75	12.11	109		
8.1-21	118	12.13-15	179	18.22-25	171
8.1-3	50	12.16-21	174, 179	18.22	135, 158, 168-70
8.1	158	12.16	171		
8.4–9.50	69	12.56	156	18.28	179
8.4-18	74	13.10-17	109	18.31-34	155, 171
8.10	54, 130	13.10	50, 109	18.31	56, 128
8.19-21	74, 75	13.18-19	75	18.35-43	155, 171
8.22–9.50	74	13.20-21	50	18.38	155
8.26-29	50	13.29	50	18.41	155
9	22	13.32-34	158	19	171
9.1-48	21	13.33-35	55, 56	19.1-10	50, 155, 171, 179
9.8	123, 138	13.33	123, 124		
9.9	155	13.34-35	139, 156	19.5-9	158
9.17	123	13.35a	37	19.8	135, 168, 170
9.19	123, 138	13.47	54		
9.47	159	13.52	123	19.9	123, 158, 172
9.51–19.44	179	14.1–18.30	22		
9.51–19.40	24	14.1	156	19.11	56
9.51–19.28	69	14.12-14	50, 163, 168, 179	19.28	56
9.51–18.14	69			19.29–21.38	69
9.51-55	50	14.12	171	19.37-38	156
9.51	55, 56, 124	14.13	158, 171	19.41–24.49	24
9.52-55	145	14.21	158, 163, 168, 171	19.43-44	37
9.53	56			19.45-46	51
9.57-60	75	14.25-33	179	19.45	69
9.61-62	145	14.33	135	19.46	54, 128, 130
10.21–13.30	22	15	173	20.1	158
10.21	158	15.1-3	50	20.9	54, 130
10.23-24	156	15.8-10	50	20.20	156
10.30-37	50	16	178, 194	21.1-4	50, 171
10.38-42	50	16.14	179	21.3	158, 168, 169
11	75	16.19-31	135		
11.14-53	156	16.19-26	50, 163	21.12	109
11.17	159	16.19-21	174	21.20-24	37
11.24	123	16.19	171	21.22	95, 128

22–24	128	12.1-8	169	4.31	158
22–23	69	12.5	169	4.32-37	135
22.7–23.16	21	12.6	169	4.34-35	177
22.37	54, 128, 130	12.8	169	4.34	165
22.47-53	128	12.42	109	5.1-11	135, 178
23.8	156	13.29	169	5.32	158
23.13	156	16.2	109	5.40-42	55
23.18	156	18.20	50, 109	6.1-6	178
23.33	128	18.23	93, 95	6.1	177
23.35	160			6.3	158
23.43	123, 158	Acts		6.5	158
23.48	156	1–12	21	6.10	158, 160
24	22, 24, 54, 69	1–2	48	7	115
		1	22, 24	7.37	123, 138
24.13-35	37	1.1-5	28	7.51	160
24.19	123, 138	1.1	21	7.52	138
24.25-26	53	1.2	158	7.57-58	160
24.26-27	123	1.3-8	52	8.1b–11.18	24, 57
24.26	128	1.5-14	53	8.4-5	55
24.27-29	123	1.8	42, 54, 56, 130	8.18-25	178
24.27	54			8.26-39	58
24.44-49	52	1.9-11	145	9.2	109
24.44	128, 129	1.12–8.1a	24	9.24	156
24.46-47	129, 139	1.12–4.23	22	9.36	178
24.46	128	1.16-20	129	10–11	145
24.47	54, 55, 128, 130, 139	1.18	178	10.1–11.18	58
		1.21-22	56	10.1-48	57, 180
24.48	56	2	128	10.2	177, 178
24.50-53	52	2.1-13	145	10.4	177, 178
24.51-53	145	2.1-11	57	10.31	177, 178
26.16	156	2.23	123	10.34-39	83
26.26	156	2.30	123	10.38	158
26.32	156	2.31	123	10.43	123, 128
26.35	156	2.40	127	11.1-18	181
26.45	156	2.41-47	178, 179	11.19–28.31	24
		2.44-45	135	11.19-21	55
John		2.45	177	11.28-30	177
2.8-9	113	3.1–4.31	27	11.29	178
4.43-45	85	3.2-10	178	12.7-8	174
4.44	81, 85	3.16	57	13–28	21, 43
6.9	173	3.18	123, 128	13.5	57, 110
6.42	80, 85	3.22-23	128, 138	13.13-44	112
6.59	50, 85, 109	3.22	123	13.14	57, 110, 132
7.7	93, 95	3.24	123	13.15	112, 122, 123, 127
7.15	80	4.8	158		
8.59	99	4.11	123	13.16-37	127
9.22	109	4.24–5.42	22	13.16	57, 110
10.39	99	4.31-35	178, 179	13.17-19	83

Index of References

13.22-23	128	18.4	57, 106, 110	Romans		
13.29-31	128	18.6-8	59	1.5	58	
13.33-35	112	18.6	57, 59	1.16-18	57, 60	
13.33	123	18.7	106	1.16	40, 57, 110, 146	
13.38-39	127	18.12–21.26	22			
13.40-41	127	18.12-13	59	3.9	40, 146	
13.42-44	59	18.12	198	9–11	23, 58	
13.43	57, 110	18.14-18	59	10.12	40, 146	
13.44-50	198	18.19	57, 110	10.14-16	57, 110	
13.45	59	18.21-23	59	11.11	58	
13.46-49	59	18.27-28	59	11.13	58	
13.46	57	19	59	11.25-26	58	
13.47	54, 130, 131, 157	19.8-10	57	15.26	166, 167, 169, 171	
		19.8	57, 110			
13.50	59	19.9-10	59	16.26	58	
13.51-52	59	19.9	59			
14	32	19.15-20	59	1 Corinthians		
14.1	57, 59, 110	20.3	198	8–10	23	
14.2-5	59	20.24	97	9.16	58	
14.3	97	20.28-35	178	9.19-23	58	
14.6-7	59	20.32	97	9.20-21	57, 110	
14.19	59, 198	21.17-26	59			
14.20-23	59	21.27–26.29	59	2 Corinthians		
15.1–18.11	22	21.27–22.29	27	3.14-15	114	
15.1-5	59	22.19	109	6.10	167, 169	
15.6-35	59	22.21	198	8.2	170	
15.6-26	181	24.12	57, 110	8.9	170, 171	
15.15-18	112, 128	24.17	177, 178	9.9	165	
15.21	112	25.6-12	27			
15.40-41	59	26.11	57, 110	Galatians		
16.13	106	26.17-18	157	1.16	58	
16.16-40	27	26.20	54, 130	2.1-10	58	
16.19-24	59	26.22-23	55, 132	2.2	58	
16.19-23	27	26.23	128, 157	2.7-9	58	
17.1-10	59	26.30–28.16	59	2.9	58	
17.1	57, 110	27	34	2.10	166, 167, 169, 171	
17.2-4	83	27.1–28.16	27			
17.2	57, 109, 112	28.4	59	3.8	58	
17.4-5	198	28.17-28	143	4.9	167, 169	
17.4	57, 59, 110	28.23-29	198			
17.5-8	59	28.24-29	59	Ephesians		
17.10-12	59	28.24	147	2.4	171	
17.10	57, 110	28.25-28	129			
17.13	59	28.26-28	155, 157	1 Timothy		
17.14-15	59	28.28-30	123	6.17	171	
17.17	57, 110	28.28	57, 143			
17.33-34	59	28.30-31	55, 60	2 Timothy		
18.4-5	59	28.30	147, 198	4.17	58	

Hebrews		2.3	167, 169, 170	2.9	170, 171
13.22	127	2.5	167, 169, 171	3.17	167, 170, 171
James		2.6	167, 169, 171	6.15	171
1.10	171			13.16	167, 170, 171
1.11	171	5.1	171		
1.22	162			21.5	202
2.2	167, 169, 170	*Revelation*			
		1.13–2.18	23		

QUMRAN

CD		3.25	166	*1QS*	
7.10	120	5.1	166	3.13–4.26	22
14.1-2	120	5.21	166	1.3	120
16.1-2	120	18.14-15	132	6.6-8	120
20.1	120			8.15-16	120
1QpHab		*1QM*			
2.1-10	120	3.4	105	*1QSa*	
		14.7	166	1.1	105
1QH					
2.32	166			*4QpPs*	
				2.11-12	166

RABBINIC WRITINGS

m. Meg.		4.5	111	32a	121
3.5	110	4.6	111		
3.6	110	4.10	111	*j. Meg.*	
4.2-3	110			74d	111, 121
4.2	111	*m. Pe'ah*			
4.3	111	8.7	173	*Lam. R.*	
4.4-5	111			3.10	174
4.4	111	*b. Meg.*			
4.5-6	111	21b	120		

PHILO

Agr.		*Poster. C.*		2.62	114
44	104	67	104		
				Vit. Cont.	
Leg. All.		*Somn.*		30–31	119
2.19-21	119	2.127	114	75–79	120
				80–81	120
Omn. Prob. Lib.		*Spec. Leg.*			
81	104	1.78	113		

JOSEPHUS

Ant.		*Apion*		*War*	
16.164	114	2.175	114	2.285-91	104
19.300	104			2.291	114
				5	37

CHRISTIAN AUTHORS

Acts of Philip		6.14.5	70	21, 60.163	31
50	105			28, 60.211	31
		Gospel of Thomas		35, 50.254	31
Apostolic Constitutions		31	85		
8.5	127			*Ign. Pol.*	
		Herm. Man.		4.2	104
Augustine		9	105		
De Consensu		11	105	*Ign. Trall.*	
Evangelistarum		13	105	3	105
1.2-3	70	14	105		
				Justin Martyr	
Eusebius		Chrysostom		*Dial.*	
Hist. Eccl.		Homily		63.5	105
3.39.15	70	1, 60.18	31		

CLASSICAL

Lucian of Samosata		Polybius		Thucydides	
1.2-5	29	12.25a.5-		1.22.1	29
		25b.1	29		

PAPYRI

Hibeh papyri		475.28	114	Tebtunis papyri	
29.21	114	476.12	114	45.5	114
92.22	114	485.49	114	186	114
		1409	114		
P. Oxy.		1556	114		
475.2	114	1573	114		

INDEX OF AUTHORS

Aletti, J.-N. 15
Alexander, L. 28, 34, 35, 62, 63, 87
Alexander, P.S. 121, 122
Anderson, H. 15, 95, 96
Ateek, N.S. 190
Aune, D.A. 20, 26, 28, 29, 35-37
Aymer, B.C.P. 16

Baarlink, H. 95
Barrett, C.K. 34
Baur, F.C. 21, 39
Beasley-Murray, G.R. 122
Bellinzoni, A.J. 71
Black, C.C. 127
Bloch, R. 116
Boismard, M.-E. 71
Bornhäuser, K. 92, 93, 95, 98
Bostock, D.G. 144
Bovon, F. 35
Brawley, R.L. 15
Brekelmans, C. 16
Brodie, T.L. 144
Brown, R.E. 48
Bruce, F.F. 45, 48
Burridge, R.A. 26, 27, 37, 38
Burrows, M.S. 185
Busse, U. 16

Cadbury, H.J. 20, 21, 34, 177
Carrington, P. 116
Cassidy, R.J. 163
Chilton, B.D. 121, 136, 138
Coggins, R.J. 175
Cohen, S.J.D. 106
Conzelmann, H. 33-35, 43, 44

Davids, P. 16
Dawsey, J. 25
Degenhardt, H.-J. 177
Dibelius, M. 32-35
Dietrich, W. 16
Donelson, L.R. 35
Draper, J. 189
Drury, J. 34, 116
Dumais, M. 16
Dungan, D.L. 71
Dupont, J. 16, 177, 178

Easton, B.S. 43
Eichhorn, J.G. 70
Ellis, E.E. 43
Esler, P.F. 16, 178, 180, 181
Evans, C.A. 83, 144, 145
Ewald, G. 71

Faierstein, M.M. 144
Farmer, W.R. 70, 71
Farrer, A. 71
Finch, R.G. 115
Fishbane, M. 120, 122
Fitzmyer, J.A. 71, 83, 84, 88, 120, 128
Foakes-Jackson, F.J. 32
Fowler, R.M. 150

Gasque, W.W. 35, 60
Gillingham, S.E. 166
Goulder, M. 71, 84, 115, 117, 118
Griesbach, J.J. 68, 70
Griffiths, J.G. 105, 107, 110
Grundmann, W. 95
Guilding, A. 115, 116
Gutiérrez, G. 186

Index of Authors

Gutmann, J. 107

Haenchen, E. 33, 35, 39, 41-43, 46, 63
Hamel, G. 166, 173-75
Hamm, D. 154 56, 172
Hanson, P.D. 51
Harnack, A. von 32
Hemer, C.J. 26, 34-36
Hengel, M. 35, 37, 103
Herder, J.G. 70
Hobbs, T.R. 175, 176
Hoenig, S. 107
Holtzmann, H.J. 70
Horsley, G.H.R. 102, 103, 108, 114, 159, 160

Jeremias, J. 93-95, 98
Johnston, L.T. 24, 25, 34, 177

Karris, R.J. 15, 163, 178, 179
Kee, H.C. 101-108, 111, 112
Koet, B.-J. 143
Kraabel, T. 107

LaVerdiere, E. 124
Lachmann, K. 70
Lake, K. 32
Le Déaut, R. 117
Leaney, A.R.C. 92
Lessing, G.E. 70
Levertoff, P.P. 115
Levine, L.I. 107
Lindsey, R.L. 71
Liu, P. 16
Lüdemann, G. 35

MacNamara, V. 192
Maddox, R. 37, 43, 44, 129
Marsh, H. 70
Marshall, I.H. 34, 43, 83, 88
Mattill, A.J. 43
Mayer, G. 104
McNamara, M. 117
Meyer, E. 32
Meyers, E. 52, 107
Mofokeng, T. 188, 189
Monshouwer, D. 132, 133, 140
Morris, L. 117

Neirynck, F. 71
Noorda, S.J. 159
Noy, D. 104

O'Fearghail, F. 95-98
O'Neill, J.C. 43
Orchard, J.B. 71
Oster, R.E. 101, 104-108, 113, 114

Parsons, M.C. 25, 38, 149, 150
Perrot, C. 117
Pervo, R. 25, 27, 29, 30, 33, 34, 37
Plümacher, E. 35
Prager, J.P. 186
Prior, M. 34, 36, 71, 78, 146, 188, 191

Ramsay, W.M. 32
Reicke, B. 137
Rorem, P. 185

Safrai, Z. 122
Sampley, J.P. 58
Sanders, J.A. 15, 52, 54, 129, 130, 136, 137, 147
Schleiermacher, F.E.D. 70
Schmidt, T.E. 177, 178
Schmitals, W. 16
Schnackenburg, R. 85
Schottroff, L. 16
Schrage, W. 102, 106
Schreck, C.J. 16
Schürer, E. 113, 114, 117
Siker, J.S. 145, 146, 150
Sloan, R.B., Jr 136
Spinetoli, O. da 16
Squires, J.T. 129
Stegemann, W. 16
Stegner, W.R. 126, 127
Storr, G.C. 70
Strange, J. 52, 107
Streeter, B.H. 70
Sugirtharajah, R.S. 187, 196

Talbert, C.H. 21-23, 25, 26, 34, 37, 43, 47, 60, 129
Tamez, E. 187
Tannehill, R.C. 24, 95, 149
Tuckett, C. 71, 84

Tyson, J.B. 129

Unnik, W.C. van 35

Vaage, L.E. 189
Violet, B. 93, 95, 98

Wechsler, A. 58
Weir, J.E. 176
Weisse, C.H. 70

West, G. 189
Wiener, A. 144
Wilkinson, J. 101
Wills, L. 127
Wilson, S.G. 43
Wright, A.G. 116
Wylie, A.B. 20, 31

Zeitlin, S. 103